DESCARTES

John Cottingham

BLACKWELL
Oxford UK & Cambridge USA

Copyright © John Cottingham, 1986

First published 1986

Reprinted 1989, 1991, 1992, 1993, 1994, 1995, 1996, 1997

Blackwell Publishers Ltd
108 Cowley Road
Oxford OX4 1JF, UK

Blackwell Publishers Inc
350 Main Street
Malden, Massachusetts 02148, USA

British Library Cataloguing in Publication Data
A CIP catalogue record for this book is available from the British Library

Library of Congress Cataloging in Publication Data
Cottingham, John, 1943–
Descartes
Bibliography: p.
Includes index.
1. Descartes, René, 1596–1650. I. Title.
B1873.C67 1986 194 86—6791
ISBN 0–631–15046–3 (pbk.)

Typeset by Columns of Reading
Printed and bound in Great Britain
by Athenæum Press Ltd, Gateshead, Tyne & Wear

This book is printed on acid-free paper

Contents

Preface

There are many worthwhile books on Descartes, and many interesting interpretations of his thought. The aims of the present volume are modest: to give a clear and straightforward account of Descartes' philosophy which does justice to the complexities of argument involved, while at the same time attempting to make the issues reasonably accessible to students who may be approaching the Cartesian system for the first time. Though difficult, such a task should not be impossible, since it was Descartes' own conviction that even the most 'sublime' aspects of his philosophy could be grasped without technical expertise, provided that the reasoning involved was laid out simply and in the proper order (AT X 497; CSM II 401).[1] Accessibility need not, I believe, mean over-simplification; indeed, I hope that at least some of what follows will have something to say to those who may have a more specialized acquaintance with the Cartesian texts.

No interpretation can claim to be wholly free of bias, but I have tried to pay attention to the intellectual climate in which Descartes' ideas were formulated, and to avoid the pitfalls of attempting to dissect his ideas as if from some timeless and ahistorical standpoint. I have not however confined myself entirely to the seventeenth-century context since part of the fascination of Descartes' work is that it illuminates philosophical issues that are still vigorously alive today. I have however tried to avoid the excessive stress on epistemological problems (connected for example with Cartesian doubt and the 'Cogito') that have preoccupied many recent writers on Descartes. No account of Cartesian thought would be complete without a proper analysis of these issues, but distortion can result if they are allowed to displace entirely discussion of Descartes' account of the physical universe or his physiological and psychological theories; for as well as being of considerable philosophical interest in their own right, Descartes' writings in these areas are of crucial

[1] For abbreviations, see p. ix below.

importance for a proper understanding of the Cartesian view of human nature. Descartes is par excellence a *systematic* philosopher, and it is vital to see how the various elements of his philosophy form an integrated whole.

Many of Descartes' arguments raise complex problems of interpretation. Although I have not tried to shirk the difficulties, I have tried to bypass unnecessary minutiae of exegesis, and to avoid breaking the flow I have relegated to the notes at the end of each chapter quite a number of qualifications and matters of detail, as well as references to some of the more technical debates in the recent literature. My own interpretations have sometimes drawn on arguments originally developed in previous articles of mine, details of which are recorded in the notes. In chapter five I have made considerable use of material from my 'Cartesian Trialism' which first appeared in *Mind* volume XCIV number 374 (April 1985) and I am grateful to the Editor and publishers for permission to include it here.

Few philosophical systems have received more intensive study than that of Descartes, and I am greatly conscious of how much I owe to a host of previous interpreters and commentators. I should also like to record my thanks to those many friends, colleagues and students from whom I have learnt in discussions. My special thanks are due to Robert Stoothoff and Dugald Murdoch who were kind enough to read the complete typescript and who made many extremely helpful suggestions and criticisms. The faults that remain are, of course, entirely my own. The entire manuscript was typed by Joan Morris, and I am most grateful to her for her careful and highly efficient work on the word-processor.

Department of Philosophy
University of Reading

Abbreviations

The following abbreviations are used in the text:

AT   *Oeuvres de Descartes* ed. C. Adam and P. Tannery. 12 vols. (Revised edition, Paris: Vrin/CNRS, 1964–76.)

CSM *The Philosophical Writings of Descartes* trans. J. Cottingham, R. Stoothoff and D. Murdoch. 2 vols. (Cambridge: Cambridge University Press, 1985.)

ALQ *Descartes: Oeuvres Philosophiques* ed. F. Alquié. 3 vols. (Paris: Garnier, 1963–73.)

K   *Descartes: Philosophical Letters* trans. A. Kenny. (Oxford: Oxford University Press, 1970; repr. Oxford: Blackwell, 1980.)

CB   *Descartes' Conversation with Burman* trans. with introduction and commentary J. Cottingham (Oxford: Clarendon, 1976). References throughout are to page numbers, *not* section numbers, of this work.

Other works are referred to in the notes by the author's or editor's name. Full details may be found in the list of references on pp. 165–7.

1

Descartes' Life and Times

Descartes' Generation: 'Science' and 'Philosophy' in the Seventeenth Century

Descartes was born in 1596, some 100 years after Columbus discovered America, some 70 years after Magellan circumnavigated the globe, and some 50 years after the publication of *De Revolutionibus Orbium Celestium*, in which Copernicus had proposed that the earth rotates daily on its axis and revolves yearly about a central sun. He died in 1650, some 40 years before Newton's formulation of the laws of mechanics and universal gravitation, some 100 years before Franklin's experiments with electricity, and some 150 years before Francis Dalton published his atomic theory of the elements.[1] The transition from the 'medieval' to the 'modern' world outlook was a lengthy, gradual and exceedingly complex affair; but if there can be said to be one generation that represents the pivotal phase of that transition, it is the generation of Descartes and his contemporaries.

The most spectacular advances of the early seventeenth century occurred in the field of astronomy. In 1610 Galileo detected the phases of Venus through his telescope – an observation that was to prove an insuperable obstacle to the Ptolemaic, earth-centred model of the universe. Earlier that year he had published *Siderius Nuncius* ('The Starry Messenger'), recording his discovery of four satellites revolving round Jupiter; again, this result clashed strikingly with the traditional Aristotelian–Ptolemaic cosmology according to which the earth was the central point of all the celestial revolutions.[2] The following year, on 6 June 1611, a poem celebrating Galileo's discovery of the moons of Jupiter was recited at the college of La Flèche in Anjou, where the schoolboy audience included the 15-year-old Descartes. A central belief of Galileo, which was to find some echoes in Descartes' conception of science, was that mathematics was the key to grasping the nature of reality: 'the grand book of the universe cannot be understood unless one first learns to comprehend the language and read the alphabet in which it is composed. It is written in the language of mathematics'.[3] It was mathematical skills that enabled the German astonomer Kepler to develop his theory that the planets move in elliptical as opposed to circular orbits: Kepler's *Tables* of 1627 provided the first accurate procedures for specifying the speeds and paths of planetary motions. As well as mathematical knowledge, however, such advances also required that other great weapon of science, the careful collection of empirical data; Kepler was able to draw on over 20 years of patient observations made by the Danish astronomer Tycho Brahe. The seventeenth century saw a great advance in new technological aids to observation – the telescope being the most important example (Descartes himself, in one of his first published essays, the *Optics*, was to devote considerable space to the problems of telescope design and lens-cutting). But as well as new instruments, the century saw a growing awareness of the importance of proper standards for conducting observations and experiments. In 1620 another near contemporary of Descartes, Francis Bacon, published his *Novum Organum*, which put forward a set of precepts for the investigation of natural phenomena and their causes, and stressed in particular the crucial importance, in finding true laws, of the search for counter-examples: 'in establishing any true axiom, the negative instance is more powerful (*major est vis negativae instantiae*)'.[4] Bacon's 'new method' of induction, setting out the techniques of tabulation, comparison, elimination and exclusion, heralded an increasing appreciation of the importance of systematic empirical research in the struggle to understand the universe.

The term 'scientific revolution' is often used to describe the great seventeenth-century upheaval in man's outlook of which Descartes, along with such thinkers as Galileo and Bacon, was a principal author. But the label 'scientific' can be misleading. First, the term in its modern sense often connotes, if not an anti-religious, then at least a secularist world view. But the outlook of the great seventeenth-century innovators (despite Galileo's notorious troubles with the Inquisition) was in many cases a strongly religious one. One cannot read the writings of Kepler, for example, without being struck by the devout, almost mystical flavour of much of his thinking. And in the case of Descartes, there is an insistence on the absolutely central role of God in any sound philosophical system. A second potentially misleading aspect of the use of words like 'science' and 'scientific' in connection with the seventeenth century is that they suggest an agreed body of standards, procedures and practices in terms of which theories are tested, evidence assessed and experiments conducted. Yet in the seventeenth century there was no such agreed corpus of rules; indeed, part of the achievement of thinkers like Descartes and Bacon was that they envisaged (though in very different ways) the possibility of developing an agreed methodology for the investigation of truth. In this sense, Descartes should be thought of not so much as being one of the inaugurators of a 'scientific revolution', but as having helped to establish the foundations for the very enterprise that was later to become known as 'science'.

Although the concept of science as we know it today did not exist in the seventeenth century, the Latin term *scientia* is frequently to be found in the writings of Descartes and other writers of the period. But it is misleading to do what is often done and translate this word as 'science'. In the philosophical Latin of the seventeenth century, the primary meaning of *scientia* (from the Latin *scire* 'to know') is simply 'knowledge'; and the cognate French term *science* is often used, in the plural, to refer to accredited branches of knowledge, such as arithmetic or geometry. (Descartes himself, as we shall see, uses *scientia* to refer to a specially privileged kind of cognition.) The seventeenth-century term which in some ways comes close to 'science' as used today is the Latin *philosophia*. When Descartes and his contemporaries need a term to describe those concerned with the investigation of the physical world, they normally speak of 'philosophers'; and Descartes himself often refers to his physical theories of the universe as his 'philosophy'. But the word has important resonances of which it is crucial to be aware. In the preface to his magnum opus, the *Principles of Philosophy*, Descartes refers back to the original Greek meaning of 'philosophy' – literally, the love of wisdom; the philosopher, for Descartes, is one who 'studies wisdom' – whose aim is to achieve a comprehensive understanding of all aspects of reality. The activity called 'philosophy' thus includes, to be sure, the whole of physics – the devising and developing of theories about the nature of matter; but it also includes, on the one hand, foundational subjects like metaphysics and epistemology which are characteristic of philosophy in the modern academic sense, and, on the other hand, detailed ground-floor work in a whole range of specific disciplines like astronomy, anatomy, meteorology and optics. The 'philosopher' welds all these elements into a systematic whole. The word 'systematic' is especially important here. True philosophy, Descartes explains, is not just a matter of amassing items of knowledge via such ordinary orthodox routes as sensory observation and booklearning; rather, it comprises 'the search for first causes and true principles which enable us to deduce the reasons for everything we are capable of knowing' (AT IXB 5; CSM I 181). From such true principles, Descartes believes, it will be possible to derive a fully inclusive system of knowledge which will have a kind of organic unity. 'The whole of philosophy is like a tree of which the roots are metaphysics, the trunk is physics, and the branches emerging from the trunk are all the other sciences' (AT IXB 14; CSM Ī 186).[5]

Scholasticism

The attempt to give a systematic and comprehensive account of the universe was not, of course, a seventeenth-century innovation; much classical and medieval philosophy had devoted itself to just such a task. Nevertheless, Descartes was regarded even by his contemporaries as breaking new ground – as propounding a philosophy which threatened to subvert the traditional approach. The fears aroused by the 'new' philosophy are vividly illustrated by the following condemnation of the Cartesian system which was issued in 1642 by the Senate of the University of Utrecht, where the lectures of Descartes' disciple Regius had aroused the hostility of the authorities:

> The professors reject this new philosophy for three reasons. First, it is opposed to the traditional philosophy which universities throughout the world have hitherto taught on the best advice, and it undermines its foundations. Second, it turns away the young from this sound and traditional philosophy, and prevents them reaching the heights of erudition; for once they have begun to rely on the new philosophy and its supposed solutions, they are unable to understand the technical terms which are commonly used in the books of the traditional authors and in the lectures and debates of their professors. And lastly, various false and absurd opinions either follow from the new philosophy or can be rashly deduced by the young – opinions which are in conflict with other disciplines and faculties, and above all with orthodox philosophy (AT VII 592; CSM II 393).

The 'traditional' philosophy referred to in this decree is what is known as 'scholasticism' – the system, derived ultimately from Aristotle, which was developed in the thirteenth century and continued, in one form or another, to dominate much of European thought right through the late medieval and renaissance periods. Scholastic philosophy is not much studied nowadays, and those commentators who do refer to it are apt to issue sweeping condemnations of its aridity and triviality; the notorious question 'how many angels can dance on a pinhead?' is often cited as a paradigm of the type of question which exercised the minds of the 'Schoolmen'. But this kind of caricature ignores the range of scholastic thought over a wide variety of important issues in logic, language and philosophy of physics; when Descartes challenged the Schoolmen he had to contend with a formidable philosophical system of considerable sophistication and power.

Scholasticism grew essentially from a fusion of the philosophy of Aristotle (known in the middle ages as '*the* Philosopher') and the doctrines of the Christian church. It was the need to reconcile the claims of 'faith' and 'reason' that produced the powerful techniques of argumentation and analysis that characterized scholastic philosophy at its best. Two principal features of scholastic philosophy as it was practised in the medieval universities should be noted here. The first was the custom of holding formal debates on set subjects (the *quaestiones disputatae*), as well as open debates where any topic could be raised (the *quaestiones quodlibetales*). The skills needed for success in these disputations were mental agility, the mastery of logical terminology, and the ability to deploy a barrage of subtle distinctions and qualifications in order to defend a position against charges either of being internally inconsistent or of clashing with some recognized authority. The second major vehicle of scholasticism was the learned critical commentary, where the great classical texts – principally those of Aristotle – were subjected to the most exhaustive scrutiny. Again, the principal object was to resolve contradictions, and reconcile the text with scriptural and other authorities.

What is important for our purposes about these aspects of scholasticism, at least as it had come to be practised by the early seventeenth century, is that in many cases skill in jargon-manipulation and the juggling of authorities had become the paramount road to academic advancement. The Utrecht decree illustrates this well – and it is doubly damning because it comes not from the critics of scholasticism but from its champions. What emerges firstly and most evidently is an unquestioned respect for authority: to show that a doctrine does not harmonize with those of the 'traditional authors' is enough to secure its condemnation out of hand. Second, there is a reverence for technical terminology – the complaint against Descartes has nothing to do with the substance of his doctrines, but with the fact that it does not employ the 'technical terms used in the lectures and debates'.

The Utrecht decree makes no direct reference to Aristotle. But there are many other sources which testify to the deep reverence with which his views were treated by many academics in the early seventeenth century. 'Aristotle', wrote one of Galileo's opponents, 'read more works than he had days, wrote more works than he counted years; *natura locutus est ex ore eius* – nature itself spoke from his mouth'.[6] The extent to which Descartes saw his doctrines as posing a direct challenge to the authority of 'the Philosopher' will emerge in later chapters; but two general points deserve a mention here. The first concerns Aristotelian logic and the theory of the syllogism – that watertight system for establishing the validity of arguments, which was arguably Aristotle's most important contribution to Western thought. It is sometimes said that Descartes' attack on scholasticism had to do with a rejection of scholastic logic – and indeed Descartes himself does often speak disparagingly of the 'logic of the schools', apparently contrasting it with his own new method for teaching the truth:

> I observed with regard to logic that syllogisms and most of its other techniques are of less use for learning things than for explaining what we already know or . . . for speaking without judgement about matters of which one is ignorant' (AT VI 17; CSM I 119).

Closer scrutiny reveals, however, that Descartes has no objection to Aristotelian syllogisms as such: 'I myself have always been prepared to use syllogisms when the occasion required it' (AT VII 522; CSM II 355). What Descartes objected to was not the logical structure of Aristotelian reasoning (which he later admitted does indeed 'provide demonstrative proofs on all subjects') but to the way in which Aristotelian logic was used in the schools (AT V 175; CB 46). Descartes frequently uses the term 'dialectic' to describe scholastic logic; by this he means, not that the reasoning involved is necessarily faulty in itself, but that it is employed in the rehearsing of 'stock arguments' and in the attempt to win debating points, rather than in any serious attempt to enlarge our knowledge (AT IXB 13; CSM I 186). Scholastic reasoning had in fact become a largely closed system – an elaborate game at which one's ability to win depended more on the skilful manipulation of terminology than on open-mindedness in the pursuit of truth.

A second feature of Aristotelian-based philosophy that Descartes came increasingly to criticize was its reliance on imprecise and often ill-defined qualitative notions:

> The majority of those aspiring to be philosophers in the last few centuries have blindly followed Aristotle . . . or else have been so saturated with his opinions in their youth that this has dominated their outlook . . . For example, there is not one of them, so far as I know, who has not supposed there to be weight in terrestrial bodies. Yet although experience shows us very clearly that the bodies we call 'heavy' descend towards the centre of the earth, we do not for all that have any knowledge of the nature of what is called 'gravity', that is to say the cause or principle that makes bodies descend in this way (AT IXB 7f; CSM I 182).

Very generally, it may be said that Aristotelian philosophy divides the things in the world into certain 'natural kinds'; ultimately, these reduce to four – earth, fire, air and water. Various objects then can be seen to behave the way they do because they are of one of these kinds; thus, fire moves upwards, and terrestrial particles move downwards, because it is of the nature of fiery and earthly matter respectively so to do. A common criticism of this type of explanation is that it is circular: to say that terrestrial particles move downwards because they are composed of earthly matter is not to explain anything but simply to redescribe the phenomenon to be explained. As Galileo acidly observed, 'to say that the wood of the fir tree does not sink because air predominates in it is to say no more than that it does not sink because it is less heavy than water'.[7] Despite such strictures, this type of explanation continued to command widespread respect throughout much of the seventeenth century. Often quoted in this connection is Molière's famous satire on the 'learned doctors' who explained the soporific power of opium by referring to its 'dormitive virtue';[8] and it is clear from the writings of such contemporaries of Molière as Robert Boyle that these 'learned doctors' were not merely stage caricatures:

> If it be demanded how snow comes to dazzle the eyes, they [the schoolmen] will answer that it is by the quality of whiteness . . .; and if you ask what whiteness is, they will tell you that it is a real entity, which they term a quality.[9]

The elimination of explanations involving 'real qualities' was one of the central planks of Descartes' scientific programme. But while Descartes evidently shared the irritation voiced earlier by Galileo and later by Boyle about the vacuity and circularity of qualitative explanations,[10] his own chief reason for rejecting such explanations is of a rather different kind. His complaint against the invoking of qualities like 'gravity' or 'heaviness' has to do with the obscurity and indistinctness of such notions: we are unable to specify in any precise way exactly what we mean by them. As he puts it elsewhere: when we say we 'perceive' such qualities in objects 'this is really just the same as saying we perceive something in the objects whose nature we do not know' (AT VIII 34; CSM I 218). It is a fundamental requirement for Descartes that all the terms used in philosophy and physics be transparently clear: they must reflect the clear and distinct perceptions of the mind when it is freed from the lumber of preconceived opinions, and guided only by careful rational reflection. Thus, instead of relying, as the scholastics did, upon a vast corpus of inherited doctrines and technical terms, Descartes proposed to 'demolish everything and start again right from the foundations', searching for simplicity, clarity and self-evidence (AT VII 18; CSM II 12). We shall see in subsequent chapters exactly how this remarkable project works out in detail.

Descartes' Early Years

The above remarks are intended as a first step to placing Descartes in the philosophical and scientific context of his times. Readers approaching Descartes from different backgrounds may find the following landmarks helpful. Descartes was born when Shakespeare was near the height of his powers; when he died, Milton was soon to embark on *Paradise Lost*. In France, Montaigne's *Essais* were published shortly before Descartes' birth, and Molière's comedies were being produced in the two decades following his death. Politically, Descartes's life spanned a period of great upheaval. His major works were published while the Civil War raged in England (we have a letter from Descartes to Princess Elizabeth of Bohemia, consoling her on the execution of her uncle, Charles I of England (letter of 22 February 1649: AT V 282; ALQ III 888)). In continental Europe, the extraordinarily bloody religious fighting known as the Thirty Years War continued during much of Descartes' adult life. Indeed, as a young man he had briefly sampled the 'wars in Germany' when he enlisted for a time with the Catholic forces. But for the most part Descartes remained detached and aloof from such events, true to his resolution to remain 'a spectator rather than an actor in the comedies of life' (AT VI 28; CSM I 125).

René Descartes was born on 31 March 1596 at La Haye, some 50 kilometers south of Tours. The house where he was born still stands, in the smallish and otherwise unremarkable town renamed La Haye-Descartes in 1802, and now known simply as 'Descartes'.[11] Descartes' family was an ancient and well-connected one, and throughout his life Descartes (whose tastes were in any case very modest) was to be free of the necessity to earn a living. His father Joachim was a parliamentary Counsellor at Rennes; his mother Jeanne died soon after his birth, and the infant René was brought up by his maternal grandmother. He was a sickly child, and he wrote later that the doctors did not expect him to reach adult life.

In 1606 he was sent to the new Jesuit college at La Flèche in Anjou, which had been founded by Henri IV in 1604.[12] Though Descartes later had some criticisms to make of the content of the curriculum, he praised the high standard of the college, which rapidly gained a reputation as 'one of the most famous schools in Europe' (AT VI 5; CSM I 113). It was at La Flèche that Descartes acquired the fluent and polished Latin in which many of his philosophical works were to be composed. He left La Flèche probably in 1614, and soon after took his *baccalauréat* and *licence* in Law, at Poitiers. At the age of 22, Descartes left France and set out on his travels. 'Resolving', he later wrote, 'to seek no knowledge other than that which could be found in myself or else in the great book of the world, I spent the rest of my youth travelling, visiting courts and armies, mixing with people of diverse temperaments and ranks . . . testing myself in the situations which fortune offered me' (AT VI 9; CSM I 115).

Descartes went first to Holland, where he made the acquaintance of Isaac Beeckman, who stimulated his interest in philosophical, mathematical and scientific questions. Descartes' first work, the brief *Compendium Musicae* (unpublished during his lifetime) was written during this year (1618), and dedicated to Beeckman. In Holland Descartes enlisted in the army of Prince Maurice of Nassau; but before long he moved to Germany and attached himself to the forces of Maximilian of Bavaria. In the summer of 1619 he visited Frankfurt to attend the coronation of Ferdinand II; but on his return later in the year to Bavaria he was delayed by adverse weather conditions, and November 1619 saw him closeted in his famous *poêle* or 'stove-heated room' probably near Ulm on the Danube:

> While returning to the army, the onset of winter detained me in quarters where, finding no conversation to divert me and fortunately having no cares or passions to trouble me, I stayed all day shut up alone in a stove-heated room, where I was completely free to converse with myself about my own thoughts (AT VI 11; CSM II 116).

After a day spent in intense philosophical speculations, Descartes fell asleep still in a state of great mental excitement; he then had three vivid dreams which he later described as having given him a sense of his mission in life. The dreams are narrated in detail by Descartes' biographer Adrien Baillet, whose account is probably based on Descartes' own early notebooks.[13]

In the first dream, Descartes felt himself assailed by phantoms, and then by a whirlwind which spun him round and prevented him standing upright. Taking refuge in a college, he attempted to reach the chapel, but was prevented by the wind. He was then greeted by a friend who gave him a message about a gift, which he assumed to be 'a melon brought from some foreign country'. On waking he felt a sharp pain which apparently made him fear that the dream was the work of some evil demon bent on deceiving him. The fear and dismay produced by the dream, reports Baillet, kept Descartes awake for two hours. When he at last fell asleep again, he immediately seemed to hear a loud thunderclap, and at once woke again in a state of terror, with the impression that the room was filled with fiery sparks. In the third and last dream, which unlike the first two was a pleasant one, he found a book on his table which he saw to be a dictionary; he was 'struck with the hope that this might be very useful to him'. Then, in another book, an anthology of verse, he found the ode of Ausonius beginning *Quod vitae sectabor iter?* ('What road in life shall I follow?'); whereupon a man appeared and spoke of another poem beginning *Est et non* ('It is and is not'). According to Baillet, Descartes began to be aware, while still asleep, that he was dreaming, and began to speculate on the interpretation of the dream. The dictionary, he reckoned, stood for all the sciences, while the anthology of poems was 'philosophy and wisdom'. Upon waking, he continued to interpret all three dreams: the poem beginning *Est et non* – the 'yes and no' of Pythagoras – represented truth and falsity in the sciences. The ode *Quod vitae sectabor iter?* spoke of his future life. The melon in the first dream he took to signify the 'charms of solitude'.

Whatever we make of these curious details, the result of his daylong meditation, and the vivid dreams that followed it, was to convince Descartes that he had a divine mission to found a new philosophical system; and forthwith he made a vow (which he probably fulfilled the following year) to go to Italy and make a pilgrimage to the shrine of the Virgin at Loretto.

Having renounced the military life, Descartes continued to travel in Germany, Holland and Italy in the early 1620s. From 1625–7 he lived in Paris, where one of his closest friends was the Franciscan friar Marin Mersenne (also a former pupil at La Flèche, though Descartes' senior by eight years).[14] When Descartes left France for Holland at the end of the decade, Mersenne was to fill something of the role of an editor or agent for Descartes in Paris; he conducted a voluminous correspondence with Descartes on a large number of philosophical topics, forwarded his letters to other scholars, and helped with the publication of his works – in particular the *Meditations*.

Towards the end of the 1620s Descartes produced his first major work, the *Regulae ad Directionem Ingenii* (*Rules for the Direction of the Mind*). This ambitious book (which was never completed and was not published in Descartes' lifetime) reveals much about Descartes' early approach to his lifelong project of establishing a universal method for arriving at the truth. From the start we find a preoccupation with a unified system of enquiry, and with the attainment of 'universal wisdom'. Knowledge is characterized as 'certain and evident cognition'; we must, says Descartes, reject what is merely probable and 'resolve to believe only what is perfectly known and incapable of being doubted' (AT X 362; CSM I 10). The main inspiration for Descartes' model of knowledge in the *Regulae* is mathematics; indeed much of the book is concerned with how to solve mathematical problems by the use of carefully designed symbols which will enable the precise nature and structure of each problem to be made transparently clear.

After an exploratory visit to Holland in 1628, Descartes decided to make that country his permanent home, and he took up residence there in the spring of 1629. He lived first at Franeker, but within a year he had moved to Amsterdam, and then, after two years, to Leiden. Altogether he was to change his address more than a dozen times in as many years: 'his place of habitation was no more fixed that than of the Israelites in the desert' observes his biographer Baillet. The restlessness may partly have been due to a desire to be left alone: Baillet notes that Descartes often kept his correspondents in doubt about his exact address, to avoid being plagued with visits. This strong desire for tranquility and solitude may have been the main reason for Descartes' departure from France in the first place, but it is also possible that he hoped that the relatively tolerant climate of Protestant Holland would enable him to pursue his scientific and philosophical studies with less danger of being embroiled in academic and theological disputes.

In the early 1630s, however, Descartes was still relatively unknown. In Holland he visited various universities and met a number of distinguished mathematicians, philosophers and medical men. While living in Amsterdam, in Kalverstraat (in the quarter where many of the city's butchers were to be found), he was able to pursue his anatomical studies by purchasing numerous carcasses for dissection. He also worked on algebra, furthering the project described in the *Regulae* of perfecting a precise notation for the solution of mathematical problems. Some of his results, published in the *Geometry* (1637), laid the foundations for what is now known as analytic or coordinate geometry. Another major interest was optics, and it was during this period that Descartes had considerable success in investigating the principles of refraction; his essay on *Optics* (*la Dioptrique*), also published in 1637, contained a tolerably accurate presentation of what is now known as Snell's law of refraction (AT VI 101; CSM I 161).[15]

Characteristically, Descartes did not keep these richly varied interests in separate compartments. As early as 1629 he had formed the idea of producing a comprehensive treatise which 'instead of explaining only one phenomenon' would explain 'all the phenomena of nature – i.e. all of physics' (letter to Mersenne of 13 November 1629; AT I 70; ALQ I 226). By 1633 this work was ready for publication. The first part, entitled *Le Monde* (*The World*) dealt with the origins and structure of the physical universe, including such topics as heat, light, fire and the nature of the stars, planets, comets and the earth; a concluding section, now known as the *Treatise on Man*, dealt with human physiology.[16]

But in June 1633 Descartes received a sharp check to his plans, when the Inquisition in Rome issued a formal condemnation of Galileo. The previous year had seen the publication in Florence of Galileo's *Dialogue on the two chief systems of the universe, the Ptolemaic and the Copernican* (*Dialogo sopra i due massimi systemi del mondo, ptolemaico e copernicano*). This had attacked a number of Aristotelian doctrines (for example the proposition that the heavenly bodies are 'ingenerable, incorruptible, unalterable, invariant and eternal') and had produced a host of arguments and observational results designed to show the superiority of the Copernican view, that the earth rotates diurnally and revolves annually about the sun, over the traditional Ptolemaic picture of an immovable central earth.[17] Galileo's previous work had already attracted adverse attention from the Holy Office. As early as 1616 it had formally condemned his defence of the proposition that the earth moves, though with the proviso that the proposition might be employed purely 'as a hypothesis' – that is to say, as an expository device that did not purport to describe the literal truth. Now, however, in the condemnation of 22 June 1633, it was implied that the heliocentric view could not be put forward even if proposed as a hypothesis.[18]

Descartes at once decided to refrain from publishing his *World*. He had been careful in that work to insist that his own explanations of the origin of the earth and solar system were purely 'hypothetical': 'My purpose is not to explain the things which are in fact in the real world but only to make up, as I please, a world which . . . *could* be created exactly as I imagine it' (AT XI 36; CSM I 92). But the new condemnation of Galileo implied that even such cautious language as this could not ensure immunity from ecclesiastical censure. 'I must tell you', Descartes wrote to Mersenne the following year,

> that all the things I explained in my treatise, which included the doctrine of the movement of the earth, were so interdependent that it is enough to discover that one of them is false to know that all the arguments I was using are unsound. Though I thought they were based on very certain and evident proofs, I would not wish for anything in the world, to maintain them against the authority of the Church. Although it might be said that not everything decided on by the Roman inquisitors is automatically an article of faith . . ., I am not so fond of my own opinions as to want to use such quibbles to be able to maintain them. I desire to live in peace and to continue the life I have begun under the motto *'Bene vixit, qui bene latuit'* (April 1634: AT I 285; K 25f).

The Latin apophthegm, from Ovid (who was in turn rendering a maxim of Epicurus), defies neat translation into English, but may be paraphrased roughly as follows: 'if you can live your life through without attracting untoward attention, you will have lived well.'[19]

Descartes' Later Years: the Major Publications

By 1637 Descartes had decided to overcome his scruples and give the public at least a sample of his work. On 8 June of that year an anonymous volume was published at Leiden containing, in French, three 'specimen essays'; the first and third of these were, respectively, Descartes' *Optics* and *Geometry* (already mentioned above); the second was his *Meteorology* (*Les Météors*), which incorporated relatively uncontroversial material from *The World* dealing with such phenomena as clouds, storms, snow and rainbows. Descartes later wrote: 'I did not want my name to appear on the title page, in order to do everything I could to protect myself from the envy and hostility which, though quite undeserved, I realized would fall on me as a result of the publication of these specimen essays' (AT VII 575; CSM II 387).

As Descartes' correspondence of 1638 shows, it was the mathematical aspects of these essays that aroused the greatest stir; the famous mathematician Pierre Fermat raised a large number of detailed objections to the *Optics*, and wrote a treatise intended to supersede the *Geometry*. From the standpoint of posterity, however, the most important part of Descartes' volume was not the three specimen essays themselves, but the introduction that preceded them, entitled *Discourse on the method of rightly conducting one's reason and seeking the truth in the sciences* (*Discours de la méthode pour bien conduire sa raison et chercher la vérité dans les sciences*).[20]

Descartes explains in a letter to Mersenne that his aim in the *Discourse* was 'not to teach the method but merely to speak about it', and that this is why he chose the label 'discourse' rather than 'treatise' (letter of 27 February 1637: AT I 349; K 30). Even a cursory inspection of the work reveals that the *Discourse* is an intensely individual work which is indeed quite unlike a conventional scholarly treatise or philosophical manual. Descartes begins by reflecting on his early years and education; next he describes the adoption of a provisional moral code for the conduct of life; after this he launches into metaphysics, and then proceeds to cover a wide range of scientific issues connected with anatomy and physiology; finally, he talks about his work in progress and future plans. But above all, the *Discourse* aims at presenting a method for reaching the truth which avoids traditional jargon and received wisdom. Descartes' appeal is not to a narrow academic audience, but to the ordinary person of simple 'good sense' – 'the most widely distributed commodity in the world' (AT VI 1; CSM I 111). The most famous section of the work, Part Four, presents a beautifully clear and accessible statement of the metaphysical core of Descartes' philosophy, and introduces the famous pronouncement '*Je pense, donc je suis*' ('*I am thinking, therefore I exist*').

From 1638–40, Descartes resided mainly in the countryside near Santpoort. In this 'corner of North Holland', he wrote to Mersenne on 17 May 1638, he could pursue his studies far more effectively than would have been possible in Paris with its 'innumerable distractions' (AT II 152; ALQ II 68). But though fond of solitude, Descartes was no hermit. Earlier, while living in Amsterdam, he had formed a liaison with his serving woman, Hélène, and the result of this union was an infant daughter, Francine, born on July 19, 1635. We know that mother and daughter came to live with Descartes during his time at Santpoort, but few details of this, or of any other aspect of Descartes' private life, are known. Apparently, Descartes planned to have his daughter educated in France,[21] but the girl died tragically of a fever on 7 September 1640. According to Baillet, the loss was the heaviest blow of Descartes' life; but the surviving letters show no noticeable interruption of philosophical activity during this period of bereavement. Descartes was later to write that 'few people have sufficiently prepared themselves for all the contingencies of life,' but that 'the chief use of wisdom lies in teaching ourselves to be masters of our passions and to control them with such skill that the evils that they cause become bearable' (AT XI 486ff; CSM I 403f).

On August 28, 1641, Descartes published his philosophical master-piece, the *Meditations on First Philosophy*. Written in Latin, the work is a dramatic and compelling account of the mind's rejection of preconceived opinions and its quest for the foundations of a reliable system of knowledge. As the title suggests, the *Meditations* are intended not as a static exposition of finished doctrines but as a dynamic series of mental exercises which the mind must follow in its journey from doubt to certainty. Thus Descartes insists: 'I would not urge anyone to read this book except those who are able and willing to meditate seriously along with me' (the argument throughout is presented in the first person); only by individually following the prescribed path will each reader be able to arrive at knowledge, first of his own existence, then of the existence of God, and finally of the essence of material things, and of the nature of the mind and its relation to the body (AT VII 9; CSM II 8).

The first edition of the *Meditations* appeared in Paris, but Descartes was dissatisfied with Michel Soly, his Paris publishers, and he arranged for a second edition to be brought out the following year by the house of Elzevir in Amsterdam. Before publication, Descartes had had the manuscript circulated to various distinguished philosophers and theologians, and had composed detailed replies to the criticisms they offered. The resulting *Objections and Replies* (seven sets in all, though the final set appeared only in the Amsterdam edition) were published together with the *Meditations* in a single volume. The authors of the Objections included the theologian Antoine Arnauld, who questioned Descartes closely on the theological implications of his views; the English philosopher Thomas Hobbes, who had fled to France for political reasons in 1640, and whose materialist account of the nature of the mind contrasted sharply with that of Descartes; and the philosopher Pierre Gassendi who offered what was virtually a line by line critique of the *Meditations*, attacking Descartes' belief in innate ideas, and taking a strongly empiricist standpoint on the origins of human knowledge. Though Descartes' replies to these objectors often display a certain testiness, he was a highly skilled debater and he was sufficiently confident of the soundness of his arguments to have deliberately sought out this opportunity to test his views. 'I shall be glad', he wrote to Mersenne (who was the principal author of two sets of Objections and was responsible for collecting most of the rest) 'if people make the strongest objections they can, for I hope that in consequence the truth will stand out all the better' (letter of 28 January 1641: AT III 297; K 93). Descartes was, however, extremely disappointed by the tone of the Seventh Set of Objections, composed by the Jesuit Pierre Bourdin. He had hoped to enlist the broad support of the Jesuits for his philosophy, and he was dismayed to read Bourdin's blisteringly hostile attack, which managed, by a combination of sarcasm, distortion and flagrant misquotation, to give the impression that Descartes' views were scarcely worthy of serious discussion.

During the early 1640s, Descartes continued to live in Holland, first at the castle of Endegeest, near Leiden, then at Egdmond op de Hoef, near Alkmaar. His time was partly occupied with unwelcome polemics – in particular with the attacks of Professor Voetius of Utrecht. In various publications Voetius had dubbed Descartes 'a foreigner and a papist', and had ominously compared his arguments with those of a notorious atheist who had been burned alive for his views earlier in the century (ALQ III 31). In 1643 Decartes published a lengthy apologia in the form of an open letter to Voetius (*Epistola at Voetium*). The letter refers to the 'wicked lies, base insults and odious calumny' of Voetius, invokes the 'religious liberty which is granted by the laws [of Holland]', and sharply contrasts Descartes' own philosophy with the scholastic doctrines it was designed to replace:

> the philosophy against which you rail with such violence . . . aims at the knowledge of the truths which are acquired by means of the natural light, and which promote the benefit of the human race; by contrast the dominant philosophy, which is taught in the schools and universities, is merely a muddled collection of opinions which are mostly open to doubts, as is proved by the debates that they occasion day after day, and which are

entirely without practical benefit, as centuries of experience have proved only too well (AT VIIIB 26; ALQ III 30).

The same year (1643) Descartes began a more rewarding exchange – his long and celebrated correspondence with Princess Elizabeth of Bohemia. The Princess, then only 24, was in exile in Holland, where her family (her mother was daughter of James I of England, her father the ill-fated Frederick V of Bohemia) had fled following the battle of the White Mountain in 1620.[22] In her letters, Elizabeth raised questions about Descartes' account of the mind and its relation to the body which pinpointed some major difficulties in Descartes' position; Descartes' detailed replies are a rich source for students of his philosophy of mind. The correspondence with Elizabeth also deals with the relationship between reason and the passions, and Descartes' thoughts on this topic were later incorporated into his major physiological-cum-psychological-cum-ethical treatise, *The Passions of the Soul* (*Les passions de l'âme*), eventually published in 1649.

It was to Princess Elizabeth that Descartes dedicated the comprehensive presentation of his philosophical and scientific system which he published in Latin in 1644 under the title *Principia Philosophiae* (*Principles of Philosophy*). Descartes planned the *Principles* as a university textbook which would rival and, he hoped, eventually replace the traditional texts based on Aristotle. The work runs to four parts, each divided into a large number of short sections or 'articles' (there are 504 in all). Part One expounds Descartes' metaphysical doctrines; Part Two sets out the principles of Cartesian physics; Part Three gives a detailed explanation, based on those principles, of the nature of the physical universe; and Part Four deals similarly with a wide variety of terrestrial phenomena. A further two parts were originally planned to deal respectively with plants and animals, and with man, but these were never completed. Much of the *Principles* was a restatement of material that Descartes had originally written for his suppressed treatise *The World*; and like *The World*, the *Principles* explicitly rejects many of the hallowed doctrines of scholasticism. There is, for example, no distinction made between terrestrial and celestial phenomena: the same mathematical and mechanical principles as are used to explain what we see here on earth are invoked to explain the workings of the sun, stars and planets. Again, the Aristotelian search for 'final causes' (purposive explanations) is stigmatized as having no place in physics: 'when dealing with natural things, we will never derive any explanations from the purposes which God or nature may have had in view when creating them. For we should not be so arrogant as to suppose that we can share in God's plans' (AT VIII 15; CSM I 202). As for the traditional geocentric account of the solar system, this is rejected out of hand: 'Ptolemy's hypothesis', observes Descartes, 'is in conflict with many observations, and is now commonly rejected by all philosophers' (AT VIII 85; CSM I 250). Descartes manages, however, to sidestep the dangerous issue of whether the earth 'really' moves, by proposing an essentially relativistic account of motion: to say that A moves and B is at rest is simply to say that there is a transfer of matter from the vicinity of one body to that of another, relative to some point which it is convenient to take as a fixed point of reference (AT VIII 53; CSM I 233). In this sense, says Descartes, it is not strictly appropriate to say that the earth moves. In spite of this manoeuvre, Descartes leaves the reader in no doubt of his commitment to the theory that the solar system is constituted by a giant 'vortex' of swiftly moving particles with the sun at its centre (AT VIII 92; CSM I 253).

In 1644, the year of the publication of the *Principles*, Descartes visited France (after an absence of over 15 years from the country of his birth). Amongst those whom he saw in Paris was the Abbé Claude Picot, an old friend who had come to stay with him at Endegeest three years earlier. Picot now embarked, with Descartes' approval, on the task of translating the *Principles* into French. The version eventually appeared in 1647, and Descartes composed an important philosophical introduction (the *Lettre Préface à l'édition française*) to mark its publication. There is also evidence that he used the opportunity of a French edition to modify or expand parts of his original Latin text.[23]

Descartes also gave his approval to a French version of the *Meditations* made by Charles-Louis d'Albert, Duc de Luynes; this was published in 1647, together with a French version of the first six sets of Objections and Replies made by Descartes' disciple Claude Clerselier. While welcoming French translations of his Latin works, Descartes was equally concerned that his French works should be published in Latin, and the year 1644 saw the publication, in Amsterdam, of a Latin version of the *Discourse* and first two *Essays* by Étienne de Courcelles. It should be remembered that in seventeenth-century Europe Latin was still the principal language of the learned world, and publication in Latin was the most efficient way to reach an international readership.

From November 1644 till the summer of 1649, apart from a further visit to France in 1647, Descartes lived continuously at Egmond Binnen near Alkmaar. He enjoyed the quiet of the countryside, keeping to a simple routine and maintaining a careful diet based largely on produce from his kitchen garden. In April 1648, a young Dutchman Frans Burman, son of a Protestant minister, came to dine with Descartes, bringing with him a large selection of queries relating to the *Discourse*, *Meditations* and *Principles*. Burman took detailed notes on Descartes' replies to his questions, and the resulting document, the *Conversation with Burman*, throws an interesting light on how the 52-year-old Descartes viewed his achievements to date. Although his discussion of topics related to the *Meditations* manifests a continued concern for clarifying the metaphysical foundations of his philosophical system, Descartes shows most enthusiasm when talking of his contribution to physics: he describes his work on the principles of celestial motion as 'the source of the greatest pleasure for him to look back on' (AT V 171; CB 39). He also talks of his continuing interest in physiology, and his projected treatise on this subject which he had been working on during the winter of 1647/48. (This treatise was never in fact completed, and was published posthumously in 1664 under the title *Description du corps humain.*) Another topic alluded to in the interview is Descartes' dispute with his former supporter Henricus Regius, who had championed Descartes' philosophy at Utrecht, but whose interpretations of his views on the nature of mind Descartes had felt obliged to disavow in the *Comments on a Certain Broadsheet*, published at the end of 1647. Throughout the interview with Burman Descartes manifests a weary distaste for academic quibbling – particularly of the theological variety: he observes that 'the theologians have made such a habit of foisting every kind of doctrine onto theologians of the opposing school and then denigrating it, that they have completely mastered the art of denigration.' Bitter experience had taught Descartes how easy it was to become embroiled in such battles, and many of Burman's questions are parried with the careful rejoinder 'We must leave that for the theologians to explain' (AT V 159 and 176; CB 21 and 47).

In February 1649, Descartes received an invitation to the royal court at Stockholm from Queen Christina of Sweden. Descartes had corresponded with the Queen for several years and had sent her an early draft of his now complete and shortly to be published *Passions of the Soul*. The Queen had also read Descartes' *Principles*, and was sufficiently impressed with his work to request that he should come to Sweden to instruct her in philosophy (AT V 290; K 246; ALQ III 897). Descartes was at first very wary of accepting. 'Experience has taught me', he wrote to Pierre Chanut, French envoy at the Swedish court, 'that very few people, even if they have an excellent mind and a great desire for knowledge, can take the time to enter into my thoughts; so I have no grounds for hoping as much of a Queen who has an infinity of other preoccupations' (AT V 327; K 247). But after much hesitation and delay Descartes finally embarked for Sweden on 1 September. It was to be his last voyage. Once installed in Stockholm, he spent a depressing autumn during which he was employed in writing a pastoral comedy and composing verses to celebrate the Queen's birthday. The following January he began his task of giving tuition to the Queen, who required him to attend on her regularly at five o'clock in the morning. Within a month he had contracted pneumonia, and he died on 11 February.

French commentators are fond of contrasting the 'warmth of Touraine', the land of Descartes' birth, with the gloom of Stockholm, where he died.[24] But Descartes was no great heliophile, and during his years in North Holland he had no doubt experienced many hard winters. A more likely immediate cause for his weakened resistance to illness was the fact that he was obliged by royal command to interrupt his lifelong sleep patterns. Even as a schoolboy at La Flèche he had received special permission to 'lie in' in the mornings, and as an adult he normally rose about eleven; he reportedly found the extra hours in bed to be a fruitful time for philosophical reflection. It does not take great imagination to appreciate the strain imposed by having to get up in the middle of the night, several times a week, to give tutorials to the Queen. In a premonition that things might not work out well for him in Sweden, Descartes had composed a rather forlorn letter to Elizabeth, shortly after his arrival in Stockholm: 'If my views do not turn out to be agreeable to the Queen', he wrote, 'I shall at least have the comfort that this will give me the chance to return that much sooner to my solitude, without which I cannot except with great difficulty make any progress in the search for truth – that search wherein consists my chief good in this life' (9 October 1649: AT V 430; ALQ III 1110).

The notion of a solitary search for truth aptly describes the character of much of Descartes' life; and in a deeper sense (as will emerge in the chapters that follow) it also signals the character of much of his philosophy. Amongst the unpublished papers found in Stockholm after Descartes' death was an important unfinished dialogue with the highly significant title *The Search for Truth by Means of the Natural Light*. The opening sentences vividly convey the intensely individualistic nature of the Cartesian method, as well as the extraordinary ambitiousness of the revolutionary programme which he bequeathed to philosophy:

> I shall bring to light the true riches of our souls, opening up to each of us the means whereby we can find within ourselves, without any help from anyone else, all the knowledge we may need for the conduct of life, and the means of using it in order to acquire all the most abstruse items of knowledge that human reason is capable of possessing (AT X 496; CSM II 400).

Notes

1 Columbus's voyage was in 1492; Magellan's circumnavigation in 1522; Copernicus's *De Revolutionibus* appeared in 1543; Newton's *Principia*, 1687;

Franklin's experiments, 1752; Dalton's theory published 1808.

2 The *Siderius Nuncius* also reported observations of the mountains on the moon, which contradicted the Aristotelian doctrine of the perfect sphericity of all celestial bodies.

3 Galileo Galilei *Il Saggiatore* ('The Assayer') 1623 in Galileo, VI 232. For Descartes' views on mathematics in science, and the extent (often exaggerated) to which they matched those of Galileo, see ch. 4, below.

4 Francis Bacon *Novum Organum* I 46.

5 The metaphor of the tree of knowledge is also to be found in Bacon; see *de Augmentiis Scientiarum* 3 i.

6 Galileo, IV 317; the opponent in question was Colombo (see further Shea, 32ff.)

7 *Discourse on Floating Bodies* (Galileo, IV 87) cf. Shea, 42.

8 Molière, *La Malade Imaginaire* (1673) Act III.

9 *The Origins of Forms and Qualities* (1672) 12–13, cited in Alexander, 42.

10 It is not clear that all qualitative explanations must ultimately be circular. The circularity will be removed if the quality invoked can eventually be explained and analysed in terms of some fine structure or internal mechanism which produces the observed effects. This is the general direction in which Bacon, Descartes and Boyle all wanted to move.

11 That the honouring of the philosopher has overreached itself may be seen from the fact that the official address of Descartes' birthplace is now 'Maison de Descartes, Rue Descartes, *Descartes*'. The house in question, aptly described by the local syndicat d'initiative as 'une honnête maison bourgeoise du XV–XVIe siècle' is now a small museum which, however, contains little of note apart from the original parish register containing the entry for René's baptism.

12 Descartes is known to have stayed at La Flèche for eight or nine years, but the exact dates of his arrival and departure are uncertain. Baillet places Descartes' admission in the year of the College's foundation (Baillet, I 18).

13 Baillet, I 81ff. For a translation of the relevant passage, see Appendix.

14 Mersenne would have finished his studies at La Flèche before Descartes' arrival (cf. AT XII 37). It is possible, however, that the friendship between the two dates from as early as 1614 when Descartes may have visited Paris (see Baillet, I 37, for this view).

15 Descartes' three essays on *Optics*, *Meteorology* and *Geometry*, prefaced by the *Discourse on the Method*, were published anonymously in 1637, though the *Essays* were all written or conceived well before the *Discourse*. See CSM I 109f.

16 For further details see CSM I 79ff.

17 The 'first day' of the dialogue attacks the Aristotelian dichotomy between celestial and terrestrial bodies. Day two discusses the rotation of the earth and day three its annual revolution. Day four puts forward Galileo's (incorrect) theory that the tides can be explained by the diurnal and annual motion of the earth. The three characters in the dialogue represent (i) Galileo himself, (ii) a supporter of the traditional Aristotelian–Ptolomaic view and (iii) an intelligent amateur sympathetic to the new Galilean approach. It is interesting to note that Descartes' own dialogue, the *Search for Truth* (probably written early in the 1640s), has a closely parallel three-

part cast consisting of (i) a figure representing Descartes himself, (ii) an Aristotelian traditionalist and (iii) an intelligent amateur sympathetic to Descartes' philosophy. Descartes saw a copy of Galileo's *Dialogues* in August 1643 (it was lent him by Isaac Beeckman). See letters to Mersenne of April 1634 (AT I 285; K 25) and 14 August 1634 (AT I 303; ALQ I 501).

18   The edict of the Inquisition noted that Galileo had persisted in a doctrine which was 'false and contrary to holy scripture', 'even though he pretended that he was putting it forward hypothetically' (*quamis hypotetice a se illam proponi simularet*). This last clause particularly worried Descartes. See letters cited above, note 17, and ALQ I 497 and 501.

19   Ovid *Tristia* III iv 25. The original Epicurean maxim λαθέ βίωσας (*lathe biosas*) means literally 'escape notice having lived'.

20   The correct short title in English is *Discourse on the Method*; the common rendering 'Discourse on Method' is indefensible since it makes nonsense of the full title. The title of Descartes' most famous work has an unfortunate history of being misquoted: a French government commemorative stamp issued in 1950 to mark the tercentenary of Descartes' death depicted a book entitled 'Discours *sur* la méthode'.

21   Cf. Baillet, II 89f.

22   The Protestant prince Frederick, Elector Palatine, had become King of Bohemia in 1619, but was swiftly deposed by Catholic forces after the Battle of the White Mountain in 1620. Though the story that Descartes was present at this battle is unfounded, it is one of the ironies of history that he was enrolled with the Catholic forces who defeated and exiled the parents of his future friend and close correspondent. (See AT XII 609, and Baillet, I chs. 13 and 14.)

23   For some of this evidence see AT V 168 (CB 35); AT IX B *Avertissement*; CSM I 178.

24   Cf. Bridoux, p. vii. In a letter to Brasset of 23 April 1649, Descartes does express reservations about going to a land of 'bears, rocks and ice'. But although he refers in passing to the 'gardens of Touraine' where he was born, the land he says he fears to leave is not France but Holland 'a land where, if there is not as much honey as God promised to the Israelites, there is probably more milk' (AT V 349; ALQ III 917).

2

The Cartesian Method

Knowledge and Intuition

Descartes' early conviction that he was destined to found a new philosophical system was not based on the belief that he had glimpsed some profound and recondite mystery about the universe. Nor (though he was not an unduly modest man) did he attribute his mission to unique or superhuman intellectual endowments.[1] His central idea was a very simple one: that the truth, so far from being shrouded in mystery, was readily accessible to the ordinary human intellect, if only it could be directed aright.

This essentially optimistic vision contrasted strongly with the prevailing belief in the sixteenth and early seventeenth centuries that the attainment of knowledge was a profoundly difficult and complex business. The search for truth was seen as a laborious attempt to uncover occult powers and forces – for example, the hidden 'virtues' of plants and minerals, and the 'sympathetic and antipathetic' influences governing natural objects and events. The following extracts from the Swiss philosopher Paracelsus (writing in the century before Descartes) give some idea of the 'magical' approach to knowledge:

> Behold the *Satyrion* root, is it not formed like the male privy parts? Accordingly, magic discovered and revealed that it can restore a man's virility and passion. And then we have the thistle; do not its leaves prickle like needles? Thanks to this sign, the art of magic discovered that there is no better herb against pricking. The *Siegewurz* root is wrapped in envelope like armour; and this is a magic sign showing that like armour it gives protection against weapons. And the *Syderica* bears the image and form of a snake on each of its leaves, and thus according to magic it gives protection against every kind of poisoning . . .[2]

The rationale behind this rather quaint pharmacopoeia is that the Creator has provided certain clues to the hidden properties of plants which the magician has managed to decipher. At its best the 'magical' approach aims to enlighten mankind by uncovering what is hidden.[3] But at its worst it can degenerate into a cult of mystery and occultism for its own sake:

> The first *arcanum* is the *prima materia*, the second the *lapis philosophorum*, the third the *mercurius vitae*, the fourth the *tinctura*. The first confers new youth, the second purifies, the third renovates, the fourth transforms everything into a noble and indestructible being . . . But to write more about this mystery is forbidden . . .[4]

The invoking of occult powers, and supposed sympathetic and antipathetic virtues, continued to flourish well into the seventeenth century, as can be seen from the following explanation of magnetism provided by the English Rosicrucian Robert Fludd (1574–1637), who crossed swords with Descartes' friend Marin Mersenne in the 1620s:

> Now since every spirit and consequently this of the Loadstone, desireth to be nourished by that which is nearest and likest unto his own nature, the which nature and spirit is only found in iron, it happeneth, for this reason, that the inward martiall spirit of the Loadstone doth draw the body of iron unto it, and after an occult manner, doth seem to suck his nourishment out of it; I conceive, therefore, that the first salt in the Iron or Loadstone is partly of a hot and dry martiall nature, and consequently of a fiery earthly condition; and partly of a cold and dry, stiptick and saturnine faculty, which also it receiveth from its earth; and therefore there concurreth two testimonies of strange attraction in the Loadstone.[5]

From the start Descartes was convinced that the sciences need not be weighed down with such occult paraphernalia; true knowledge was open rather than hidden, simple rather than complex, clear and certain rather than murky and full of doubt. 'The sciences are at present masked' he wrote in an early notebook, 'but if the masks were taken off they would be revealed in all their beauty' (AT X 215; CSM I 3).

Philosophical knowledge as conceived by Descartes in his early writings has three main features, which we may label *unity*, *purity* and *certainty*. By insisting on the *unity* of knowledge, Descartes rejected the scholastic conception of science as a set of separate disciplines, each with its own methods and level of precision. The extent to which this 'separatist' view had become an entrenched dogma by the early seventeenth century is shown by the way in which Galileo was criticized by the Italian scholastics for using mathematical reasoning in natural science:

All the sciences and arts have their own principles and their own causes by means of which they demonstrate the special properties of their own object. It follows that we are not allowed to use the principles of one science to prove the properties of another. Therefore everyone who thinks he can prove natural properties with mathematical arguments is simply demented.[6]

In place of this separatist conception, which claimed to draw its authority from Aristotle, Descartes (whether or not he was consciously influenced by Plato) reverted to the older Platonic notion of philosophy as a unified system.[7] For Descartes, the various elements of the system are as coherent and interlinked as a set of theorems in mathematics. 'If we could see how the sciences are linked together', he wrote while still in his early 20s, 'we would find them no harder to grasp than the series of numbers' (AT X 215; CSM I 3). 'I had the idea', he later wrote of this period, 'that all the things that can fall under human knowledge are interconnected'; the connecting chain might be long but – as with a geometrical argument – each link in the chain could be quite simple and straightforward (AT VI 19; CSM I 120).

As for *purity*, Descartes felt that prevailing doctrines, though they might contain some elements of truth, were corrupted by a large mixture of incoherence and inaccuracy; what was needed was a system that was 'free from any taint of falsity' (AT X 364; CSM I 12). In his earliest major work, the *Regulae*, or *Rules for the Direction of the Understanding*, Descartes stresses that some truths of the requisite degree of purity have already been discovered by mankind – viz. those of arithmetic and geometry: 'They alone are concerned with an object so pure and simple that they make no assumptions that experience might render uncertain' (AT X 365; CSM I 12). The high standards characteristic of mathematics (in his later metaphysics Descartes claimed actually to have surpassed them[8]), were to remain an important inspiration for much of Descartes' philosophical work.

The notion of *certainty* brings us to what is probably the most discussed aspect of Descartes' conception of knowledge. In ordinary usage, one may often be said to 'know' something without being certain – at any rate 100 per cent certain – of its truth. But Descartes is not primarily concerned with 'epistemology' in the modern academic sense – with investigating the logical grammar of epistemic verbs, or with uncovering the standard criteria for knowledge claims. The philosopher, for Descartes, is the seeker after wisdom or understanding, one who *supra vulgus sapere cupit* – desires a level of knowledge that is above the ordinary (AT VII 32; CSM II 21). In the *Regulae* Descartes introduces the Latin term *scientia* as what is virtually a technical term to denote the kind of knowledge he is after. All *scientia*, he asserts, is 'certain and evident cognition' (Rule Two: AT X 362; CSM I 10). Later on in the same passage he enlarges on what is meant by certain cognition, contrasting it with that which is merely probable. Much scholastic philosophy, he remarks, is based on debating techniques which use 'probable syllogisms'; by this he seems to mean that although the arguments employed may be valid in the sense that they conform to acceptable logical patterns, the initial premises from which the arguments proceed have a status which is no better than probable. Descartes' own proposal is that, rather than starting from received opinions or from merely probable conjectures, we should begin from premises whose truth we can *intuit* (Rule Three: AT X 366; CSM I 13).

The term 'intuit' can mislead the modern reader into supposing that some mysterious non-rational faculty is involved; but what Descartes means by intuition is intellectual cognition of the simplest and most direct kind. For the educated seventeenth-century reader, the primary connotation of the Latin verb *intueri* which Descartes uses here would have been the quite literal and ordinary meaning of to 'see', 'gaze at', or 'look upon' which the verb has in classical usage. Descartes, then, is drawing on an implicit comparison between mental apprehension and ordinary ocular vision. The general comparison between understanding and seeing has a long ancestry: it is to be found in Plato and Plotinus, and plays a prominent role in the writings of Augustine.[9] In Descartes it is not confined to the use of *intueri*, but recurs in a number of different guises throughout his writings; its most striking manifestation, to be found again and again in both the early and the mature works, being the use of phrases like *lumen naturale, lumen naturae* and *lux rationis* ('natural light', 'light of nature', 'light of reason') to describe the mind's innate cognitive powers.[10]

If we cash out the comparison between mentally 'intuiting' and seeing with the eyes, it works something like this. Our vision is, to be sure, sometimes blurred or hazy; but in good light, when we look carefully at something which is 'right there' in front of us, we have a direct kind of awareness that seems quite simple and unproblematic. There is a proviso here: if the object has a very detailed structure, or is compounded of elements which I cannot discern clearly, or is in some other way complex, then what I 'see' may not be so straightforward a matter; but when the object in question is very simple, then my seeing – at least as far as my own internal awareness is concerned – is as straightforward as can be. There is the object in front of me: I see a cup, I see a table, I see that the cat is on the rug. So it is, Descartes' metaphor implies, with certain kinds of cognition.[11] As he later put it, 'I call a [mental] perception *clear* when it is present and accessible to the attentive mind –

just as we say that we see something clearly when it is present to the eye's gaze, and stimulates it with a sufficient degree of strength and accessibility' (*Principles* I, 45: AT VIII 22; CSM I 207). Here is the full definition of 'intuition' given in the *Regulae*:

> By 'intuition' I do not mean the fluctuating testimony of the senses, or the deceptive judgement of the imagination as it botches things together, but the conception of a clear and attentive mind, which is so easy and distinct that there can be no room for doubt about what we are understanding. Alternatively, and this comes to the same thing, intuition is the indubitable conception of a clear and attentive mind which proceeds solely from the light of reason . . . Thus everyone can mentally intuit that he exists, that he is thinking, that a triangle is bounded by just three sides and a sphere by a single surface, and the like (AT X 368; CSM I 14).

This early account of knowledge based on direct mental apprehension or intuition is not offered simply as a piece of conceptual analysis. The object is a practical one: Descartes' purpose in the *Regulae* is, as the title suggests, to provide a methodology, a set of principles for guiding or regulating the intellect in its quest for the truth. The essentials of the method are stated in Rule Five:

> The whole method consists entirely in the ordering and arranging of the objects on which we must concentrate our mind's eye if we are to discover some truth. We shall be following this method exactly if we first reduce complicated and obscure propositions step by step by simpler ones, and then, starting with the intuition of the simplest ones of all, try to ascend through the same steps to knowledge of all the rest (AT X 379; CSM I 20).[12]

One may be forgiven, however, for wondering exactly how helpful all this really is. The injunction to start with what is simplest may be sound enough, but there is a curious blandness and generality about it. Have we really got a new and exciting method of discovering the truth here? The growing impression, as one reads through the *Regulae*, of a rather pedestrian and obvious set of maxims, is reinforced when we arrive at Rule Eight, which tells us that 'if in the series of things to be examined we come across something which our intellect is unable to intuit sufficiently well, we must stop at that point and refrain from the superfluous task of examining the remaining items' (AT X 392; CSM I 28). Rule Nine tells us, hardly more excitingly, to 'concentrate our mind's eye on the smallest and easiest of matters and dwell on them long enough to acquire the habit of intuiting the truth distinctly and clearly' (AT X 400; CSM I 33). The message is clear – that the truth is within our grasp if we go for what is clear and simple, and avoid what is convoluted and obscure; but how exactly does the method function in practice?

Descartes does proceed to provide a number of examples of his method at work, but in the extant portions of the *Regulae* they are confined to what he calls 'perfectly understood problems'. These are, in effect, those problems which can be expressed in terms of a mathematical equation where all that is required for the solution is contained somewhere in the data. Now, 'reduce the problem to its simplest essentials and proceed step by step' may be sound advice when operating within 'closed' and formal disciplines such as arithmetic or algebra but the reader is bound to be left wondering whether Descartes has any warrant for supposing such a procedure can be 'extended to the discovery of truths in any field whatsoever' (AT X 374; CSM I 17).

The underlying worry here is about whether Descartes' concept of intuition has any useful application outside the mathematical sphere. It is, perhaps, reasonable to say that the intellect just 'sees' the truth of very elementary mathematical propositions such as 'a triangle has three sides', since the 'self-evidence' involved seems to depend directly on the definitions of the terms involved. But do we have any corresponding 'intuitions' of a non-mathematical kind which will serve as the basis for the solution of substantive philosophical or scientific problems? Part of the answer emerges in Rule Twelve, where Descartes introduces his doctrine of 'simple natures' – items which, we are told, the intellect recognizes as 'self-evident and never containing any falsity' (AT X 420; CSM I 45). The language which Descartes uses to talk about his simple natures is, by modern philosophical standards, somewhat imprecise. Sometimes they appear as fundamental concepts or conceptual categories, sometimes as the 'things' or 'objects' to which those concepts refer, and sometimes as elementary propositions or truths. What is clear is that Descartes divides the 'natures' into three main classes. First, there are 'intellectual' natures which the mind 'recognizes by a sort of innate light without the aid of any corporeal image'; it is recognition of these natures that enables us to understand what knowledge is, or what doubt or ignorance is, or what volition is. Second, there are 'corporeal' natures, such as shape, extension and motion, which are are 'recognized to be present only in bodies'. And thirdly there are 'common' natures such as duration and existence, which (as their name implies) may be ascribed either to corporeal or to intellectual items; the common natures also include 'common notions' – elementary logical truths such as 'things that are the same as a third thing are the same as each other' (AT X 419–20; CSM I 44–5). These various 'natures' function, according to Descartes, as the elementary building blocks from which all our knowledge is systematically constructed: 'The whole of human knowledge consists uniquely in our achieving a distinct perception of how all these simple natures contribute to the composition of other things' (AT X 427; CSM I 49).

The doctrine of the intuition of the simple natures by the intellect contains the germ of many developments to be found in Descartes' mature metaphysics. But as it stands, the doctrine has an unsatisfyingly static quality. The human mind, we are told, can achieve systematic and certain knowledge by starting with the cognition of what is self-evident. But beyond the insistence on the simplicity of the objects of such primary intuition, there is no mechanism offered for pointing the mind in the right direction, no procedure for weeding out the false from the true, no sense of movement, of the mind's struggle to get closer to the truth. Some ten years later, however, by the time he came to write the *Discourse on the Method*, Descartes had developed a more vivid sense of what was involved in the quest for true knowledge. In Part Two of the *Discourse*, to be sure, we have a recapitulation of the bland prescriptions of the *Regulae*, compressed into four rules; the third rule, for example, requires us to direct our thoughts 'in an orderly manner, beginning with the simplest and most easily known objects in order to ascend little by little, step by step, to knowledge of the most complex' (AT VI 18; CSM I 120). But in Part Four of the *Discourse*, what is presented in a remarkably concise paragraph is the outline of a new and much more dynamic philosophical approach. The key to this is what has come to be known as Descartes' 'method of doubt'; Descartes shows how the systematic rejection of beliefs which are open even to the slightest doubt can serve as a vehicle for the discovery of a reliable starting point for philosophy.[13] The celebrated passage is worth quoting in full:

> Since I now wished to devote myself solely to the search for truth, I thought it necessary to . . . reject as if absolutely false everything in which I could imagine the least doubt, in order to see if I was left believing anything that was entirely indubitable. Thus because our senses sometimes deceive us, I decided to suppose that nothing was such as they led us to imagine. And since there are men who make mistakes in reasoning, commiting logical fallacies concerning the simplest questions in geometry, and because I judged that I was as prone to error as anyone else, I rejected as unsound all the arguments I had previously taken as demonstrative proofs. Lastly, considering that the very thoughts we have while awake may also occur while we sleep without any of them being at that time true, I resolved to pretend that all the things that had ever entered my mind were no more true than the illusions of my dreams. But immediately I noticed that while I was trying thus to think everything false, it was necessary that I, who was thinking this, was something. And observing that this truth 'I am thinking, therefore I exist' was so firm and sure that all the most extravagant suppositions of the sceptics were incapable of

shaking it, I decided that I could accept it without scruple as the first principle of the philosophy I was seeking (AT VI 32; CSM I 127).

The Role of Doubt in Descartes' Philosophy

The doubts sketched out in the above passage are augmented and presented in much greater detail in the *Meditations*, published four years after the *Discourse*. The whole of the First Meditation is devoted to the discussing 'What can be called into doubt'. Descartes' dramatic presentation of the successive waves of doubt which engulf him may be divided, for convenience, into twelve phases.

1 Firstly, Descartes rejects the testimony of the senses: 'From time to time I have found that the senses deceive, and it is prudent never to trust completely those who have deceived us even once.'

2 But this doubt is limited in scope: the senses may deceive concerning tiny or distant objects, but there are some sense-based judgements which it seems I would be mad to doubt, e.g. that I am holding this piece of paper, or that I am sitting by the fire.

3 But now a fresh doubt arises: 'How often asleep at night, am I convinced of just such familiar events – that I am here in my dressing-gown, sitting by the fire – when in fact I am lying undressed in bed!' If it is possible that I am now dreaming, then even such seeming straightforward judgements as 'I am now sitting by the fire' may be open to doubt.

4 But dreams are presumably composed of elements originally drawn from real life, just as paintings of imaginary objects are made up of elements based on reality. So the world must presumably contain such general kinds of things as heads, hands and eyes.

5 Perhaps, however, just as a painter may produce a wholly imaginary creation, so the items which appear in my dreams may be utterly imaginary and unreal.

6 Yet it seems that even the most fictitious compositions must conform to certain very simple and universal categories, such as extension, shape, size, number, place and time; these items, at least, must surely be real.

7 From this it seems that 'arithmetic, geometry and other subjects of this kind which deal only with the simplest and most general things, regardless of whether they exist in nature or not, contain something certain and indubitable. For whether I am awake or asleep, two and three added together are five, and a square has no more than four sides.'

8   Yet now an even more worrying doubt occurs: could not God, since
    he is omnipotent, make me go wrong every time I add two and three
    or count the sides of a square?
9   Or perhaps there is no God. But in that case I was created not by a
    perfect God but from a series of chance events or some other
    imperfect chain of causes; and if my origins are so imperfect, it
    seems I have even less reason to be confident that my judgements
    are free from error.
10 The conclusion is that 'there is not one of my former beliefs about
    which a doubt may not be properly raised.'
11 In the closing stages of the Meditation, Descartes reflects that
    although, in the light of his reasoning so far, he ought to suspend all
    his previous beliefs, this is easier said than done: 'my habitual
    opinions keep coming back and despite my wishes they capture my
    belief which is at it were bound over to them as a result of long
    occupation and the law of custom.'
12 As an aid to maintaining his suspension of belief, Descartes
    therefore proposes to imagine that there is a 'malicious demon of the
    utmost power and cunning' who employs 'all his energies' in order
    to deceive him. Thus the whole external world may be a sham: 'the
    sky, the air, the earth, colours, shapes, sounds and all external
    things are merely the delusions of dreams which he has devised to
    ensnare my credulity.' The conclusion of the Meditation sees
    everything in doubt. In the metaphor which opens the Second
    Meditation, the whirlpool of doubt is all engulfing and bottomless –
    until Descartes manages to find his first firm foothold, the
    proposition 'I exist'.

Almost every phase of the above argument has been subjected to
exhaustive criticism by commentators; but many of the standard
objections are curiously irrelevant to what Descartes is actually trying to
do. In the case of the argument about the senses, for example, it is often
asked whether it is right wholly to reject the testimony of the senses
merely because *some* sensory data are unreliable; indeed, is not our very
ability to judge that the senses sometimes deceive us parasitic on the fact
they are sometimes non-deceptive? (For example, I find that the stick in
water is not really bent by taking it out and inspecting it or feeling it –
the later sensory data correct the earlier.)[14] This type of objection
scarcely touches Descartes, however, for his reasoning does not require
the premise that the senses are always deceptive. Indeed, he explicitly
asserts that, despite my experience that the senses sometimes deceive,
there are many sense-based beliefs about which doubt seems quite
unreasonable – for example the belief that I am sitting by the fire (AT VII

18; CSM II 12). At this stage of the argument, then, Descartes is not concerned to impugn all sensory judgements, but merely to raise the preliminary worry that they are not always reliable.

Nevertheless, there is no doubt that Descartes does see the general aim of the First Meditation as that of 'drawing the mind away from the senses' (Synopsis: AT VII 12; CSM II 9); and his *eventual* philosophical position on the role of sense-perception will severely downgrade the importance of the senses in favour of the intellect. Thus even when (as in the bent-stick-in-water case) an initial misleading sensory perception is apparently 'corrected' by a later reliable one, Descartes insisted in reply to his critics that 'the sense of touch alone does not suffice to correct the visual error; in addition we need to have some degree of reason which in this case tells us we should believe the judgement based on touch rather than that elicited by vision . . . Thus it is the intellect alone which corrects the error of the senses' (Sixth Replies: AT VII 439; CSM II 296). The senses alone, then, merely provide data for judgement; reason or intellect is needed to adjudicate when (as often happens) the data are contradictory.[15] It is worth adding, moreover, that Descartes' *final* verdict on the senses whill be even more radically dismissive than this. For he will eventually argue that even under optimum conditions, when the senses are doing their job properly and are in perfect working order, they are still in many cases an inherently confused and unreliable instrument for establishing the nature of the external world. But this is to take us far beyond the doubts of First Meditation, and into Descartes' general theory of our knowledge of the material world, which will be examined later on.[16]

The second main argument of Meditation One, the so-called 'dreaming argument', has also provoked considerable criticism. Some philosophers have tried to deny that the supposition that I might be dreaming makes sense; for my very ability to entertain self-conscious doubts about whether I am dreaming entails, so the objection runs, that I am not dreaming but awake. Thus, according to Norman Malcolm, 'If a person affirms, doubts, thinks or questions that he is sound asleep, then he is not sound asleep . . . If a person is in *any* state of consciousness, it follows that he is not sound asleep'.[17] This objection can be demolished quite swiftly. Dreams do occur, and however we describe them there is no avoiding the fact that they involve mental experiences which occur during sleep. Modern science, moreover, has been able to supply considerable detail about the frequency, duration, and physiological accompaniments of these experiences. A now well-established phenomenon is the 'false awakening', where the dreaming subject supposes that he has woken up and started his day (e.g. got dressed and ready for work), when in reality he is still asleep in bed. This strikingly supports

Descartes' contention that one may believe oneself to really Xing (e.g. sitting by the fire) when in fact one is asleep (and only dreaming one is Xing). As to the possibility of 'affirming, doubting, thinking and questioning' while asleep, considerable evidence has come to light in recent years about the curious phenomenon of the 'lucid dream', where some part of the dreamer's consciousness may be struck by some incongruous or bizarre feature of his dream experience, and he may begin, while still dreaming, to entertain doubts about whether he is awake. Subjects in sleep-laboratories have actually been able to signal to experimenters, by the use of a distinctive pattern of previously agreed eye-movements, the onset of this lucid-dreaming state; remarkably, they are able to produce such signalling when, from a physiological point of view, they are sound asleep.[18] Of course people vary widely as to the vividness and coherence of their dreams, and only a minority, it seems, have lucid dreams (Descartes himself may well have been such a one).[19] But what these cases clearly show is that it is possible to have a dream experience which includes the experience of wondering whether one is awake. It follows that the fact that a person has the experience of entertaining doubts about whether he is awake is no guarantee that he is in fact awake.

Other critics of the dreaming argument have taken issue with Descartes' insistence that 'there are never any sure signs by which being awake can be distinguished from being asleep' (AT VII 19; CSM II 13). The Oxford philosopher J. L. Austin reportedly maintained that there were about 50 such signs.[20] But again, this criticism hardly touches Descartes' actual position. For Descartes himself admits (later in the Sixth Meditation) that there are many tests which are serviceable for ordinary purposes for distinguishing dreaming from waking experiences (AT VII 89; CSM II 61). From the standpoint of the First Meditation, however, where the position is that we are not entitled to rely on anything that is not absolutely certain and indubitable, the ordinary criteria simply will not do: they fall short of providing an indubitable guarantee. Though Descartes himself does not go into this, there is a general objection to any proposed test T which is supposed to guarantee that I am awake (e.g. pinching myself and seeing whether it hurts), namely that it will always be conceivable that I should dream that T is satisfied; and so it follows that, as far as the individual doubter is concerned, the subjective experience of performing the test and finding it to be satisfied will not be sufficient to allay the doubt.[21]

Perhaps the most striking and dramatic doubt-inducing device which is introduced in the First Meditation is the supposition of the malicious demon bent on universal deception. This has drawn fire from philosophical critics who have complained that the supposition is empty:

if the demon's operations are undetectable, if all the sensory data which he produces in my mind are identical to those produced by the real world, then is there really any content in the suggestion that 'the earth, the sky and all external things' are merely illusions which he has devised to ensnare my judgement?[22] But long-term questions about the verifiability or factual content of the demon hypothesis are in a sense irrelevant to the perspective of the First Meditation, which is 'temporally indexed' – it is essentially linked to the 'here and now'. Descartes' scenario is confined to the first-person, present-tense reflections of the solitary doubter. From my perspective as a solitary doubter, all that is available to me here and now is a collection of subjective sensations, impressions and memories. True, my memory may tell me that this chair or this room or this house was here yesterday, or last week, or last year; but if the demon is at work then it is possible that 'my memory tells me lies, and none of the things it reports ever happened' (AT VII 24; CSM II 16). The introduction of the demon is a dramatic way of making the point that, from the subjective standpoint, I have no guarantee, here and now, that my present experience is anything more than a series of fleeting and insubstantial chimeras, with no basis in any stable and enduring reality.[23]

The doubts so far discussed all relate, in one way or another, to my knowledge of the nature or existence of the material world. And this is certainly Descartes' primary emphasis in the First Meditation, which he describes in his Synopsis as providing 'possible grounds for doubt about all things, *especially material things*' (AT VII 12; CSM II 9). But in the course of the Meditation he does mention one other, quite different kind of doubt – a doubt concerning my knowledge of mathematics – a subject which deals only with very simple and general terms 'without bothering whether they exist in the world or not'. Mathematical truths seem to survive the doubts raised by the dreaming argument, for 'whether I am awake or asleep two and three added together are five, and a square has no more than four sides' (AT VII 20; CSM II 14).[24] Descartes goes on to suggest, however, that although mathematical truths are immune from doubts about the existence of external objects, there may still be room for error in my intuition of such truths. Is it not possible that I could be made to 'go wrong every time I add two and three or count the sides of a square, or in some even simpler matter, if that is imaginable?' The apparent possibility of doubting even the most elementary truths of mathematics raises a new and fascinating set of difficulties; but because the problems involved affect the whole status of Descartes' reasoning in the *Meditations*, it will be best to postpone discussion of these difficulties until we come to assess the general structure of Descartes' system of knowledge in chapter 3.[25]

At this point it will be useful to pause and reflect on Descartes' purposes in constructing the complex barrage of doubts which we find in the *Discourse* and, more elaborately, in the *Meditations*. Particularly in the latter work, Descartes' dramatic manner of presenting the doubts is vividly original; but the arguments themselves are far from novel. There was a long history, going back as far as Plato, of argument and counter-argument concerning the reliability of the senses and the distinction between dreams and waking experiences – so much so that Thomas Hobbes, author of the Third Set of Objections to the *Meditations*, complained that Descartes had done less than justice to himself by dredging up this 'ancient material' (AT VII 171; CSM II 121). The scenario of the malicious demon may have been novel, but various forms of extreme (or 'Pyrrhonian') scepticism had been closely debated in the late sixteenth century (for example by Montaigne), and we know that varieties of such scepticism were still fashionable when Descartes wrote the *Meditations*.[26]

Descartes' intentions in presenting these arguments were frequently misunderstood – sometimes deliberately and maliciously so. His enemies went so far as to accuse him of giving comfort to the cause of atheism by raising excessive doubts (for example by suspending even his belief in God, in the First Meditation); Descartes replied that to accuse him of supporting the sceptics was as absurd as to accuse a doctor of promoting disease: the disease had to be described if it was to be cured (AT VII 574; CSM II 387). But in his desire to avoid the slur of scepticism, Descartes sometimes went a little too far the other way in presenting himself as the arch anti-sceptic. When goaded beyond endurance by the wilful misinterpretations of Pierre Bourdin, author of the Seventh Objections, Descartes retorted by describing himself as 'the first philosopher ever to overturn the doubts of the sceptics' (AT VII 550; CSM II 376). In fact, however, Descartes' true purpose was not to contribute to the philosophical debates over scepticism. He stressed many times that there was a sense in which the doubts he raised were not meant to be seriously entertained; they were 'hyperbolical' or 'exaggerated' – temporary expedients, eventually to be discarded with relief (AT VII 89; CSM II 61). But equally, many of the counter-arguments for allaying the doubts later on in the *Meditations* were regarded by Descartes as in one sense superfluous: 'the point of my arguments is not, in my view, that they prove what they establish – namely that there really is a world, and that human beings have bodies and so on – since no sane person has ever seriously doubted these things' (Synopsis: AT VII 16; CSM I 11). The crucial point about 'Cartesian doubt' is that it is essentially a means to an end; it is a mechanism for the production of first principles. Only by pushing doubt to its limits can we discover what is incapable of being doubted; and by discovering what survives even the most extreme and exaggerated doubts, we can establish foundations for philosophy that are unshakeably firm. That the point of the whole exercise is the search for first principles is made clear by Descartes at the outset of the *Meditations*: 'I realized that it was necessary, once in the course of my lifetime, to demolish everything completely and start again right from the foundations if I wanted to establish anything at all in the sciences that was stable and likely to last' (AT VII 17; CSM II 12). But how can it be proved that the foundations are sound? 'This is shown', Descartes later wrote, 'by the way in which I discovered them, namely by rejecting everything in which I could discover the least occasion for doubt; for it is certain that principles which it was impossible to reject in this way when one attentively considered them, are the clearest and most evident that the human mind can know' (Preface to *Principles*: AT IXB 9; CSM I 183).

First Principles

Probably the best known fact about Descartes' philosophy is that its starting point is the realization 'I am thinking, therefore I exist'. The famous dictum first occurs in its French form, *je pense, donc je suis*, in the 1637 *Discourse on the Method* (see passage quoted above, p. 28); a few years later, the even better known Latin formulation *cogito ergo sum* appears in the *Principles of Philosophy* and in the Latin translation of the *Discourse* (both published in 1644). But the most illuminating exposition of the train of thought which uncovers Descartes' first firm foothold occurs in the *Meditations* of 1641.

> I have convinced myself that there is absolutely nothing in the world, no sky, no earth, no minds, no bodies. Does it follow that I too do not exist? No: if I convinced myself of something then I certainly existed. But there is a deceiver of supreme power and cunning who is deliberately and constantly deceiving me. In that case I too undoubtedly exist if he is deceiving me; and let him deceive me as much as he can, he will never bring it about that I am nothing so long as I think that I am something. So . . . I must finally conclude that this proposition, *I am, I exist*, is necessarily true whenever it is put forward by me or conceived in my mind (AT VII 25; CSM II 17).

It will be noted that the famous canonical phrase *cogito ergo sum*, 'I am thinking therefore I exist', does not occur here; instead what is stressed is my knowledge of the simple and bald proposition *I exist*. But the connection with thinking is made readily apparent: what guarantees the certainty of 'I exist' is, Descartes suggests, a process of thought; the proposition 'I exist' is true *whenever it is conceived in the mind.*

Reflection on the phrase just quoted should make it clear that the correct English translation of *cogito/je pense*, when these words occur in Descartes' discussion of the certainty of his existence, should employ the so-called continuous present – 'I am thinking' – rather than the simple present, 'I think'. For what makes me certain of my existence is not some static or timeless fact about me – that I am one who thinks; rather, it is the fact that I am at this moment engaged in thinking. And so long as I continue to be so engaged, my existence is guaranteed. As Descartes puts it later on in the Second Meditation, 'I am, I exist – that is certain: but for how long? For as long as I am thinking' (AT VII 27; CSM II 18). As he puts it elsewhere, 'It is a contradiction to suppose that what thinks does not, *at the very time when it is thinking*, exist' (Principles I 7: AT VIII 7; CSM I 195).

This 'temporary' nature of the guarantee of my own existence explains much about the structure of 'the Cogito' (as Descartes' argument is standardly labelled nowadays).[27] Most logicians are accustomed to think of validity predominantly in terms of timeless, non-tensed propositions, and many commentators – Descartes' own contemporaries as well as modern critics – have managed fundamentally to distort Descartes' argument by trying to construe it 'blackboard fashion', as an exemplification of some timelessly valid formal structure. Thus Frans Burman, who interviewed Descartes in 1648, was much exercised over the question of whether the Cogito was syllogistic – that is, whether the reasoning exemplified the standard Aristotelian triadic pattern of a major premise, minor premise and conclusion, as follows:

> (i) Whatever is thinking exists (major)
> (ii) I am thinking   (minor)
> therefore (iii) I exist   (conclusion)

But Descartes had already made it clear in his Reply to the Second Set of Objections that this was not what he had in mind:

> When someone says 'I am thinking therefore I am, or I exist', he does not deduce existence from thought by means of a syllogism but recognizes it as something self-evident by a simple intuition of the mind. This is clear from the fact that if he were deducing it by means of a syllogism he would have to have had previous knowledge of the major premise 'Everything which is thinking is, or exists'; yet in fact he learns it from experiencing in his own case that it is impossible that he should think without existing. It is in the nature of the mind to construct general propositions on the basis of our knowledge of particular ones (AT VII 140; CSM II 100).

In his comments to Burman, Descartes enlarges on this somewhat. It is possible, he admits, to regard a major premise as 'implicitly presupposed' when I arrive at knowledge of my own existence. But the meditator is certainly not explicitly aware of any such premise. When I infer my own existence, says Descartes, 'I attend only to what I experience inside myself – for example *I am thinking therefore I exist*. I do not pay attention in the same way to the general notion *whatever is thinking exists*' (AT V 147; CB 4).

The message is clear: that as far as the individual meditator is concerned, arriving at knowledge of one's existence is a matter of recognizing a particular fact that is true in one's own case; there is no need for the meditator to construct any formal syllogism. (This does not, of course, explain *how* the certainty of the meditator's train of thought is guaranteed; this remains to be examined.)

Some modern commentators have suggested that the validity of the Cogito hinges on a concealed premise of even greater generality than 'Whatever is thinking exists' – namely the principle that whatever has attributes must exist. On this view, the Cogito argument could be set out as follows:

$$\text{(i) } (x)(F)(Fx \rightarrow (\exists y)(x = y))$$

              Roughly: if any item has an attribute, then the subject of that attribute exists

$$\text{(ii) } Fa$$

              I have the attribute of thought

$$\text{therefore (iii) } (\exists y)(a = y)$$

              I exist

Now it is undeniably true that Descartes does elsewhere record his allegiance to the standard logical maxim, *Nihili nulla sunt attributa*, – 'Nothingness has no attributes' (AT VIII 8; CSM I 196). So he would agree that there cannot be 'floating' attributes or properties; a property cannot belong to nothing but must be assigned to some subject. But it is highly implausible to suppose that he is relying on this maxim when he infers his own existence in the Second Meditation. For he explicitly asserts, later on in the *Meditations*, that there are objects (e.g. triangles) to which we can assign properties *without committing ourselves to their actual existence* (AT VII 64; CSM II 45). So the maxim 'Nothingness has no attributes' cannot entail that all property attribution presupposes an actually existing subject; all it implies is that properties must belong to subjects of some kind – though these may well be items like triangles or unicorns which perhaps fall short of having actual existence.

There is good reason, then, to suppose that Descartes would have rejected a 'formalized' interpretation of the Cogito of the type just discussed. And even in the case of the syllogistic interpretation, where he seems to concede that the Cogito *could* be represented in terms of some formal syllogistic pattern, he appears to want to say that such a formulation is a distortion of the way in which the meditator actually arrives at knowledge of his existence. But this stress on the particularity of the individual meditator's cognition of his existence still leaves some questions unanswered. The formal approach, whatever its failing, does at least attempt to give an account of how the conclusion 'I exist' gets its validity. And if the formal approach is rejected as a distortion of Descartes' intentions, then it seems that some work will have to be done to show exactly how Descartes is entitled to claim that the pronouncement 'I am thinking so I exist' has a special self-evidence and certainty.

The most striking feature about the accounts Descartes himself gives of the Cogito argument is that the certainty involved stems from the fact that the meditator has pushed his doubt to the limit. The final wave of doubt in the First Meditation involved the exaggerated hypothesis of the demon bent on universal deception: any of my beliefs might be false, because the demon might be deceiving me. But if I am in doubt, if I am entertaining the possibility that I might be deceived, then the very fact that I am around to entertain the doubt shows that I must exist. As Descartes puts it in his dramatic dialogue *The Search for Truth*, which was probably composed about the same time as the *Meditations*: 'You exist, and you know that you exist, and you know this just because you are doubting' (AT X 515; CSM II 410). The point is reinforced later on, as follows:

> If it is true that I am doubting (I cannot doubt that), it is equally true that I am thinking, for what is doubting if not thinking in a certain kind of way? . . . I exist, and I know this fact because I am doubting, i.e. because I am thinking (AT X 521; CSM II 415).

The crucial point here is, that *doubting is a special case of thinking*. So, the proposition 'I am thinking' is indubitable in a special way: doubting it confirms its truth. This special feature explains Descartes' frequent insistence that various other premises for deriving the conclusion 'I exist' will not do. I cannot say 'I am breathing therefore I exist' or 'I am walking therefore I exist', since it is possible to doubt the premises involved. (I may be dreaming, in which case I am not walking, but lying in bed; I may not have a body at all, in which case 'I am breathing' would be false.) But it is not only premises with corporeal implications that are suspect. Even a mentalistic premise like 'I am willing' or 'I am hoping' would not, it seems, have the required kind of indubitability. 'I doubt that I am hoping' is not indubitable in the relevant sense: doubting that one is hoping does not entail that one is hoping, since doubting is not a case of hoping. Only a premise which refers to an act of *thinking*, construed narrowly as a piece of 'cogitation' will have the property of having its truth confirmed by the very act of doubting it. The validity of the Cogito argument may now be defended, as follows. First, the premise 'I am thinking' has a special kind of indubitability, along the lines just explicated. Second, given that I am indubitably aware that I am at this moment thinking, then my own existence necessarily follows. For so long as I am actually engaged on this activity, then I cannot possibly not exist.

On the above interpretation of *cogito ergo sum*, which may be called a 'narrow' or 'restricted' interpretation, the premise of the argument must be construed as referring to a 'cogitative' act – an act of a specifically intellectual kind. *Volo ergo sum* ('I am willing therefore I am') or *sentio ergo sum* ('I am having a sensation therefore I am') will not do; for since 'I doubt that I am willing' does not entail 'I am willing' and 'I doubt that I am having a sensation' does not entail 'I am having a sensation', neither of these non-intellectual acts have the right kind of indubitability. Many commentators, however, support a much wider interpretation of the argument according to which any mental act whatsoever will do as a premise for the Cogito. In favour of the wide interpretation is the fact that Descartes often defines the concept of 'thought' (Lat. *cogitatio*; Fr. *pensée*) in a broad way, so as to include in its scope all conscious acts. In the formal definition provided in the Second Replies he says: 'I use the term *thought* to include everything that is within us in such a way that we are immediately aware of it. Thus all the operations of the will, the intellect, the imagination and the senses are thoughts' (AT VII 160; CSM II 113). And most tellingly, in the *Principles*, Descartes seems specifically to commit himself to saying that any mental act will do as a premise for the Cogito.

> By the term *thought*, I understand everything which we are aware of as happening within us, in so far as we have awareness of it. Hence, thinking is to be identified here not merely with understanding, willing and imagining, but also with sensory awareness. For if I say 'I am seeing or I am I walking therefore I exist', and take this as applying [not to bodily activities but] to the actual sense of awareness of seeing or walking, then the conclusion is quite certain, since it relates to the mind, which alone has the sensation or thought that it is seeing or walking (*Principles* I, 9: AT VIII 7; CSM I 195).

On the wider interpretation, what guarantees the certainty of the premise 'I am Xing' (where 'Xing' refers to any mental activity) is that Descartes takes it as true by definition that the mind has evident awareness of all its actions (this is sometimes called the doctrine of the 'perfect transparency of the mind'). A 'thought', in the wide sense, is *defined* as that of which I am immediately aware. Thus, if I have a visual sensation, or a sensation of walking, or if I am consciously willing or hoping or believing something, then in all these cases activity is going on of which I have an immediate and self-evident awareness. Hence I can with certainty assert 'cogito' (in the wide sense) which comprises any conscious experience, and then proceed to infer my existence.[28]

This interpretation is philosophically less satisfying than the narrow interpretation for two reasons. First, it rests on the doctrine of the perfect epistemological transparency of the mind, which is a doctrine for which one might have expected Descartes to *argue*. No such argument is to be found in the various presentations of the Cogito. Yet why should *all* my mental states be impervious to the demon's wiles? Why is it not conceivable that the demon might deceive me into believing I have a desire or a hope, when this is not in fact the case? In the various discussions of the Cogito we find no attempt to rule out this worry. Secondly, the wide interpretation somehow fails to capture the sense in which the certainty of the Cogito is directly 'extruded' as it were, from the method of doubt. It is hard to read the definitive presentations of the Cogito, in the *Meditations* and *Discourse*, as designed to convey the impression that certainly of one's existence arises from *any* mental activity; the natural and most obvious impression is that the certainty arises from the meditator's specifically intellectual activities of reflecting, pondering and doubting.

But in spite of these unsatisfactory features attaching to the 'broad' interpretation, there seems no getting round passages like those quoted above from the *Principles* which imply that any mental act will do. In order to reconcile this conflict between the narrow and the broad interpretations of the Cogito argument, it is necessary to ask *why* Descartes, when explaining what he means by the term 'thought', defines it in such broad terms. It is sometimes suggested that Descartes was simply following ordinary seventeenth-century practice which allowed *pensée* in French and *cogitatio* in Latin to be used in a wider sense than the English 'thought'. Yet there is plenty of evidence from the correspondence that Descartes' use of *pensée* and *cogitatio* was puzzling to his contemporaries; he frequently had to stipulate that he was using the terms in a specially wide sense, in order to avoid being misunderstood.[29] But for all that, the stipulation Descartes makes is not a case of an arbitrary or perversely idiosyncratic redefinition. The reason he has for classifying such widely varied activities as understandings, willings, lovings, hatings, imaginings and sensings as kinds of 'thought', is that in each case there is a narrowly intellectual act of awareness involved. Thought is defined in the passages just quoted above from the Second Replies and the *Principles* as that which is within us in such a way that we are aware (*conscius*) of it, or have awareness (*conscientia*) of it. Now the crucial point is that this awareness will not of course be a volition, or an act of imagination or a case of loving or hoping or fearing; it will be a specifically intellectual, reflective activity.[30]

Following the full implications of Descartes' wide definition of 'thought' thus turns out, in the end, to lend support to a narrow interpretation of what gives the Cogito argument its certainty. Whatever mental act the meditator engages upon, there will always be a narrowly intellectual element involved – an act of reflective awareness. And such reflection will be indubitable in the strict sense already explained: doubting that one is reflecting is impossible, since doubting is itself a case of reflection. So whether the meditator starts from *cogito* in the broad sense, which includes any mental conscious act, or *cogito* in the narrow sense which refers to the reflective activities of the intellect, his mental activity will always comprise *thinking* in the strict and narrow sense; and being unable to doubt that he is thinking (since doubting is a species of thinking) he has an indubitable premise from which to derive the certain conclusion that he exists.

Although the above reconstruction of 'I am thinking therefore I exist' does not formally invoke any concealed premises, in order for the meditator to be able to arrive at knowledge of his own existence by the route sketched some prior knowledge on his part must be presupposed. First, in order to know indubitably that he is thinking, he will have to know what is meant by thinking, and he will have to know that doubting is an instance of such thinking. And second, in order to infer the necessity of his existing so long as he is thinking, he will have to know that in order actually to be engaged on the activity of thinking, it is necessary to exist. This may seem quite a bit to presuppose; but when discussing the Cogito argument in the *Principles*, Descartes readily admits that this kind of prior knowledge is indeed required:

> When I said that the proposition *I am thinking therefore I exist* is the first and most certain of all to occur to anyone who philosophizes in an orderly way, I did not in saying that deny that one must first know what thought, existence and certainty are, and that it is impossible that that which is thinking should not exist (*Principles* I 10: AT VIII 8; CSM I 196).

This last point brings out an important and insufficiently appreciated feature of Descartes' argument. The Cogito is only the 'first step' of Descartes' system in the sense that it is the first *existential* truth that he arrives at; it is the first sure information he has about what actually and really exists. But this information does not, as it were, come out of a complete vacuum. In order to arrive at such knowledge, indeed in order to meditate at all, the Cartesian doubter must already have at his disposal

a whole apparatus of fundamental concepts which he can manipulate
clearly and rationally. He must know what thought is, what doubt is,
what existence is, and so on. The necessity for possessing these
fundamental conceptual (or linguistic)[31] intuitions is never questioned by
Descartes; and this in turn shows that the doubts of the First Meditation
are not intended to be as radical as is sometimes supposed. Descartes is
not trying to 'validate reason' or to reconstruct the entirety of human
cognition from the bottom up – that would be a wildly impossible
project. His goal is the more modest one of establishing secure
foundations for the sciences, and showing that it is possible, without
making any existential presuppositions, to achieve systematic knowledge
of the world, of what exists. And by engaging in a systematic programme
of doubt he manages, successfully, to show that there is one being –
himself – whose actual existence cannot be doubted.[32]

But Descartes' first insight, reliable though it is, has, as we have
already noted, a curiously temporary and provisional character. The
meditator has knowledge of his own existence only as long as he
continues to reflect on his thinking and continues the (unsuccessful)
attempt to doubt that he is thinking. The monumental task which still
faces Descartes is to transform this isolated act of cognition from a
fleeting insight into the basis for a solid and permanent system of
knowledge. The job of the next chapter will be to examine how he
attempts this task and to decide how far he is successful.

Notes

1   In the opening of the *Discourse* Descartes observes: 'I have never presumed
   my mind to be in any way more perfect than that of the ordinary man' (AT
   VI 2; CSM I 111). This is not merely a conventional gesture towards
   modesty: the point is that each man has, for Descartes, an equal share of the
   'natural light' – an innate, God-given power of reason whereby we may
   distinguish the true from the false. The reason so many go astray, Descartes
   explains, is that they do not direct their reason aright. See letter to Mersenne
   of 16 October 1639 (AT II 598); *Conversation with Burman*, (AT V 175; CB 45
   and 113–4); and *Search for Truth* (AT X 495–8; CSM II 400–1).
2   Paracelsus, I/13 (translated in Jacobi, 197).
3   'It is God's will that his secrets should become visible; it is his will that they
   become manifest and knowable through the works of man who has been
   created in order to make them visible' (Paracelsus, I/12 59; Jacobi, 183).
4   Paracelsus, I/13 138; Jacobi, 222.
5   From *Philosophica Moysaica* (1638) quoted in Craven 191. Mersenne in his
   Commentary on Genesis (1628) had accused Fludd of heresy and unlawful
   magic. For details of the controversy see Craven, ch. 4. For a discussion of
   occultism in the seventeenth century see G. McD. Ross, 'Occultism and

Philosophy' and S. Schaffer, 'Occultism and Reason' in Holland, 95ff (where it is argued that the seventeenth-century context was such as to make it difficult to draw a clear contrast between 'Scientific' and 'Occultist' thinking).

6   *Considerazioni . . . da Accademico Incognito* (Pisa, 1612) in Galileo, IV 385; cited in Shea, 1972, 34/5.

7   For Aristotle, each subject has its own methods and level of precision or *akribeia*. See *Nicomachean Ethics* Bk I ch. 2. For the unity of knowledge in Plato see *Republic* 511.

8   'If you were to go to the mathematicians and cast doubt on all the things I cast doubt on in my metaphysical enquiries, then absolutely no mathematical proof could be given with certainty; whereas I went on to give metaphysical proofs in spite of the doubt. So the proofs in metaphysics are more certain than those in mathematics' *Conversation with Burman*: AT V 177; CB 49.

9   See Plato *Republic* 514–8; Plotinus *Enneads* III viii 11 and V iii 17; Augustine *De Trinitate* XII xv 24: 'the mind when directed to intelligible things in the natural order, according to the disposition of the Creator, sees them in a certain incorporeal light which is *sui generis*, just as the corporeal eye sees adjacent objects in the corporeal light.'

10 *Lumen naturale* and *lumen naturae* are the phrases most commonly found in the *Meditations* and *Principles*. For the phrase *lux rationis* ('light of reason') see *Rules for the Direction of the Understanding*: AT X 368; CSM I 14. Commenting on the 'light' metaphor Descartes observed to Hobbes: 'As everyone knows, a "light" in the intellect means transparent clarity of cognition' (AT VII 192; CSM II 135).

11 As will emerge, Descartes in fact maintains that the perception of the intellect is in fact vastly superior to anything that could be provided by the sense of vision, or indeed any of the senses. See below ch. 4, p. 80 and ch. 6, p. 136.

12 It should not be supposed that Descartes' doctrine of intuition is entirely original. The standard Aristotelian account of demonstrative knowledge is that it begins with *nous* (intuition) of first principles or axioms and then proceeds by *apodeixis* (deduction) to establish their logical consequences (*Posterior Analytics* 13a). Descartes seems to follow this terminology when he says in Rule Two that in addition to intuition there is another mode of knowing, deduction 'by which we mean the inference of something as following necessarily from other propositions' (AT X 369; CSM I 15). Each step in the deductive chain must, however, be directly intuited if the reasoning is to be valid. For an interesting view of the contrasts between Descartes' and Aristotle's accounts of intuition and deduction, see Marion (I), 60ff.

13 Although in the *Regulae* Descartes does mention indubitability as a feature of genuine knowledge (e.g. in Rule Two, title), he does not there exploit its use as a touchstone in establishing the foundations of knowledge.

14 The bent stick example is raised by the authors of the *Sixth Objections* (AT VII 418; CSM II 282).

15 The crucial role of reason shows that Descartes' opening comment in Meditation One, 'Whatever I have so far accepted as true I have acquired

from or through the senses' (AT VII 18; CSM II 12) is very far from representing his final and considered view on the origins of human knowledge. In the First Meditation Descartes is merely canvassing the views of 'the man who is only just beginning to philosophize' (see *Conversation with Burman*: AT V 146; CB 3).

16 See below, chs 4 and 6, pp. 80ff and 136ff.

17 See Norman Malcolm, 'Dreaming and Scepticism', *Philosophical Review* LXV (1956) 14–37. Reprinted in Doney, 61–2.

18 See Celia Green, *Lucid Dreams* (Green, chs 1, 4 and 13). Lucid dreams, like ordinary dreams, occur during so-called 'paradoxical' or 'REM' sleep when normal muscular activity is suspended – except for eye movements. It is this exception that gives rise to the possibility of the sleeper's being able to signal the onset of the lucid dreaming state. In the experiments conducted by M. Schatzman and P. Fenwick at St Thomas's Hospital, London, subjects were asked e.g., to glance to the left five times in quick succession when they became aware that they were dreaming. The subjects on waking reported that they had complied, during their dreams, and records of their eye movements showed, during the REM sleep, a characteristic pattern of five swerves to the left. (See P. Fenwick et al., 'Lucid Dreaming', *Biological Psychology* (1984) 243–52).

19 See appendix.

20 J. L. Austin, cited in Kenny, 29; cf. Austin, 48.

21 According to Green, lucid dreamers sometimes begin to wonder whether they might be dreaming but 'decide' (wrongly) that they are awake. See Green, ch. 13.

22 See O.K. Bowsma, 'Descartes' Evil Genius', *Philosophical Review* LVIII (January 1949).

23 Compare Meditation Two: 'I will suppose that everything I see is spurious . . . Body, shape, extension, movement and place are chimeras' (AT VII 24; CSM II 16). It should be noted, however, that the precise role of the malicious demon in Descartes' reasoning is a matter of debate. Some see the hypothesis as designed (in part) to cast doubt on the truths of logic and mathematics; for this view see Frankfurt, 75ff. For the view expressed in the text, that the demon's role is principally to reinforce doubts about the external causes of my present experience, see J. G. Cottingham, 'The role of the malignant demon', *Studia Leibnitiana* VIII (1976), 257ff. See also Gouhier, 150ff, and ALQ II 408ff.

24 Descartes' Jesuit critic Pierre Bourdin objected that 'there are no limits to what a dreamer may not "prove" or believe'; and he cites the case of a man who 'when falling asleep, heard the clock strike four and shouted out "That clock must be going mad; it has struck one o'clock four times!" ' (AT VII 457; CSM II 306). Descartes in reply acknowledges that dreams may be indistinct and confused, but insists that if one *does* manage to have a clear and distinct thought (e.g. of the kind 'two and three make five'), then it must be true, irrespective of any doubts about whether one is awake (AT VII 461; CSM II 310).

25 See below, ch. 3, pp. 66ff.

26 For the dreaming argument, cf. Plato *Theaetetus*, 158. For more information on fashionable varieties of scepticism in the sixteenth and seventeenth

centuries see Popkin, chs. II and III, and Curley, chs. I and II. Professor Curley sees Montaigne as a possible source for the deceiving God hypothesis (though the passages he cites contain little more than the barest hint of the idea; Curley, 38). It seems possible that Augustine's argument *si fallor sum* ('if I am deceived I exist') – (*De Libero Arbitrio* II iii 7) may have suggested to Descartes the possibility of constructing a scenario of systematic and universal deception in order to establish the irrefutable certainty of one's own existence.

27 Since Descartes does not always employ the formulation *cogito ergo sum*, and since there is dispute among commentators as to how exactly to construe Descartes' reasoning (e.g. is he *inferring* existence from thought, or simply recognizing his existence as self-evident?), it is convenient to have a general non-question-begging label for the procedure whereby Descartes establishes the certainty of his own existence. The somewhat awkward label 'the Cogito' meets this need, and is probably here to stay. (What Descartes would have made, however, of some of the wilder ways in which the phrase '*le Cogito*' is used by some of his modern compatriots, one shudders to think. Compare Gueroult: 'The Cogito, as a substance – in the epistemological sense – is, according to Cartesian terminology, something "concrete" and something complete' (Gueroult, 30). Here 'the Cogito' means something like 'the self'; but only a few sentences away Gueroult uses it as a label for an *affirmation* (the affirmation of one's own existence).)

28 For the wide interpretation, see Kenny, 45f. For the kind of analysis which points towards a more restricted interpretation, see B. Williams, 'The Certainty of the Cogito' in Doney, 88ff. In evaluating different interpretations of the Cogito, it is important to distinguish two quite different properties of mental states: *transparency* (the fact that if I am in a given state then I am automatically aware of being in that state), and *self-confirmingness* (the fact that if I am aware of being in a given state then that awareness must be correct, since doubting it confirms the truth). Any conscious state will of course be transparent; but only narrowly intellectual acts such as thinking and doubting will be self-confirming. (Cf. Bernard Williams's distinction between *evidence* and *incorrigibility* in Williams, ch. 3, where there is an elegant discussion of the epistemological status of various mentalistic propositions.)

29 For the view that Descartes' usage was in accordance with tradition see Anscombe and Geach, xxlvii; but for Descartes' need to explain his wide use of the term, cf. letter to Reneri for Pollot of April 1638 (AT II 36; K 51). For further discussion of this issue see J. Cottingham, 'Descartes on Thought', *Philosophical Quarterly* 29 (July 1978) 551–55.

30 Cf. Descartes' reported comment in the *Conversation with Burman*: 'to be conscious is to think and to reflect on one's thought' (*conscium esse est cogitare et reflectere supra suam cogitationem*; AT V 149; CB 7).

31 That the solitary Cartesian thinker is making use of linguistic concepts might be thought already to presuppose a public world outside – public conventions and rules of language – in which case Descartes' attempt to start from his own consciousness and move outwards to establish the existence of an external world is self-defeating. This criticism is suggested by Ludwig Wittgenstein's celebrated argument against the possibility of a private

language, according to which there can be no language without public criteria for the correct use of terms (Wittgenstein, I 243). Descartes' (shaky) position appears to be that linguistic terms are merely the outward clothing of inner thoughts which are directly manifest to the thinker. Cf. his reply to Hobbes at AT VII 178; CSM II 126.

32   The limited 'success' ascribed to Descartes here remains subject to the criticism referred to in note 31, above. That Descartes' principal aim is to establish solid foundations for the sciences is suggested by the opening paragraph of Meditation One. The view that he has in mind the more radical task of 'validating reason' is expounded in H. Frankfurt, 'Descartes' Validation of Reason', *American Philosophical Quarterly* II (April 1965), reprinted in Doney. The question of whether Descartes ever calls into doubt the intellect's intuition of fundamental logical and conceptual truths is discussed more fully in chapter 3 below.

3

From Self to God to Knowledge of the World

The proposition 'I am thinking, therefore I exist' which Descartes says he can 'accept without scruple' as the 'first principle' of the philosophy he is seeking (AT VI 32; CSM I 127), does not on the face of it look a very promising starting point for developing an entire system of knowledge. If Descartes is to remain true to his resolve – to 'be so careful and precise as to take nothing as true if I am not as sure of it as I am of the certain fact that I exist and am thinking' (AT X 526; CSM II 419) – then there seems a risk that he will remain isolated in the secure but ultimately unproductive realm of subjective self-awareness, unable to proceed any further without risk of error. In the words of the imaginary objector in Descartes' dialogue *The Search for Truth*: 'You seem to me like an acrobat who always lands on his feet, so constantly do you go back to your "first principle". But if you go on in this way, your progress will be slow and limited. How are we always to find truths such that we can be as firmly convinced of them as we are of our own existence?' (AT X 526; CSM II 419).

Descartes' way forward is not to launch directly into an attempt to establish the existence and nature of the external world. Rather, he takes what may seem to the modern reader to be the curiously indirect route of seeking first to prove the existence of God – the 'true God, in whom all the treasures of wisdom and the sciences lie hid' (AT VII 53; CSM II 37). His line of thought is this: If I am *not* the creature of a perfect and benevolent God, but owe my existence to a chain of imperfect causes, my nature might, for all I know, be such that I am deceived even in matters which seem to me most evident (AT VII 21; CSM II 14. Cf. AT VII 36; CSM II 25). But if, on the other hand, it can be established that I was brought into existence by a perfect creator, then it will follow that my fundamental innate ideas or notions must have some foundation of truth: 'for otherwise it would not be possible that God, who is all perfect and all truthful, should have placed them in me' (AT VI 40; CSM I 131).[1] Given this 'foundation of truth', Descartes has hopes of developing a reliable corpus of knowledge about the world around him.

The point is *not* that, if I can prove the existence of a benevolent creator, the achievement of knowledge will suddenly become easy and unproblematic; for many of the beliefs we have formed since childhood are confused or erroneous and Descartes insists that it will still need diligence and effort to eradicate them (AT VIII 35ff; CSM I 218ff). But if we are careful to restrict our judgements to 'clear and distinct perceptions', relying on the fundamental innate truths which God has implanted in us, then there is hope of moving forward without being plagued at every stage by obsessive doubts about whether our perceptions are true. The way is open, says Descartes, for achieving 'full and certain knowledge of countless matters' – not just concerning myself but concerning 'corporeal nature' (AT VII 71; CSM II 49). Knowledge of God opens up the possibility of our being able to achieve understanding of the fundamental principles of the entire physical universe. (It might be objected at the outset that the task Descartes has set himself here is an impossible one: if there can be no reliable knowledge until after God's existence is proved, then how will it be possible to construct a reliable proof of God's existence in the first place? This fundamental objection to Descartes' procedure will be looked at later on, after the details of Descartes' arguments for God's existence have been examined.)

The Trademark Argument

Descartes' first argument for God's existence (first in the 'order of discovery' which is followed in the *Discourse* and the *Meditations*)[2] follows on directly from his initial awareness of his own existence. Not yet being assured of the existence of any external world, Descartes cannot take the most popular traditional route of the theologians – viz. that of starting from observed effects in the world (such as motion, or order) and inferring the existence of God as their cause (e.g. as prime mover or orderer). As it turns out, Descartes' approach *is* a causal one; but the 'effects' which it focuses on belong entirely within the mind of the meditator. His argument, which has been nicknamed the 'Trademark Argument', because it invokes the idea that God has placed within us the idea of himself 'to be as it were the mark of the craftsman stamped on his work' (AT VII 51; CSM II 35), may be set out in four phases, as follows:

1 The meditator starts by making an inventory of the ideas which he finds within himself. Amongst these he finds the idea of 'a supreme God, eternal, infinite, omniscient, omnipotent and the Creator of all things that exist apart from him' (AT VII 40; CSM II 28). The presence of this idea of a perfect being is the first premise of the

argument (so far, of course, there is nothing to show that anything corresponding to this idea actually exists).

2 The second premise of the argument is a principle which Descartes says is self-evident or 'manifest by the natural light', namely that 'there must be at least as much reality in the efficient and total cause as in the effect of that cause' (AT VII 40; CSM II 28). This principle, which may be called the 'Causal Adequacy Principle' implies that if there is some item X having the property F, then the cause which produced X, whatever it may be, must possess at least as much F-ness as is to be found in X itself. Thus 'a stone', says Descartes, 'cannot be produced except by something which contains . . . everything to be found in the stone; similarly heat cannot be produced except by something of at least the same order of perfection as heat' (ibid.). In defending his principle Descartes remarks that it is a version of the fundamental axiom *Ex nihilo nihil fit* ('Nothing comes from nothing'): 'For if we admit that there is something in the effect that was not previously present in the cause, we shall also have to admit that this something was produced by nothing' (Second Replies: AT VII 135; CSM II 97).

Before proceeding to stage 3, it is necessary to explicate some technical terminology which Descartes now introduces. Ideas are conceived of by Descartes as, in one respect, like pictures – they have a certain representational content (for example, I may have an idea of the Eiffel Tower which, like a picture of the Eiffel Tower, contains features which depict or represent some of the actual properties of the Tower). Following scholastic jargon, Descartes calls the representational content of an idea its 'objective reality'. Thus if an idea A represents some object X which is F, then F-ness, which may really be present in the actual object X, is said to be present in the idea merely 'objectively' or 'representatively'. (So if my idea of the Eiffel Tower represents it as having the property of tallness, say, then tallness, which really belongs to the actual tower, will be said to be present 'objectively' or 'representatively' in my idea.) It should be clear at once that this use of 'objective' has nothing at all in common with the modern sense of the term: 'objective reality' in Descartes' sense is *not* something which applies to independent objects outside the mind. Quite the reverse: 'objective reality' in Descartes' sense belongs within the mentalistic realm of ideas and representations.

3 Descartes now proceeds to argue that the Causal Adequacy Principle does not only apply to ordinary items like stones, but is also applicable to the realm of ideas, and, most importantly, to the

features which are depicted as part of the 'objective' or representative content of an idea. Thus, if an idea A represents some object which is F, then the cause of the idea, whatever it may be, must itself really and actually contain as much reality (as much F-ness) as is to be found merely 'objectively' or 'representatively' in the idea. In the *Principles of Philosophy*, Descartes clarifies this by means of an example: 'If someone has within him the idea of a highly intricate machine, it would be fair to ask what was the cause of his possession of the idea: did he somewhere see such a machine made by someone else, or did he make such a close study of mechanics, or is his own ingenuity so great that he was able to think it upon his own, although he never saw it anywhere? All the intricacy which is contained in the idea merely objectively, as in a picture, must be contained in its cause, whatever kind of cause it turns out to be' (*Principles* I, 17: AT VIII 11; CSM I 198).

4   To complete the argument: given (1), that I have an idea of God which represents him as a being who is eternal, infinite, omniscient, omnipotent, etc., it follows from the results established under (2) and (3) that the cause of this idea must be something which really and actually contains in itself all the features which are to be found merely objectively or representatively in my idea. Now since I am clearly a finite and imperfect being (as is shown e.g. by the fact that there are many things of which I am ignorant), then clearly (by the Causal Adequacy Principle) *I* cannot be the cause of this idea: 'All the attributes represented in my idea of God are such that, the more carefully I concentrate on them, the less possible it seems that the idea I have of them could have originated from me alone' (AT VII 45; CSM II 31). Nor can the idea merely have been put together from various other ideas of mine. For 'although one idea may perhaps originate from another, there cannot be an infinite regress here; eventually one must reach a primary idea, the cause of which will contain formally and in fact all the reality or perfection which is present only objectively or representatively in the idea' (AT IX 33; CSM II 29).[3] Hence the ultimate cause of my idea of God must be something which really possesses all the perfections represented in the idea. From this 'it must necessarily be concluded that God exists' (AT IX 36; CSM II 31).

The feature of the above argument which perhaps appears most dubious to the modern reader is the Causal Adequacy Principle (described under 2 above). To say that whatever produces a stone must itself have all the features to be found in the stone seems to imply a kind of 'heirloom' view of causation – that the only way an effect can have come to possess some property is by inheriting it, heirloom fashion, from its causes. Descartes' principle is supposed to apply to 'efficient' causes (roughly, an efficient cause is the productive agency or power which gives rise to some change, or brings something into being); but as Descartes' critic Gassendi pointed out, what plausibility the heirloom view possesses seems to depend on a consideration not of efficient causes but of 'material' causes, or ingredients (AT VII 288; CSM II 201). For example, if we find a bridge which is very strong, then we might argue that the material ingredients which went to make up the bridge (the girders, the rivets) must possess at least as much strength as is to be found in the bridge; for it might seem that if the bridge did not get its strength from its causes, it would have got it from nowhere, which is absurd.

Even in the favourable case of 'material' causation, however, the heirloom principle seems open to counter-examples. Helium has properties which were not present in the hydrogen from which it was formed by fusion. Or (if an example taken from modern science seems unfair to Descartes) consider the case of a sponge cake: this has many properties – e.g. its characteristic sponginess – which were simply not present in any of the material ingredients (the eggs, flour, butter). To invoke the principle 'Nothing comes from nothing' here, in order to defend the heirloom doctrine, would seem to be a muddle. Of course, the sponginess does not arise *ex nihilo*; it emerges from the complex chemical changes produced by the mixing and the baking. But this fact simply does not support the conclusion that the sponginess was somehow present in some form in the materials from which it arose. (One may be tempted to say that the sponginess must have been 'potentially' present in the materials, but this seems to defend the Causal Adequacy Principle at the cost of making it trivially true. In any case, Descartes could not concede that the features found in an effect might be present only potentially in its cause, for his argument requires that the cause of my idea of God be something that not merely potentially but *actually* possesses all the relevant perfections (AT VII 47; CSM II 32).

The problem of 'new' or emergent properties seems even more acute when we move from the case of 'material' causation to that of productive agency, or 'efficient' causation. Descartes' friend and critic Mersenne pointed in this connection to the example of the generation of life. If we take the efficient causes of life to be the action of the sun and rain on the earth, then living animals can arise from non-living causes, and so, Mersenne concluded, 'it does happen that an effect may derive from its cause some reality, which is nevertheless not present in the cause' (Second Replies: AT VII 123; CSM II 88). Descartes has a two-pronged reply to this. First, animals (which he considered to be simply mechanical automata) 'have no perfections which are not also present in inanimate bodies'. Second, the Causal Adequacy Principle is formulated in terms of the efficient *and total* cause of an effect. Hence, if animals do possess perfections which are not to be found in the sun and the rain etc., then we can be sure that these things are not the *total* causes of animal life (AT VII 134; CSM II 96). The trouble with this manoeuvre is that Descartes seems to be making his position immune from criticism by baldly denying the possibility of genuine emergent properties. Thus, evolutionary biologists would necessarily be wrong, in Descartes' view, to suppose, for example, that consciousness can emerge from non-conscious forces. Yet this is clearly a controversial issue and was a matter for debate even in Descartes' time and indeed long before (the Greek atomists, with whose work Descartes was perfectly familiar,[4] had argued for just such emergence). Whatever the truth about the origins of life and consciousness may be, the very existence of a long-standing debate on these issues seems enough to undermine Descartes' claim that the truth of the Causal Adequacy Principle is just 'manifest by the natural light'.

The aspect of Descartes' proof which caused most scepticism among his contemporaries, however, was the application of the Causal Adequacy Principle to the realm of ideas (phase 3 of the argument as described above). The author of the First Set of Objections, for example, complained that an idea is simply a subjective aspect of my thought, rather than an actual object or entity requiring a cause: 'Why should I look for a cause of something which is not actual, and which is simply an empty label, a non-entity?' (AT VII 93; CSM II 67). Descartes replied that although ideas have no existence outside the intellect, that does not in any way remove the need for causal explanation of an idea's having a certain content. In this he seems quite correct, and indeed the Causal Adequacy Principle actually seems on *firmer* ground when applied to ideas than when applied to the physical world. Recall Descartes' example of the 'highly intricate machine'; and for the sake of simplicity let us follow Descartes' own comparison between ideas and pictures, and consider the case of a drawing or a picture rather than an idea. Suppose a five-year-old child produces a highly complicated design for a computer – a design which we know could only be produced by a highly skilled mathematician with a mental age vastly superior to the child's. The fact that the design is only a drawing and not an actual computer does not block the causal question: the representative or 'objective' intricacy of the design still has to be accounted for. Of course, the child might simply have copied down the drawing from a book. But this simply pushes the argument one stage further back. We are, it seems, justified in asserting that somewhere along the line of causation there must be an actual entity or being that really does possess sufficient complexity to account for the complexities which are to be found in the design. And what goes for the drawing goes equally for an idea: complex representational content requires a complex cause.

The suggestion that the child might simply have copied down the design, e.g. from a book, parallels an objection that many critics are initially inclined to raise about Descartes' argument: need my idea of God have been placed in me by God himself? Could not its presence in my mind be the result of its having been passed on to me, e.g. by parents and teachers? As Mersenne commented: 'You have derived the idea from earlier preconceptions, or from books or conversations with friends and so on, and not simply from your mind or from an existing supreme being' (AT VII 124; CSM II 88). Descartes' answer is that this simply postpones the question of the original cause of the idea: 'if I ask these other people (from whom I have allegedly got this idea) whether they derive it from themselves or from someone else, the argument proceeds in the same way' (AT VII 136; CSM II 98). Eventually one must reach a primary idea, the cause of which will be like an 'archetype' which really contains all the perfection represented in the idea (AT IX 42; CSM II 29). Somewhere down the line we will have to suppose a being of sufficient perfection to account for the perfection represented in the idea.

At this stage, it will be useful to mention a refinement in Descartes' formulation of the Causal Adequacy Principle which has been omitted up till now. The principle asserts that whatever is found in an effect must be present in its cause; but Descartes adds that it may be present *either formally or eminently* (AT VII 41; CSM II 28; cf. AT VIII 11; CSM I 199). The jargon has worried some commentators[5] but it is straightforward enough. If an item possesses some feature F *formally*, it possesses it in the literal and strict sense; if it possesses F *eminently*, then it possesses it in some higher or grander form. The French version of the Third Meditation cashes this out in the case of the stone example as follows: 'Whatever is the cause that produced the stone, it must be something that possesses either formally or eminently whatever enters into the composition of the stone; that is, it must possess in itself *either the self-same things* as are in the stone, or *more excellent things* (AT IX 32; CSM II 28). The notion of 'eminence' has particular relevance when we are dealing with 'objective' or representative reality. In our computer diagram example, the ordered pattern in the circuit design could be caused by its having been copied from a previous blueprint, in which case the organization was 'formally' or literally present in the original. Alternatively, the child's hand might have been guided by a master mathematician, in which case the organization manifest in the diagram would be derived from a cause which possessed that organization not 'formally' but 'eminently'; that is, the organization in the drawing would be derived from a higher kind of organization – the complex pattern of thoughts in the consciousness of the mathematician.

If the 'objective complexity' to be found in the circuit diagram supports, as it seems to, the inference of a being who actually possesses (formally or eminently) at least as much complexity as that found in the diagram, does this vindicate Descartes' inference from the 'objective perfections' to be found in my idea of God to the actual existence of a being possessing the relevant perfections? One crucial disanalogy between the two cases seems to be this. In the case of the diagram, the supposition was that it depicted a wealth of positive detail and intricacy which it was simply not possible that the five-year-old child could have produced on his own. But the idea of a perfect God, it seems, is altogether more vague and hazy. If the child had simply drawn a mysterious black box and labelled it 'supremely complicated computer', we would hardly have been so inclined to insist that the representational content of the drawing required us to posit a cause of greater complexity than the child's mind.

In following up the question of just how clear our idea of God is, some of Descartes' critics went so far as to deny that we have any idea of God at all. 'We have no idea or image corresponding to the sacred name of God,' wrote Thomas Hobbes in the Third Set of Objections (AT VII 180; CSM II 127). Descartes replied that an idea, though it may in some respects be *like* a picture or an image, is not *actually* an image; the word 'idea', he said, refers simply to 'that which is immediately perceived by the intellect' (AT VII 181; CSM II 127). So the very fact that we understand what is meant by the infinite perfections of God shows, according to Descartes, that we do have a true idea of God, even if we are unable to picture, imagine or otherwise 'grasp' his perfections:

> It does not matter that I do not grasp the infinite, or that there are countless additional attributes of God which I cannot in any way grasp, and perhaps cannot even reach in my thought . . . It is enough that I understand the infinite' (AT VII 46; CSM II 32).

In Descartes' terminology, one can *know* or *understand* something without fully *grasping* it.[6] He remarks elsewhere that 'the mere fact that I express something in words and understand what I am saying makes it certain that I have within me an idea of what is signified by the words in question' (AT VII 160: CSM II 113).

It seems hard to deny that we do indeed have an idea of infinite perfection in this sense – we understand what is meant by the terms involved. But need this idea have been implanted by an actually infinite being? Could we not have formed the idea by some process of projection or extrapolation – by starting from an idea of a limited or finite being, which we can get from ourselves, and then going on to construct the idea of a being who is *not* thus limited? (Our own imperfections are apparent, as Descartes elsewhere remarks, simply from the fact that we are doubtful and ignorant of many things (AT VII 47: CSM II 32).) Descartes' reply to this objection is as follows:

> I must not think that, just as my conceptions of rest and darkness are arrived at by negating movement and light, so my perception of the infinite is arrived at not by means of a true idea, but merely by negating the finite. On the contrary, I clearly understand that there is more reality in an infinite substance than in a finite one, and hence that my perception of the infinite, that is God, is in some way prior to my perception of the finite, that is myself (AT VII 45; CSM II 31).

But what does this 'priority' of the infinite amount to? Questioning Descartes about his passage, Frans Burman objected that the meditator is described as recognizing his own imperfection *before* he arrives at knowledge of God, so could the idea of God really be said to be 'prior'? Descartes replied that, whatever the order of discovery might be, the infinite perception of God must in reality be prior to our imperfections, since imperfection is a 'negation of the perfection of God' (AT V 153; CB 13). The trouble with this, however, is that Descartes at no point succeeds in providing a convincing independent criterion for distinguishing what is a 'negation' from what is a 'positive' attribute. It is of course true that in order to understand the term 'finite' we have to understand that it is the negation of 'infinite'. But the converse is also true: in order to understand what is meant by 'infinite' we have to understand what is meant by 'finite'. Pairs of opposites like these seem to rank equally, inasmuch as understanding one member of the pair automatically implies an understanding of the other. If this is right, then Descartes' claim to the 'priority' of the concept of the infinite cannot be made good, and his argument therefore fails.[7]

Coda: the Trademark Argument, Second Version

Applying the label 'the Trademark Argument' to the reasoning which has just been discussed is potentially misleading, since Descartes does in fact offer us two apparently distinct ways of inferring the existence of God from the objective perfection of our idea of God. The second, shorter, argument appears as a brief endpiece to the Third Meditation (AT VII 48ff; CSM II 33ff). Given that I possess the idea of God, could I exist, asks Descartes, if no such being actually existed? No, he replies:

for in that case I would have either to be self-creating (to derive my existence myself), or else to derive my existence from my parents, grandparents and so on – that is, from a chain of imperfect causes; and either supposition, Descartes argues, runs into a contradiction. If I were self-creating, then I would surely have given myself all the perfections which I know by experience that I lack. As for the other alternative, to suppose I owe my existence to a chain of imperfect causes is impossible:

> As I have said before, it is clear that there must be at least as much reality in the cause as in the effect. And therefore whatever kind of cause is eventually proposed, since I am a thinking thing and have within me some idea of God, it must be admitted that what caused my idea is itself a thinking thing, and possesses the idea of all the perfections I attribute to God (AT VII 49; CSM II 34).

As the above (highly compressed) summary shows, the second version of the Trademark Argument cannot work without relying on the results supposedly achieved by the first version. Amongst other things, it takes for granted that the reader understands and accepts the Causal Adequacy Principle (that there must be at least as much reality in the cause as in the effect); and in particular it relies on the notion, supposedly established in the first argument, that this principle can be applied to the representational content (or 'objective reality') of the idea of God: whatever caused me, it is claimed, must ultimately be sufficiently perfect to account for the perfections depicted in my idea of God.

Despite this close continuity between the two arguments, some of Descartes' critics, both ancient and modern, have wanted to construe the second line of reasoning as a new and logically distinct proof. The author of the First Set of Objections claimed that it was, in effect, a version of the Second of Aquinas's celebrated 'Five Ways' of proving God's existence: viz. the argument that the series of causes in the world must ultimately lead to an uncaused cause (AT VII 94; CSM II 68).[8] Descartes brusquely replied that there was no real parallel. Firstly, the Cartesian argument does not start from a succession of causes in the world, for at this stage of the *Meditations*, the meditator is not reliably assured of the existence of anything apart from himself. Second, although Descartes does inquire about his causal origins, he notes that: 'in inquiring what caused me, I was not simply asking about myself as a thinking thing; principally and most importantly I was asking about myself in so far as I observe amongst my other thoughts, that there is within me the idea of a supremely perfect being . . . This idea shows me not just that I have a cause, but that this cause contains every perfection and hence that it is God' (AT VII 107; CSM II 78). So the second argument is not so much a distinct proof as a further development of the line of reasoning contained in the first. And as with the first version, the pivot of the argument is the 'objective perfection' represented in my idea of God. As Descartes comments in the First Set of Replies:

> The entire luminous power of the argument depends on the fact that this ability to have within us the idea of God could not belong to our intellect if the intellect were simply a finite entity (as indeed it is) and did not have God as its cause. Hence I went on to inquire 'whether I could exist if God did not exist'. But my purpose here was not to produce a different proof from the preceding one, but rather to take the same proof and provide a more thorough explanation of it (AT VII 105; CSM II 77).

Despite its dependence on the earlier version, the second version of the Trademark Argument has some interesting features in its own right, which have attracted considerable attention from the commentators.[9] The purpose of this chapter, however, is not to scrutinize every detail of the Third Meditation, but to move towards an overall assessment of Descartes' prospects for constructing a systematic body of knowledge, on the foundations of his awareness of his own existence and his recognition that he was created by a perfect being. Since it has already been argued that the first version of the Trademark Argument fails, and since the second version must fail to carry conviction if the first version is rejected, it will therefore be best to proceed without more ado to the entirely distinct and separate argument for God's existence which Descartes offers later on in the Fifth Meditation; this is an argument which has nothing to do with causal considerations, but is based on a purely *a priori* analysis of the concept of God.

The Ontological Argument

The term 'Ontological Argument' was invented after Descartes' death; the argument itself, or at least a version of it, was around long before his birth. The label 'Ontological Argument' is due largely to Kant, who distinguished a special type of proof of God's existence where 'abstraction is made from all experience', and the existence of a supreme being is 'inferred *a priori* from concepts alone'.[10] Descartes himself, though he did not use the label 'ontological' did in fact draw a firm distinction between the causal approach to proving God's existence which he adopted in the Third Meditation, and the purely *a priori* approach taken in the Fifth Meditation:

[The Third Meditation involves the] sort of argument that can taken some effect of God [namely the idea of God] as a premise from which the existence of a supreme cause, namely God, can subsequently be inferred. By contrast the other argument in the Fifth Meditation proceeds *a priori* and does not start from some effect (AT V 152; CB 12).[11]

Descartes' *a priori* proof, which he regarded as 'at least as certain as any geometrical proof' (AT VI 36; CSM I 129) starts from the standard medieval and scholastic distinction between essence and existence. Traditionally, the question *Quid est?* ('What is it?'), a question about something's nature or essence, was regarded as prior to the question *An est?* ('Is it?'), a question about something's existence. We can, for example, discuss the nature of a triangle and investigate the properties which necessarily belong to it, without having to confront the question of whether any triangles actually exist in the world. Descartes puts it as follows:

When, for example, I imagine a triangle, even if perhaps no such figure exists, or has ever existed, anywhere outside my thought, there is still a determinate nature or essence or form of the triangle which is immutable and eternal and not dependent on my mind. This is clear from the fact that various properties can be demonstrated of the triangle, for example that its three angles equal two right angles, that its greatest side subtends its greatest angle and the like; and since these properties are ones which I clearly recognize whether I want to or not, even if I never thought of them at all when I previously imagined the triangle, it follows that they cannot have been invented by me (AT VII 64; CSM II 45).

The two key points here are, first, that a triangle has a determinate 'nature' or 'essence' (the two terms are synonymous in Descartes) whether or not it exists; and second, that the essence must be independent of me, since I recognize certain properties (e.g. that the angles equal 180°) 'whether I want to or not'. Modern readers may be suspicious of the second of these notions, the supposed 'independence' of geometrical objects and their properties. For we are nowadays familiar with the idea that it is possible to vary the axioms of geometry and get different results; we can, for example, construct non-Euclidian geometries in which the angles of a triangle will be greater, or less, than 180°. But though Descartes did not question the prevailing pre-nineteenth-century assumption that there was only one geometry, namely Euclid's,[12] his argument does not hinge on that assumption. Even if one grants the possibility of non-Euclidian triangles with different properties from those of Euclidian ones, it remains true that a Euclidian triangle necessarily has, in virtue of its essence or nature, certain determinate properties, and that these properties are not dependent on me. Irrespective of whether I am capable of deducing them, the properties do follow inevitably from the way in which a Euclidian triangle has been defined; and once I have been shown that they so do follow, I must acknowledge them 'whether I want to or not'.

Having set up this standard notion of essence, as illustrated by the case of the triangle, Descartes now turns to the special case of God:

> It is quite evident that existence can no more be separated from the essence of God than the fact that its three angles equal two right angles can be separated from the essence of a triangle . . . It is . . . a contradiction to think of God (that is, a supremely perfect being) lacking existence (that is, lacking a perfection) (AT VII 66; CSM II 46).

The argument is extraordinarily brief, and, on the face of it, extraordinarily simple. First, God is defined as a supremely perfect being. No questions are begged here: as with the triangle, one can talk about the essence or nature of something without committing oneself to its actual existence. Second, it is claimed that supreme perfection implies existence. A totally perfect being must possess all perfections, and hence if one listed the perfections of God, then, along with omnipotence, omniscience and so on, one would have to include existence. And so, without more ado, Descartes concludes that God exists.

But *why* must existence be included in the list of divine perfections? 'It is necessary' writes Descartes, 'that I attribute all perfections to [the supreme being]. And this necessity plainly guarantees that, when I later realize that existence is a perfection, I am correct in inferring that the supreme being exists' (AT VII 67; CSM II 47). Clearly then, Descartes' argument depends on the premise that, just as omnipotence and omniscience are perfections, so existence is a perfection. It is this premise that has probably been the major focus of interest for critics of Descartes' argument. First of all, if existence is to count as a perfection, then it must be a property of some kind; yet reflection suggests it is a rather odd kind of property. If I tell you I have a colleague in my department who is tall, you have learned something about him; but if I tell you that he exists, this hardly seems to increase your stock of information. When questioned about whether existence was a property, Descartes was quite explicit: 'I do not see', he said, 'why existence cannot be said to be a property just like omnipotence – provided of course that we take the word "property" to stand for any attribute, or for whatever can be predicated of a thing' (AT VII 382; CSM II 263). Descartes seems on reasonably firm ground here. It seems quite possible to mention objects (triangles, or for that matter unicorns) without committing ourselves as to whether they exist; so if, having started talking about unicorns, we went on to find that they actually existed (suppose we find one in a remote part of South America), then one quite plausible way of describing what had happened would be to say that we began with a subject (the unicorn) possessing attributes (e.g. that of having a crumpled horn), and then went on to predicate actual existence of that subject. It is often said by modern commentators that even though existence may function as a *grammatical* predicate in this type of case, it still does not have the status of a *logical* predicate. Yet the notion of a 'logical predicate' is itself in need of clarification; and even if it can be explicated satisfactorily by reference to modern symbolic logic, it is still not clear that there is the basis here for a knock-down objection to Descartes' procedure.[13]

If it is granted that existence may function as a property in Descartes' broad sense of 'whatever may be predicated of a thing', this still does not explain why it is supposed to be a *perfection*. The originator of the Ontological Argument, St Anselm (Archbishop of Canterbury from 1093 to 1109), explains this rather neatly, somewhat as follows. If we define 'God' as 'a being than which nothing greater can be conceived', then there are two possibilities with regard to the question of his existence. Either he actually and really exists, or else he is a fictitious being who exists only in the minds of deluded theists. Let us for simplicity (the labels are not Anselm's) call the first kind of existence (i.e. real, actual existence) 'Grade A existence'; and let us call the second kind of existence – the kind of shadowy, imaginary existence which Father Christmas and other mythological beings have – 'Grade B existence'. Now if God merely possessed Grade B existence, he would not be the greatest being we could conceive of, so this supposition leads to a contradiction. It follows that God, given that he is defined as the greatest being we can conceive of, must have Grade A existence – he must really and actually exist.[14]

Although Descartes does not defend the premise that existence is a perfection precisely along these lines (indeed, in the Fifth Meditation he takes the premise largely for granted), we do find in the *Principles* a distinction between grades or kinds of existence. The distinction drawn, however, is not a distinction between actual and imaginary existence, but one between necessary and contingent existence. My idea of a table or a triangle involves the idea of merely possible or contingent existence (that is, the triangle may happen to exist, or it may not; there is nothing about the concept of a triangle that enables me to decide whether triangles exist). But in the idea of a supremely perfect being, 'the mind recognizes existence – not merely the possible and contingent existence which belongs to the ideas of all the other things which it distinctly perceives, but utterly necessary and eternal existence' (*Principles* I 10: AT VIII 10;

CSM I 197). The train of thought here seems to be that if the supremely perfect being merely 'happened' to be around, or if he existed merely temporarily, then he would by definition not be the supremely perfect being. Once we have defined something as supremely perfect, then it follows that it necessarily and eternally exists.

But there may be an equivocation, or a confusion, in Descartes' linking of the terms 'necessary' and 'eternal' here. It is certainly true that a being who existed temporarily – who had just popped into existence, or who might cease to exist at some time – would not be the most perfect being we could conceive of. So supreme perfection does indeed seem to imply eternal existence – the kind of existence which is 'necessary' in the sense that we cannot suppose that a supremely perfect being has not always existed or will one day cease. But it does not follow from this that such a being has 'necessary' existence in the logical sense that it is a contradiction to deny that there is such a being in the first place. In fact, Descartes' central comparison with the triangle suggests that the claim that God has 'necessary existence' is supposed to be the claim that existence is a logically inseparable property of the perfect being, just as the property of having angles equalling 180° is a logically inseparable property of a triangle. But if that is the argument, then it is subject to a serious difficulty – one that is pointed out by the author of the First Set of Objections:

> Even if it is granted that a supremely perfect being carries the implication of existence in virtue of its very title, it still does not follow that the existence in question is anything actual in the real world; all that follows is that the concept of existence is inseparably linked to the concept of a supreme being (AT VII 99; CSM II 72).

This criticism (which is based on that of Aquinas[14]) in effect concedes the Anselmian point that supreme perfection implies existence; but it denies that anything follows from this about what does or does not exist in the real world. True, *if* there is anything which qualifies as 'supremely perfect', then the very fact that it meets this qualification implies that it actually exists; but we have yet to be shown that there is, in fact, anything which qualifies for this title in the first place. In his comments in the First Replies, Descartes does not succeed in coping with this objection, but resorts instead to the unsatisfactory equivocation over 'necessary' described above (AT VII 119; CSM II 85). And indeed ultimately the objection seems unanswerable.

The objection we are discussing is related to a general worry which many people intuitively feel on being confronted with the Ontological Argument, namely that the argument tries to 'define God into existence' by a kind of verbal conjuring trick. In Humean terminology, one may express this worry by saying that 'relations of ideas' are one thing, 'matters of fact' quite another.[16] Examining definitions may help us to draw out the logical implications of the concepts we employ, but can hardly entitle us to draw substantive conclusions about the real world.

In the Fifth Meditation Descartes seems ready to cope with the spirit of this objection, which he proceeds to formulate in the following terms. 'It does not seem to follow from the fact that I think of God as existing that he does exist. For my thought does not impose any necessity on things; and just as I may imagine a winged horse even though no horse has wings, so I may be able to attach existence to God, even though no God exists.' Descartes replies to his imaginary objector as follows:

> It is not that my thought makes it so, or imposes any necessity on things; on the contrary, it is the necessity of the thing itself, namely the existence of God, which determines my thinking in this respect. For I am not free to think of God without existence (that is, a supremely perfect being without a supreme perfection) as I am free to imagine a horse with or without wings (AT VII 67; CSM II 46).

But this is not entirely satisfactory. It is true that the concept *equus* (horse) does not imply anything about wings. But what of the concept *Pegasus*? Anything which is Pegasus is, by definition, a winged horse (that is, it is necessarily true of Pegasus that he has wings). The 'necessity' here is, it seems, at least partly a function of how the definition is set up. This worry in turn gives rise to what may be called the 'overload' objection to the Ontological Argument. We have already moved from *equus* to *Pegasus*; now let us move one step further and consider *Superpegasus*. Let Superpegasus be defined as a being which has all the properties of Pegasus, plus the property of actually existing. It will now be necessarily true of Superpegasus that he exists. This example does not constitute a criticism of the Ontological Argument in the sense that it pinpoints a logical flaw in or a non-sequitur in Descartes' reasoning; but it does undermine the credibility of the argument by showing that, if the Ontological Argument for God's existence is valid, then we can overload the universe by constructing parallel arguments for the existence of all sorts of fantastic and unlikely entities such as necessarily-existing-winged-horses.

The 'overload' objection was never directly put to Descartes in this form, but he was sensitive to the kind of difficulty which specially defined entities might pose to the structure of his argument. In the First Replies, he points out that only some of our ideas correspond to true and immutable natures; other ideas depict fictitious or invented natures which are merely 'put together by the intellect':

We must notice a point about ideas which do not contain true and immutable natures but merely ones which are invented and put together by the intellect. Such ideas can always be split up by the same intellect, so that *any ideas which the intellect cannot split up in this way* were clearly not put together by the intellect (AT VII 117; CSM II 83–4; italics supplied).

The trouble with this criterion is that it seems too generous (since it allows all sorts of weird imaginary beings to possess true essences). Even an imaginary being like a chimera has essential properties which cannot be 'split off' by the intellect; for there are some features (e.g. the property of having a lion's head) which are logically inseparable from the concept of a chimera. When confronted with this example, Descartes replied that 'even if we can with the utmost clarity imagine the head of a lion joined to the body of a goat . . . we do not perceive the link, so to speak, that joins the parts together' (AT V 160; CB 23). Apparently this means that a complex idea does not depict a 'true nature' if the parts of that complex are not necessarily or analytically linked together. But unfortunately for Descartes, he finds himself wanting to say elsewhere that there are composites with separable components – e.g. a triangle inscribed in a square – which *do* depict true natures (First Replies AT VII 118; CSM II 84). The reason why he has to say this is that there are mathematical properties that can be demonstrated to hold of the composite 'triangle in a square'; and the fundamental criterion in the Fifth Meditation for X's having a true nature is that properties can logically be demonstrated to hold of X (AT VII 64; CSM II 45). Descartes seems to be in an impossible dilemma here. The whole Ontological Argument depends on the notion that some of my ideas represent objects (God, triangle) which have essences independent of me; and this notion is backed up by the fact that such objects have logically demonstrable properties which I must recognize whether I want to or not. So, on this showing composites like the triangle-in-a-square cannot be excluded from the class of objects having true essences. But, now, to include such composites as having true essences even though (as is the case with the triangle in the square) the components are not themselves analytically linked, appears to allow objects like Superpegasus to have true essences, and so leaves Descartes open to the 'overload' objection to the Ontological Argument.[17]

Some critics have suggested that Descartes was not entirely satisfied with the Ontological Argument, or at least that he regarded the argument as less certain than the Trademark Argument, or perhaps even logically dependent on it.[18] But in the summary of his metaphysics which Descartes offers in the *Principles of Philosophy*, both arguments rank equally; indeed the order of the *Meditations* is reversed and the Ontological Argument is presented first. There seems no convincing reason for doubting that Descartes considered the two arguments to be equally and independently valid. If the various criticisms expounded above are sound, then both are equally and independently flawed.

The Avoidance of Error

Descartes' arguments for God's existence have considerable interest in their own right. But to study them in isolation is to ignore the crucial structural role they play in Descartes' philosophical system. The attempt to prove God's existence is, for Descartes, not merely one item on a list of projects for expanding our knowledge of reality. Rather it is the only way in which the Cartesian meditator can progress beyond the narrow confines of subjective self-awareness: 'From this contemplation of the true God, in whom all the treasures of wisdom and the sciences lie hidden, I think I can see a way forward to the knowledge of other things' (AT VII 53; CSM II 37).

The first step in the way forward is the realization that God cannot deceive:

> To begin with, I recognize that it is impossible that God should ever deceive me. For in every case of trickery or deception some imperfection is to be found . . . The will to deceive is evidence of malice or weakness and so cannot apply to God (Fourth Meditation: AT VII 54; CSM II 37).

It is inconceivable, then, that a perfect God should deceive us. And yet the fact remains that we do often go wrong. And this presents Descartes with a problem which is rather like the traditional theological problem of evil. Just as, if God is good and the omnipotent creator of all, it seems odd that there should be evil in the world, similarly, if God is good and the source of truth, it seems odd that there should be error. More specifically, if God created me and gave me a mind which is, in principle, a reliable instrument for the perception of truth (AT V 148; CB 5) how does it happen that I often go astray in my judgements?

A standard theological move in coping with the problem of evil was to put the blame on man's exercise of his free will; and Descartes makes the selfsame move in explaining away error. Human error, Descartes now proceeds to argue, is not due to the intellect with which God has endowed us; for this, though finite and therefore limited in its perceptions, is nevertheless a reliable instrument for arriving at the truth. Rather the source of error lies in our will. Not that the will is defective – far from it: it is in our unlimited and unrestricted freedom of the will that we come close to sharing in divine perfection. But the very unrestricted scope of the will means that on any occasion we have the power to jump in and give our assent to a proposition even though the intellect may not have perceived it clearly:

> The source of my mistakes is that the scope of the will is wider than that of the intellect; but instead of restricting it within the same limits, I extend its use to matters which I do not understand (AT VII 58; CSM II 40).

But this analysis of the causes of error itself suggests a rule for arriving at the truth: 'If, whenever I have to make a judgement, I restrain my will so that it extends to what the intellect clearly and distinctly reveals, and no further, then it is quite impossible for me to go wrong' (AT VII 62: CSM II 43).

How exactly does this strategy for the avoidance of error work? An example from astronomy which Descartes employs elsewhere in a slightly different connection explains what he has in mind. If I look up in the sky, I might be tempted to judge that the sun is a fiery ball much smaller than the earth (AT VII 39; CSM II 27). But I do not clearly and distinctly perceive its size; all I can say for sure is that the sun *looks* a certain size when seen from the earth. So what I should really do in such cases is to suspend judgement until I find a watertight argument, of the kind which a mathematical astronomer can provide, that will clearly establish the true size of the sun on the basis of clear and precise reasoning.

The choice of a piece of mathematical reasoning as an example of the application of clear and distinct perception is highly appropriate: mathematical properties are frequently cited by Descartes as paradigm cases of properties which the intellect can clearly and distinctly perceive (AT VIII 33; CSM I 217). To restrict our judgement to the sphere of pure mathematics is thus (with certain provisos) a reliable strategy for avoiding error. But this in turn suggests a way forward to knowledge of the physical universe. For many aspects of the physical world, in particular the shapes and sizes of ordinary three-dimensional objects, can be characterized in purely mathematical or geometrical terms. Corporeal nature *qua* extended stuff – that which has length, breadth and height – is a proper subject for mathematical reasoning. So the way is now open for us to apply our God-given and therefore reliable intellectual perceptions to the structure of the physical world:

> Thus I see plainly that the certainty and truth of all knowledge depends uniquely on my knowledge of the true God, to such an extent that I was incapable of perfect knowledge about anything else until I knew him. And now it is possible for me to achieve full and certain knowledge . . . *concerning the whole of that corporeal nature which is the subject of pure mathematics* (AT VII 71; CSM II 49; italics supplied).

The Cartesian Circle

This high vision of a sure road to a true understanding of the world – in many ways a paradigm of rationalist optimism about the attainment of knowledge – is beset at the outset with a major structural difficulty. Descartes' strategy is premised on the reliability of the human intellect, and the certainty of its clear and distinct perceptions: 'a reliable mind was God's gift to me' (AT V 147: CB 5). But if the reliability of the intellect is guaranteed only after we have established the existence of a perfect creator who endowed me with my intellect, then how can the existence of such a creator be established in the first place? For clearly I must rely on my intellect in order to perceive the validity of the proof of God's existence, and the truth of the premises of that proof. How can I know that these perceptions of the intellect are not fundamentally flawed? Any appeal to the veracity of God at *this* stage – when I have not yet proved he exists – is clearly ruled out. The position thus seems to be that I need to trust my intellect in order to prove God's existence, yet without prior knowledge of God's existence I have in principle no reason to trust my intellect. This, in brief, is the notorious problem of the 'Cartesian Circle'.

The problem is given special piquancy by Descartes' own statement (in the passage from the Fifth Meditation quoted above) that 'the certainty and truth of all knowledge depends on my knowledge of the true God'. If *all* knowledge depends on God, then can I know the premises I need to prove God's existence without first knowing God? Come to that, can I even know I exist without first knowing God? When asked about his statement in the Fifth Meditation and the threat of circularity it seemed to present, Descartes replied quite straightforwardly as follows:

> When I said that we can know nothing for certain until we are aware that God exists, I expressly declared that I was speaking only of knowledge of those conclusions which can be recalled when we are *no longer attending* to the argument by means of which we deduced them' (AT VII 140; CSM II 100; italics supplied).

The clear implication here is that at the time when I am clearly and distinctly perceiving a proposition, I do not need knowledge of God in order to be sure of its truth, and at the time when I am actually attending to an argument I do not need knowledge of God to be sure of its validity.

That Descartes says this should be no surprise. In his discussion of the Cogito he had expressly said that the proposition 'I am, I exist' is true '*as often as it is put forward or conceived in my mind*' (AT VII 25; CSM II 17; see above pp. 35f). Nothing was said here about any need for a general guarantee (whether divine or otherwise) of the reliability of the intellect. Each of us just perceives in his own case that it is impossible that he should think without existing (AT VII 140; CSM II 100). And as long as I focus on this truth, then not even the extreme and hyperbolical doubt introduced by the hypothesis of the malicious demon can shake my certainty: 'he can never bring it about that I am nothing so long as I think I am something' (AT VII 25; CSM II 17). Nor is awareness of my own existence the only case where Descartes seems to claim that I have reliable cognition independently of knowledge of God. In the case of the proposition 'two and three make five', I realize, says Descartes, that the demon could never bring it about that two and three added together are more or less than five – so long, that is, as I 'turn to' the proposition, or keep it in focus (AT VII 36; CSM II 25). And the selfsame point applies, Descartes is reported as saying, to the axioms needed to prove God's existence: 'I know I am not deceived with regard to them, since I am actually paying attention to them. And as long as I do pay attention to them, I am certain that I am not being deceived and I am compelled to give my assent to them' (*Conversation with Burman*: AT V 148; CB 6).

It seems clear, then, that Descartes' way out of the Circle Objection was to claim that there are some propositions of which I can enjoy self-evident knowledge, so long as I continue to attend to them, without any need for a divine guarantee. But how could there be, as it were, 'self-guaranteeing' cognition of this sort? The notion is in fact not as odd, or as ambitious as might at first appear. Consider exactly what Descartes means by 'clear and distinct perceptions'. A clear perception is defined as one which is 'present and open to the attentive mind'; a distinct perception is one which contains *nothing but* what is clear (*Principles* I, 45: AT VIII 22; CSM I 207). Explaining this, Descartes observes that a perception may be clear without being distinct. For example, if I say 'I have a pain in my leg' there is something which I am clearly aware of – a feeling of discomfort; but the proposition which I have asserted has implications which take me beyond that of which I am directly aware. (One such implication, for example, is the proposition that I have a leg; yet as Descartes' example of 'phantom limb' pain shows, it is possible for people to suppose that their leg is hurting when in fact their leg has been amputated (AT VIII 320; CSM I 283)). Moreover, even the basic presupposition that I have a body in the first place could be called into question by the doubts of the First Meditation. But in the case of a very simple proposition such as 'I am thinking' or 'two plus three is five', then there are no such 'extraneous' implications, doubt about which could lead me to reject or withdraw my assertion. For I am committing myself to nothing beyond what I am directly aware of; I have, right there before my mind, all I could possibly need in order to be sure that the proposition is entirely true.

This last point explains the importance of mental *attention* which Descartes constantly harks back to in discussion of the Circle Objection (AT VII 140, 460; CSM II 100, 309). For it seems that as long as I hold a proposition like 'two and three make five' in front of my mind – as long as I know what I mean by the symbols involved – then there is nothing that the demon can *do* to bring it about that what I am asserting is false. Let him, if he wishes, eliminate the entire physical universe; let him, if he wishes, alter the conventional meanings of the symbols, so that though I take the symbol '+' to stand for addition, the rest of mankind understands it as the symbol for subtraction. None of this affects the fact that when I now assert '2 + 3 = 5', what I am asserting is a true proposition.

An objection to the interpretation just presented of Descartes' escape route from the circle is that Descartes does seem, at one stage in his argument, to cast doubt even on the mind's perception of such simple and distinct propositions as 'two and three make five'. In the First Meditation, after raising the possibility of an omnipotent deceiver, Descartes asks: 'Since I sometimes believe that others go astray in cases where they think they have the most perfect knowledge, may I not similarly go wrong every time I add two and three or count the sides of a square?' (AT VII 21; CSM II 14). And in the Third Meditation he recapitulates: 'Whenever my preconceived belief in the supreme power of God comes to mind, I cannot but admit that it would be easy for him, if he so desired, to bring it about that I go wrong in even those matters which I think I see utterly clearly with my mind's eye' (AT VII 36; CSM II 25; cf. *Principles* I 5: AT VIII 6; CSM I 194). These passages have led some commentators to suggest that the systematic doubts raised by Descartes extend even to the simplest intuitions of the mind when it clearly and distinctly perceives something (let this be called the 'extreme' view of Cartesian doubt).[19]

It cannot be denied that in the Third Meditation Descartes does reflect on the possibility that I might be caused to go wrong 'even in those matters I think I see utterly clearly with my mind's eye.[20] But immediately afterwards he counters with a riposte:

> When I turn to the things themselves which I think I perceive very clearly, I am so convinced by them that I spontaneously declare: let whoever can do so deceive me, he will never bring it about . . . that two and three added together are more or less than five (AT VII 36; CSM II 25).

It is sometimes suggested that in this passage Descartes is simply recording his subjective conviction of the truth of 'two and three make five', not claiming that he has any guarantee of its actual truth.[21] It is true that the meditator is described as experiencing a spontaneous feeling of conviction; but he is also said to declare that there is nothing a deceiver could possibly *do* to render this proposition false. And this suggests that Descartes' riposte is not just a declaration of subjective conviction, but has epistemic implications: so long as the meditator focuses on the proposition in question, then there is nothing that could be done to undermine its self-evident truth. I conclude that the doubt raised here about the possibility of a deceiving God (what Descartes goes on to call this 'very slight and metaphysical reason for doubting') does not impugn my knowledge of a proposition like 'two plus three is five', at the time when I am perceiving it. The doubt remains a nagging background worry that still needs to be dispelled; for 'my nature is such that I cannot fix my mental vision continually on the same thing so as to keep perceiving it clearly' (AT VII 69; CSM II 48); so the moment I let my attention slip, the 'deceiving God' scenario might cause me to doubt whether the cognition I have just achieved is accurate. But at the actual moment when I am perceiving a simple truth such as 'two and three make five', then so long as I keep it in focus, I know it to be true.[22]

There is, in any case, a strong reason for rejecting the 'extreme' view (that Cartesian doubt extends even to my present intuition of clearly and distinctly perceived truths). If Descartes is indeed introducing a legitimate doubt about whether I can know the truth of such a simple proposition as 'two plus three is five' at the time when I am intuiting it, then there can be no hope of setting up the axioms needed to prove God's existence. The circle will indeed be insoluble – indeed so hopelessly and obviously so that it is hard to believe that Descartes can seriously have intended the doubt to go this far. In the face of this, some commentators have defended what may be called a 'fall-back' position: that Descartes is not really concerned to establish an objectively true system of knowledge, but merely to show we have certain fundamental beliefs that carry such firm subjective conviction that we can confidently expect them to remain unshaken by any further inquiry. Though this position has been worked out with considerable sophistication, to construe Descartes as foregoing any claim to have reached objective truth seems to me to involve viewing his work from a far too 'modern' or relativistic a perspective. Descartes, throughout his writings, describes the meditator as, par excellence, the seeker after *truth*.[23]

Another objection to the 'extreme' view is that not only does it make it impossible for the meditator to break out of the circle and establish a true system of knowledge, but it makes it difficult to see how meditation could even get started in the first place. Even to reach the most basic stage of awareness of my own existence, I must be able to trust the fundamental intuitions of my intellect with respect to the contents of my thoughts. I must, for example, know what I mean by 'thought' and 'doubt'; I must, as Descartes insists, know the basic proposition that 'it is impossible for me to think without existing' (*Principles* I 10: AT VIII 8; CSM I 196). To raise the possibility that I might be in error at the time when I am actually intuiting a proposition like 'in order to think one must exist', or 'two and three make five', is in effect to raise the spectre of my being unable to keep a grip on the simplest ideas I employ. But that would make all thought impossible.

The Role of God

Descartes' view, then, is that the meditator's cognition of such elementary truths as 'two plus three makes five' or 'I am thinking, therefore I exist' is indeed self-guaranteeing. Such cognition is an exception to the principle that all knowledge depends on God, for so long as we are attending to these truths, we recognize that there is nothing that could possibly render them false. But if such self-guaranteeing cognition is available (and, as will appear, Descartes admits that even an atheist can have it) then what is the importance of God in Descartes' system? How do we construe Descartes' frequent assertions that God is the source and guarantor of all knowledge?

The answer lies in the very temporary nature of the self-guaranteeing flashes of intuition which the meditator enjoys. The guaranteed recognition of truth lasts, for any given proposition, only so long as the meditator holds that proposition in front of his mind; as soon as his attention wanders, even for a moment, the guarantee vanishes. Now if our capacity for attention were infinite, or if we could focus simultaneously on an infinite number of propositions, this would be no problem. We could perhaps intuit all truth in one blinding flash of cognition. But unfortunately our experience makes it only too clear first that our attention often wanders, and second, there is a limit to the number of propositions we can hold in our mind at any one time. (The parallel with vision, Descartes' favourite metaphor for cognition, is instructive here: if I try to keep more than a few objects in my field of vision, some of them are bound to go out of focus.)[24]

Once God's existence is established, however, then we have the possibility of progressing beyond such isolated flashes of cognition and building up a systematic body of knowledge. As Descartes puts it, we can move from *cognitio* (mere cognition) to *scientia* (stable knowledge) (AT VII 141; CSM II 101). How is this possible? First, the nagging background doubt about whether I may be systematically deceived even in the simplest cases is eliminated. If when my attention wanders from some proposition, I am assailed by this nagging doubt, then I only have to run through the proof of the existence of a perfect and benevolent God in order to put it to rest. Second, I can begin to rely (with due caution) on all the props and aids which finite beings need in order to gather their fleeting intuitions together and weld them into a systematic whole. This is partly a matter of being able to call on my memory of what I intuited a moment ago, or half an hour ago; but it is not the case, as is sometimes suggested, that once God's existence is established, I can start to rely uncritically on my powers of memory.[25] Even after proving God's existence, I will need to check and recheck my results; I will need to remind myself (if need be by the use of notes and other kinds of aide-mémoire) of the results I have established earlier. I will need to keep all my arguments under review, struggling to make sure I have not included anything that was not clearly and distinctly perceived. And I will continue the attempt to eliminate any residual preconceived opinions which may be infecting my judgement (cf. *Principles* I, 68–75: AT VIII 33ff; CSM I 217ff). But provided I go carefully, and restrict myself at any given stage to what I clearly and distinctly perceive, then I have reason to hope, given the perfection of God and the general reliability of the intellectual equipment he has given me, that my project of developing a systematic body of knowledge has some hope of success.

The general interpretation offered here seems to be confirmed by what Descartes has to say about atheists and geometry. Commenting on Descartes' remark that 'all knowledge depends on God', Mersenne had objected that an atheist is surely able to perceive clearly and distinctly that the three angles of a triangle equal two right angles (AT VII 125; CSM II 89). Descartes, in his reply, *does not dispute this*. But the *cognitio* of the atheist, he points out, does not amount to true *scientia*, since nothing that can be rendered doubtful seems fit to be called *scientia* (AT VII 141; CSM II 101). Now as we have already seen, at the time when the atheist is actually perceiving a simple proposition such as that about the triangle, then no divine guarantee is needed. And Descartes makes it quite clear elsewhere that such cognition is perfectly genuine, and involves a successful grasp of the truth, not merely a conviction of truth: 'if something is clearly perceived, then no matter who the perceiver is, it is true and does not merely seem or appear to be true' (Seventh Replies: AT VII 511; CSM II 348). But the atheist, it seems, will never be able to progress beyond such isolated awareness of individual truths. He can never move to *scientia*, since from minute to minute, his attention will lapse and he will then be back to a state of potential doubt, unable to make constructive use of the results he has established. Nor can he even be confident, once he allows his attention to wander, that he *has* established any firm results; for at any moment he may be assailed by the nagging background doubt about whether his fundamental intuitions are reliable (AT VII 146; CSM II 104). The Cartesian theist, by contrast, can put this doubt to rest by focusing his mind on the proof of the existence of a benevolent God. The proof, Descartes insists, is short and simple enough to be held in front of the mind in its entirety (AT V 149; CB 6). And so the circle is broken.

The above remarks are intended, first, to provide a plausible interpretation of how Descartes responds to the Circle Objection, and, second, to show that his strategy does succeed in avoiding circularity. But this, of course, is still very far from constituting a vindication of the actual steps which Descartes takes in developing his system of knowledge. For even if there are some propositions of such simplicity and distinctness that while I continue to attend to them I can be sure of their truth, it is very hard to accept that the premises needed for the proofs of God's existence fall into this category. We have seen for example, how the Causal Adequacy Principle – that there must be at least as much reality in the efficient and total cause as in the effect – has implications that are, to say the least, complex and controversial; and the same goes even for the apparently simpler premises of the ontological proof – for example the premise that existence is a perfection. Descartes may sincerely have believed that he intuited these premises clearly and distinctly; but as he himself acknowledged, people can sometimes be wrong in thinking that they clearly and distinctly perceive something. 'It requires some care', he admitted in reply to his Jesuit critic Pierre Bourdin, 'to make a proper distinction between what is clearly and distinctly perceived and what merely appears to be' (AT VII 462; CSM II 310).

Descartes might well point out in his own defence that he never promised the road would be easy. 'In metaphysics' he wrote in the Second Replies, 'there is nothing which causes so much effort as making our perception of the primary notions clear and distinct' (AT VII 157; CSM II 111). Yet the contrast which Descartes himself draws in this passage with his with first love, geometry, has disturbing implications for the success of his metaphysical project. There can be no possible doubt of the distinctness of a primary geometrical proposition as 'a triangle has three sides'. But this distinctness, it seems, is bought at the cost of absolutely minimal content.[26] When we come to metaphysics, and in particular when we progress beyond the minimal awareness of our own existence to the more 'meaty' premises needed to establish the existence of God, then it is clear, on Descartes' own admission, that great effort is required to make sure nothing dubious has crept in. And it seems that the Cartesian is never in a position to know with absolute certainty that a little more effort would not reveal a hitherto unnoticed element of indistinctness. Descartes' problem here lies in the very austerity and strictness of his requirements for the foundations of knowledge. As he attempts to progress from his minimal base of indubitable self-awareness to ever richer and more contentful results, it is going to be ever more likely that he will need premises that are too rich to satisfy his austere test of distinctness – of not containing anything that is not 'present and open to the attentive mind' (*Principles* I 45). The ultimate objection to Descartes' strategy is not that it is circular but that it is over-ambitious.

Notes

1 Compare Second Replies: 'Since God is the supreme being, he must also be supremely good and true, and it would therefore be a contradiction that anything should be created by him which positively tends towards falsehood' (AT VII 144; CSM II 103).

2 In the *Principles of Philosophy* the proofs of God's existence are presented in a different order, which Descartes describes as the 'order of exposition'. In the *Meditations* (and *Discourse*) the order followed is the 'order of discovery', which characterizes the route which the individual meditator will most naturally take, given that he is aware only of his own existence and of the ideas within him. Cf. *Conversation with Burman*: AT V 153; CB 12 and 69ff. It should be noted that before proceeding to the question of God's existence (in Meditation Three), Descartes devotes considerable space, in Meditation Two, to a preliminary investigation of his nature as a 'thinking thing' (*res cogitans*). For a discussion of his reasoning on this matter see below, ch. 5, pp. 111ff.

3 The translation here follows the 1647 French version of the *Meditations*, which is by the Duc de Luynes (cf. CSM II 1ff). Though not entirely reliable, and sometimes less precise than the Latin, the French version sometimes provides explanatory glosses which clarify Descartes' meaning. Thus in the passage quoted, the explanation of 'objectively' as 'representatively' is supplied in the French version.

4 Cf. Descartes' comments on Democritus, in *Principles* IV 202: AT VIII 325; CSM I 287.

5 E. Anscombe and P. Geach remark that these scholastic terms had 'degenerated to mere jargon by Descartes' time' (Anscombe and Geach, 81). But this is misleading if it is taken to imply that Descartes is carelessly allowing these conventional labels to slip into his work without giving them a precise job to do.

6 'To grasp something is to embrace it in one's thought; to know something it suffices to touch it, just as we can touch a mountain but not put our arms around it' (letter to Mersenne of 27 May 1630: AT I 152; K 15).

7 In discussing our ideas of rest and darkness which are arrived at 'by negating movement and light', Descartes says that such ideas are 'materially false' –

that is, they represent as 'things' (*res*) objects which are really non-entities or absences (AT VII 43 and 46; CSM II 29 and 31). But this suggests a further objection to Descartes' argument which is closely related to the one raised in the text: how do we have a guarantee that the idea of God is not 'materially false'? May we not be wrong in supposing that what is represented is in fact something real and positive? Cf. Arnauld's challenge to Descartes on the definition of material falsity (AT VII 206; CSM II 145), and Descartes' somewhat confusing reply (AT VII 232; CSM II 162). See also *Conversation with Burman*, where Descartes says that my idea of whiteness may be materially false since I may (wrongly) suppose that what is represented is a real thing or quality (AT V 152; CB 11). For an acute discussion of Descartes' contortions over the issue of material falsity see Wilson, 108ff.

8   In the passage cited, Caterus (author of the First Objections) states the argument thus: 'I am thinking, therefore I exist; indeed I am . . . a mind. But this mind derives its existence either from itself or from another. If the latter, then we continue to repeat the question – where does this being derive its existence from? And if the former, if it derives its existence from itself, then it is God.' Note that this formulation does not mention the *idea* of God at all. Of the modern critics who treat the second argument as a distinct proof in its own right, cf. Alquié (ALQ II 448f); Gueroult, ch. VI; Curley, 138ff. Contrast Williams, 151.

9   There is for example a much discussed paragraph where Descartes notes that even if he had always existed, he would still require a cause which 'preserved' him, or maintained him in existence from moment to moment (AT VII 49; CSM II 33). For a dicussion of the principle of the 'discontinuity of time' which Descartes seems to invoke here, see Gueroult, 193ff; Kenny, 143f.

10   Kant, A591/B619.

11   Since Kant, the term *a priori* has been used by philosophers to mean (roughly) 'independently of experience'. (Thus, truths which can be known *a priori* are contrasted with those which have to be established empirically.) In the passage quoted here, however, *a priori* is used in the older sense (found in, e.g., Aquinas), meaning (roughly) 'from cause to effect'. In this particular context, the ancient and modern uses of *a priori* converge, since what is envisaged is a proof of God's existence which does not rely on observed effects of God, but which starts, as it were, from God himself – from an analysis of his nature or essence. For Descartes' own use of the term *a priori* (which is not always particularly clear), see AT VII 155; CSM II 110.

12   Descartes does however hold that the laws of logic and mathematics are, like everything else in the universe, dependent on the will of God; so there is for him a sense in which geometrical truths could have been otherwise (had God so decreed) (see letters to Mersenne of 15 April and 27 May 1630; AT I 145 and 152). Descartes insists, however, that God's decrees once made are eternal and unalterable and that we are unable to conceive how they might have been otherwise (see letter to Arnauld of 29 July 1648: AT V 224; and *Conversation wtih Burman*: AT V 160; CB 22 and 90).

13   Modern logicians, instead of treating existence as a 'first-order' property that applies directly to objects or individuals, treat it as a 'second-order' notion: assertions of existence are taken as saying that certain other properties are

instantiated. Thus, to say 'horses exist' is to say that equine properties find exemplification in the world. Accordingly, in the modern Frege–Russell logical notation, existence is symbolized not by a predicate letter but by a quantifier; that is, it appears as a 'sentence opener', introducing a subject for predication, rather than as a symbol for a predicate or property. Thus 'the ruler of kings exists' is symbolized as $(\exists x)(y)(Ky \rightarrow Rxy)$ or ('there exists an x such that for all y, if y is a king, x rules over y'). (Strictly speaking, further symbols would have to be added to convey that there is only one such ruler.) But it is not enough for the defenders of the view that existence is not a predicate simply to point to the notation employed by modern symbolic logic. There is nothing sacrosanct about this notation (we could, for example, produce a subject–predicate expression 'Fn' such that 'F' symbolizes the verb 'exists' and 'n' designates the subject 'the ruler of kings'). What those who deny that existence is a logical predicate must show is that there is something philosophically suspect about treating existence as a first-order property; they have to show that there is something suspect in a logic which allows us to introduce 'pure' objects (such as 'the ruler of kings' or 'the chief unicorn') to which it is possible to ascribe, or deny, actual existence. For some objections to such pure objects see Kenny, 168; as E. M. Curley has shown, however, these are far from decisive (Curley, 153/4).

14 See Anselm *Proslogion* II. Having defined God as 'that than which nothing greater can be conceived' (*aliquid quo nihil maius cogitari potest*) Anselm goes on to argue that it would be a contradiction to suppose that such a being merely existed in the mind or intellect of man. The argument is discussed, and rejected, by Aquinas, *Summa Theologica*, P.1, Q.2, art. 1.

15 Aquinas, *Summa Theologica*, P.1, Q.2, art. 1.

16 See David Hume, *Enquiry concerning Human Understanding* (1748) IV 1.

17 For further criticism of the argument – in particular the problem of whether the idea of a supremely perfect being is coherent, see Curley, 167ff.

18 For this view cf. Gueroult, 248. 'the ontological proof . . . cannot be sufficiently established until the validity of all mathematical demonstrations is established, that is, generally, the validity of all the necessary relations included in clear and distinct ideas.' But the need for a guarantee of the validity of clearly and distinctly perceived relations would seem to be a problem which applies equally to the causal argument and to the Ontological Argument. See the discussion of the 'Circle' later in chapter 3, pp. 66ff, above.

19 For the extreme view cf. Frankfurt, 166: 'Descartes . . . asserts without any qualification . . . that so long as he is ignorant of God's existence he must fear a proposition is false even though he perceives it quite clearly and distinctly.' Cf. M. Wilson's remarks on the deceiving demon hypothesis in Wilson, 36/7.

20 Cf. *Principles* I 5: 'Our doubt will also apply . . . even to the demonstrations of mathematics and even the principles which we hitherto considered to be self-evident . . . For we do not know whether God may have wished to make us beings of the sort who are always deceived even in those matters which seem to us supremely evident' (AT VIII 6; CSM I 194).

21 Cf. Frankfurt, 167. See also note 23, below.

22 The analysis here follows that sketched in my introduction to *Descartes'*
    Conversation with Burman (CB xxvi). Criticizing that analysis, Professor
    Wilson has objected that if there is nothing even an omnipotent God could
    do to make it now false that two plus three equals five, this would be 'a
    striking limitation on God's power' (Wilson, 134); and Descartes, she
    argues, would not have allowed such a limitation. Certainly, there are several
    passages where Descartes puts forward the thesis of 'metaphysical
    voluntarism' (as it is sometimes called), claiming that all things – even truths
    of mathematics – are subject to the power of God: 'it is because God willed
    that the three angles of a triangle should necessarily equal two right-angles
    that this is true and cannot be otherwise' (AT VII 432; CSM II 291; cf. note
    12, above.) But does Descartes' metaphysical voluntarism entail that there
    are no logical limitations *at all* on God's power? Clearly God could have
    created a world without me in it, but so long as I am thinking, could he
    make it *now true* that I do not exist? Similarly, God could, on Descartes'
    view, have made the essence of a triangle somehow different, but could he
    now make false the proposition I am at this moment intuiting when I say 'a
    triangle has three sides'? I know of no passage where Descartes' pious
    acknowledgement of the power of God goes *this* far (indeed, if the analysis
    presented in the text is correct, he specifically implies that it does not go this
    far). Descartes' reported comments when he was questioned about his
    metaphysical voluntarism are significant here: while piously acknowledging
    that there is nothing God could not have brought about, Descartes draws
    back from the claim that there is nothing he could not *now* bring about (AT
    V 159; CB 22).

23 For what I have called the 'fallback' position, see Frankfurt, 180ff. One
    place where Descartes seems at first to come close to asserting that subjective
    indubitability rather than absolute knowledge is what he is after is a passage
    in the Second Replies:

> As soon as we think that we correctly perceive something we are spontaneously
> convinced that it is true. Now if this conviction is so firm that it is impossible
> for us ever to have any reason for doubting what we are convinced of, then
> there are no further questions for us to ask: we have everything we could
> reasonably want. What is it to us that someone may make out that the
> perception whose truth we are so firmly convinced of may appear false to God
> or an angel, so that it is absolutely speaking false. Why should this 'absolute
> falsity' bother us, since we neither believe in it, nor have even the smallest
> suspicion of it? For the supposition which we are making here is of a
> conviction so firm that it is quite incapable of being destroyed; and such a
> conviction is clearly the same as the most perfect certainty (AT VII 145; CSM
> II 103).

On the 'fallback' view Descartes is in effect saying here that if we have a
firm and unshakeable conviction of something then this is all that can be
asked for; we need not bother about the possibility that our beliefs are
objectively or 'absolutely' false. But the context of the passage quoted shows
that so far from foregoing a claim to objective truth, Descartes is here
defending the thesis that 'what we clearly and distinctly perceive must be
completely accepted as true and certain' (AT VII 144). And later he goes on

to say that 'the evident clarity of our perceptions does not allow us to listen to anyone who makes up this kind of story (viz. the story that our perceptions might fall short of attaining to objective truth). (For further discussion of this see Kenny, 195, and Williams, 199).

An alternative fallback position, which is strongly influenced by Frankfurt's analysis, is that of Curley, who argues that in attempting to *prove* his results, Descartes is 'working with a concept of proof for which it does not hold that if there is a proof of P, then P is true'. According to Curley, Descartes is 'implicitly redefining the concept of proof' in such a way that a proposition is held to be proved merely if (i) it compells our assent so that we are incapable of doubting it; and (ii) we have no valid grounds for doubting it (Curley, 118–9). This 'subjectivist conception of proof', is, says Curley, 'tailored to meet the requirements of the skeptical dialectic' (115); Descartes is trying to beat the sceptic at his own game, by showing that the sceptic can produce no reasonable ground for doubting his (Descartes') arguments. Though ingeniously worked out, this interpretation seems to me to reduce Descartes' stature by locating his philosophical goals too narrowly within the context of the moves and counter-moves of the historical debates over scepticism. Further, although Curley 'subjectivizes' Descartes less than Frankfurt, his interpretation still appears to do insufficient justice to Descartes' central and highly ambitious goal of achieving '*knowledge of the truth* by means of first principles' (AT IXB 4; CSM I 181); see further *Principles* I 1 (title), 4 (first sentence), and *The Search for Truth*: AT X 495-6 (passim); CSM 400f.

24 'It is impossible for us to see more than one object distinctly at one time' *Optics* (AT VI 621). 'The mind cannot think of a large number of things at the same time' (*Conversation with Burman*: AT V 148; CB 6).

25 On the so-called 'memory' view of how Descartes escapes circularity, God's role is not to guarantee our clear and distinct intuitions at the time we are having them, but to guarantee the reliability of our memories. In fact the first, negative, part of the memory thesis is quite correct: no divine guarantee is needed for our present intuitions. But the second part is highly implausible. If Descartes had claimed that once God's existence is established the accuracy of our memory is guaranteed, then he would be flying in the face of common sense, since it is notorious that human memory is weak and fallible. Moreover, Descartes himself explicitly acknowledges this, by advising those who are worried about their powers of memory to take notes to help them (AT V 148; CB 5). What originally gave rise to the 'memory' view was the fact that references to 'remembering' and 'recalling' constantly crop up in Descartes' discussions of the circle problem. (Cf. Second Replies: 'When I said that we can know nothing for certain until we can know that God exists, I expressly declared that I was speaking merely of those conclusions which can be recalled when we are no longer attending to the reasoning which led us to their deduction' (AT VII 40; CSM II 100). But careful scrutiny reveals that Descartes' purpose in making these references to memory is to stress that the self-guaranteeing intuition of primary truths is never timeless but always temporally indexed. Once our attention lapses, we can no longer be sure of the truth of the proposition intuited. For further discussion of the memory view see W. Doney, 'The Cartesian Circle',

Journal of the History of Ideas XVI (1955), and CB xxviiff.

26 See Hume, *Enquiry concerning Human Understanding* IV 1: the propositions of geometry which are 'discoverable by the mere operation of thought' provide no information about 'matters of fact' but merely express 'relations of ideas'.

4

The Material Universe

Our Knowledge of the World: the Intellect and the Senses

Once the Cartesian meditator is assured of the existence of a benevolent God, he can swiftly conclude that an external world exists. As I survey my ideas I find various sensory ideas (visual, tactile, auditory etc., impressions) which appear to come from corporeal objects distinct from myself; and 'I do not see how God could be understood to be anything but a deceiver if these ideas were transmitted by a source other than corporeal things. It follows that corporeal things exist' (AT VII 80; CSM II 55).[1]

But having established this result in the Sixth Meditation, Descartes immediately injects a note of caution. Physical objects 'may not all exist in a way that exactly corresponds with my sensory grasp of them, for in many cases the grasp of the senses is very obscure and confused' (ibid.). Even back in the Second Meditation, when still in a state of doubt about whether anything existed apart from himself, Descartes had expressed serious reservations about the kind of information provided by the senses. His example, a famous one, concerns a piece of wax:

> Let us take . . . this piece of wax. It has just been taken from the honeycomb; it has not yet quite lost the taste of the honey; it retains some of the scent of the flowers from which it was gathered; its colour, shape and size are plain to see; it is hard, cold and can be handled without difficulty; if you rap it with your knuckle it makes a sound (AT VII 30; CSM II 20).

All this looks straightforward enough and seems to provide us with 'everything which appears necessary to enable a body to be known as distinctly as possible'. But immediately this confidence is dispelled:

> Even as I speak, I put the wax by the fire, and look: the residual taste is

eliminated, the smell goes away, the colour changes, the shape is lost, the size increases; it becomes liquid and hot, you can hardly touch it, and if you strike it, it no longer makes a sound.

So a distinct understanding of the wax, Descartes suggests, cannot be based on any of the features arrived at via the senses – for all these features are subject to alteration. He goes on to argue that if I concentrate carefully, and subtract 'everything which does not belong to the wax', I am left simply with the conception of something spatially *extended* – a three-dimensional object which is capable of undergoing countless changes in shape. This conception of the wax as an extended thing, which is capable of being now square, now round, now triangular, etc., is not based on the senses, or even on imagination; for 'I can grasp that the wax is capable of countless changes of this kind, yet I am unable to run through this immeasurable number of changes in my imagination.' It follows, says Descartes, that the true nature of the wax as an extended thing is in no way revealed by the senses or the imagination; it is perceived 'by the mind alone':

> The perception I have of the wax is a case not of vision or touch or imagination – nor has it even been, despite previous appearances – but of purely mental scrutiny; and this can be imperfect and confused, as it was before, or clear and distinct as it is now, depending on how carefully I concentrate on what the wax consists in (AT VII 31; CSM II 21).

There is much that is curious about this argument. Descartes seems correct in his claim that our conception of the wax as an object that can be extended in indefinitely many ways goes *beyond* what we can actually observe, or even picture in the imagination; but this does not at all licence the inference that a clear and distinct conception of the wax is based on *purely* intellectual scrutiny – that the senses play no role at all. Descartes seems to overreach himself here (and in fact his eventual conception of scientific inquiry will allow a considerable role for sensory observation); but we nonetheless get a glimpse in this passage of a thesis which is central to Descartes' entire conception of our knowledge of the material world. The essence of material things, Descartes holds, consists not in those qualitative features which we arrive at by sensory observation, but in their underlying geometrical structure – in the attribute of being extended in three dimensions. And for an understanding of this we must look not to the senses, but to abstract mathematical reasoning. My sensory grasp of physical things may be obscure and confused, but, says Descartes in the Sixth Meditation, 'at least they possess all the properties which I clearly and distinctly understand – that is, all those which, viewed in general terms, are comprised within the subject matter of pure mathematics' (AT VII 80; CSM II 55).

But *is* the information of the senses as 'obscure and confused' as Descartes suggests? The wax argument places great weight on the changeability of sensory properties: the wax is now hard, now soft. But why does the fact that sensible properties change imply that there is anything indistinct in what our senses grasp? The answer is that Descartes is searching for the *essential* properties of material things, and there is a longstanding philosophical model, having its roots in Plato and Aristotle, which requires that essential properties be stable and immutable properties – properties that are eternally and necessarily true of their objects, rather in the way that the property having its angles equal to two right angles is eternally and necessarily true of a triangle.[2] This conception, moreover, is by no means confined to classical philosophy. A pervasive assumption of modern physics is that in order to achieve scientific understanding we must go beyond temporary fluctuations and local variations to an investigation of the permanent structural properties of things.[3]

The permanence requirement, however, is not of itself enough to entitle Descartes to disdain 'sensible' properties (i.e. properties whose ascription is directly based on visual, auditory, tactile, olfactory or gustatory data.) It is true that being hard is not a permanent property of wax, but what about being hard at 10° Celsius? It seems that if we are careful enough to specify our background conditions, then sensible qualities like hardness may indeed appear in the specification of permanent properties of things. So has not Descartes been too hasty in downgrading sensible properties as 'not really belonging' to the wax?[4] Any misgivings which the reader may feel on this score are largely left unanswered in the *Meditations*; for Descartes' purpose here is not to propound a theory of the physical universe, but to establish the metaphysical and epistemological foundations for such a theory. Thus the Sixth Meditation, having established the existence of an external world, gives us little information about its nature; all Descartes will assert is that human beings can achieve clear and distinct knowledge of *res extensa* – 'extended stuff' – in so far as it is the subject matter of pure mathematics (AT VII 70, 78; CSM II 50, 54). In the remainder of the Meditation, Descartes' main preoccupation is with the phenomenon of human error; he wishes to explain the fact that human beings are frequently mistaken in the judgements they make about the world in a way which does not reflect adversely on the benevolence and goodness of God.[5]

For further information about our knowledge of the material world we must turn to Descartes' mammoth philosophical-cum-physical treatise, the *Principles of Philosophy*. Part One of this work covers some of the same metaphysical and epistemological ground as the *Meditations*; but in Part Two, we find a great deal of detailed philosophical discussion on the nature of matter, and how it can be known. Right at the start of Part Two, Descartes asserts that 'sensory perception does not show us what really exists in things':

> The nature of matter, or body considered in general, consists not in its being something which is hard or heavy or coloured, or which affects the senses in any way, but simply in its being something which is extended in length, breadth and depth. For as regards hardness, our sensation tells us no more than that the parts of a hard body resist the motion of our hands when they come into contact with them. If, whenever our hands moved in a given direction, all the bodies in that area were to move away at the same speed as that of our approaching hands, we should never have any sensation of hardness. And since it is quite unintelligible to suppose that, if bodies did move away in this fashion, they would thereby lose their bodily nature, it follows that this nature cannot consist in hardness. By the same reasoning it can be shown that weight, colour, and all other such qualities that are perceived by the senses as being in corporeal matter, can be removed from it, while the matter itself remains intact; it thus follows that its nature does not depend on any of these qualities (*Principles* II 4: AT VIII 42; CSM I 224).

And Descartes goes on to argue that the true nature of matter or 'body considered in general' consists solely in extension (*Principles* II 5). The curious phrase 'body considered in general' (in Latin, *corpus in universum spectatum*, or *corpus in genere sumptum*[6]) is highly revealing. In the wax example Descartes had considered a particular object and pointed out that any one of its sensible properties might change. Here in the article from the *Principles*, however, he abstracts from all particulars, and simply considers what is true of matter in the most general sense. Materiality or corporeality in general cannot require hardness, since we can imagine bodies which recede as fast as our hands approach them (indeed, there actually are such bodies – air corpuscles).[7] Again, materiality cannot involve colour, since (as Descartes says in a subsequent article from this part of the *Principles*) 'there are objects which are so transparent as to lack all colour'; heaviness is also excluded, since fire, for example, is extremely light yet still counts as corporeal (*Principles* II 11: AT VIII 46; CSM I 227). In short, the properties which Descartes is looking for are properties which are true of matter in all its manifestations and under all conceivable conditions; and what this leaves us with, in Descartes' view, is mere extension; matter is simply that which has dimensions, which occupies space.

What is it about this highly abstract conception of matter that enables us to achieve a clear and distinct understanding of a kind that was not possible in the case of a conception based on sensible properties? The answer is that matter conceived simply in terms of extension can be characterized in strictly geometrical terms, and hence our reasoning concerning it can enjoy the simplicity, precision and certainty of a geometrical demonstration. We shall be able to confine ourselves to simple, self-evident propositions that we can clearly and distinctly perceive, and the conclusions which we draw will be deduced as following self-evidently. All this is strongly reminiscent of the mathematical model of knowledge that Descartes had originally proposed in Rules Two and Three of the *Regulae*;[8] and his continuing commitment to it is affirmed nearly 20 years later in Part Two of the *Principles*:

> I am assuming that my readers know the basic elements of geometry already, or have sufficient mental aptitude to understand mathematical demonstrations. For I freely acknowledge that I recognize no matter in corporeal things apart from that which the geometers call quantity, and take as the object of their demonstrations, i.e. that to which every kind of division, shape and motion is applicable. Moreover, my consideration of such matter involves absolutely nothing apart from these divisions, shapes and motions; and even with regard to these, I will admit as true only what has been deduced from indubitable common notions so evidently that it is fit to be considered as a mathematical demonstration (*Principles* II 64: AT VII 78; CSM I 247).

Sensible properties like hardness and redness, then, have no place in Descartes' model of scientific knowledge. First, there is no way – or at least no obvious way – that they can be expressed quantitatively; they are *qualia* rather than *quanta* – they tell us what something is 'like', but are not susceptible of the kind of simple and exact measurement which applies to properties such as length, breadth and depth.[9] Second, Descartes suggests elsewhere that, though we are lavish enough in our use of such qualitative labels, we do not properly understand exactly what we mean by them. We may say that a body is 'heavy', but 'we do not for all that have any knowledge of the nature of what is called "heaviness"' (AT IXB 8; CSM I 182; cf. Sixth Replies: AT VII 442; CSM II 298). Or again, in the case of colour, 'when we say that we perceive colours in objects, this is really just the same as saying that we perceive something in objects whose nature we do not know, but which produces in us a certain . . . sensation which we call the sensation of colour' (*Principles* I 70: AT VIII 34; CSM I 218). Third (and this is closely connected with the second point), Descartes holds that properties like hardness, heaviness, redness and so on will turn out under scrutiny to be not really *in* objects at all. For according to Descartes our ideas of the so-called sensible qualities are simply confused sensations arising in our minds as a result of the impinging of extended matter on our nervous systems (*Principles* IV 189–98: the details of this last claim will be considered when Descartes' views on physiology and psychology are examined in the following chapter.)

Extended Substance

Physics, then, is presented by Descartes as the study of matter *qua* that which is extended – matter in so far as it can be characterized in terms which permit of clear and distinct geometrical analysis. Descartes uses various terms to refer to matter so conceived. As we have seen, he often calls it 'body' (*corpus*) with the qualifier 'in the general sense'. Frequently he calls it simply *res extensa*, literally 'extended thing' (the term is contrasted in the *Meditations* with *res cogitans* ('thinking thing'). But in the *Principles*, which was specifically intended to serve as an academic textbook, the more technical notion of *substance* is generally employed. Extension, says Descartes, 'constitutes the nature [or essence] of corporeal substance' (Latin, *substantia corporealis*, *Principles* I 63: AT VIII 30; CSM I 215). A substance, as understood in the Aristotelian–scholastic tradition in which Descartes grew up, is, in the first place, simply a subject of predication, a bearer of attributes. But the term also carried the connotation of something which has independent existence, which can stand or subsist on its own.[10] In this strict sense, Descartes points out, only God qualifies as a substance: 'By *substance* we can understand nothing other than a thing which exists in such a way as to depend on no other things for its existence. And there is only one substance which can be understood to depend on no other thing whatsoever, namely God' (*Principles* I 51: AT VIII 24; CSM I 210). Corporeal substance, however, while not being independent in the sense that it is self-creating or self-sustaining, is independent of everything else apart from God. It is 'incorruptible, and cannot ever cease to exist unless reduced to nothingness by God's denying his concurrence to it' (Synopsis: AT VII 14; CSM II 10).[11] Thus, though it may undergo indefinitely many changes or modifications, corporeal substance or 'body' in the general sense, never perishes.

There is a clear contrast here with the traditional Aristotelian conception of the world as composed of a large number of individuals, each of which is regarded as a particular substance (for Aristotle, an individual horse or tree or chair qualifies as a substance).[12] Instead Descartes offers a radically monistic view of corporeal substance. The physical universe is a single indefinitely extended thing: 'The world, that is the whole universe of created substance, has no limits to its extension'; 'the matter whose nature consists simply in its being an extended substance occupies all imaginable space' (*Principles* II 21 and 22: AT VIII 52; CSM I 232). Individual items – planets, horses, trees – are thus construed simply as local modifications of the single extended substance. Just as the investigation of the wax showed that it could take on indefinitely many shapes, but these shapes were all modifications or 'modes' of the single attribute of extension, so corporeal substance in general, as defined by the attribute of extension, can be modified in indefinitely many ways: 'There are various modes of extension, or modes which belong to extension, such as all shapes, the positions of parts and the motions of the parts (*Principles* I 65).[13]

This curious notion of the universe as a single, indefinitely modifiable, infinitely extended thing led Descartes to make a number of what appear now – and seemed to many of his contemporaries – to be serious errors in physics. For example, the familiar idea that a given portion of matter (e.g. a given quantity of air) can be rarefied or condensed, so as to occupy a greater or lesser volume of space, is ruled out by Descartes as incoherent. When we say that a body expands, all this can mean, according to Descartes, is that some of its pores which were previously closed up are now filled with new matter (as the pores of a sponge become filled with water). There is no true increase in extension here, for the total extension of the particles of sponge remains the same; all that has happened is that water has moved from its original location to occupy the pores of the sponge (*Principles* II 6). The model of the sponge is taken by Descartes to be applicable in all cases – even where we are dealing with minute particles like those of air, where the 'pores' Descartes admits, are too small to be detectable (*Principles* II 7). For Descartes, there can be no contraction of any fluid or vapour without displacement of matter from its interstices to the environment, and no expansion without an incursion of new matter from the environment to the interstices.

Part of the reason why this sounds so wrong-headed to us now is that we are used to the idea that a quantity of gas (e.g. of hydrogen) can be condensed (e.g. in a star), but can equally be spread out (e.g. as a rarefied cloud over vast areas of empty space). But for Descartes the notion of truly empty space is incoherent; for 'the extension constituting the nature of a body is exactly the same as that constituting the nature of a space' (*Principles* II 11). Hence it is a contradiction to suppose there could be a vacuum 'in the philosophical sense of that in which there is no substance whatsoever':

There is no difference between the extension of a space . . . and the extension of a body. For a body's being extended in length, breadth and depth in itself warrants the conclusion that it is a substance, since it is a complete contradiction that a particular extension should belong to nothing; and the same conclusion must be drawn with respect to a space that is supposed to be a vacuum, namely that since there is extension in it, there must necessarily be substance in it as well (*Principles* II 16: AT VIII 49; CSM I 229).

Ironically, Descartes was writing this in the same decade that Pascal, using Torricelli's barometer, was performing experiments which strongly supported the view that a vacuum was possible – and indeed could be artificially created here on earth.[14] Descartes' friend Marin Mersenne had earlier raised not an actual case but a thought-experiment, which none the less seemed decisive in establishing at least the logical possibility of a vacuum: could not God, at least, remove all the matter from a room while at the same time preventing any new matter from taking its place? Descartes replied:

> If you make this supposition you will have to suppose *eo ipso* that the walls of the room will touch each other, otherwise you will be thinking a self-contradictory thought. Just as you cannot imagine God flattening all the mountains in the world while leaving all the valleys, so you cannot think that He removes every kind of body and yet leaves space behind (9 January 1639: AT II 482; K 62).

The argument is purely *a priori*, and depends on the fundamental definition of matter or 'body' in Descartes' system. Something is matter if and only if it has extension; extension is synonymous with dimensionality; hence a space, being dimensional, cannot be empty of matter. Descartes put the matter very neatly in a letter to Chanut of 6 June 1647:

> When I examine the nature of . . . matter, I find it to consist merely in its extension in length, breadth and depth, so that whatever has three dimensions is a part of this matter; and there cannot be any completely empty space, that is, space containing no matter, because we cannot conceive such a space without conceiving in it these three dimensions, and consequently matter (AT V 52; K 221).

So abstract is Descartes' conception of matter that one initially wonders how the purely geometrical feature of three-dimensional extension can possibly yield any of the familiar items – the rocks and stones and trees and oceans – which make up the world around us. Is not Descartes' matter too abstract to be genuinely *material*? A certain amount of 'corporeality' is given by the fact that the geometrical model with which Descartes is working is three-dimensional rather than two-dimensional; that is, we are dealing with solid rather than plane geometry. It follows from this that matter is to be understood as entirely impenetrable: 'the true extension of a body is such as to exclude any interpenetration of the parts' (Sixth Replies: AT VII 422; CSM II 298).[15] 'Let us conceive of matter', Descartes writes in his earlier treatise on physics *Le Monde*, 'as a real, perfectly solid body which uniformly fills the entire length, breadth and depth of . . . space' (AT XI 33; CSM I 91). But this seems to give us nothing more than an entirely bland and homogenous universe – a kind of universal, impenetrable three-dimensional dough. Descartes asserts, however, that, though matter is impenetrable, portions of it move at different speeds from other portions, and this is enough to give differentiation and variety to the universe. The different motions of parts of matter enable it to be classified into three 'elements' which are characterized as follows in Part Three of the *Principles*:

> The first element is made up of matter which is so violently agitated that when it meets other bodies it is divided into particles of indefinite smallness. The second is composed of matter divided in spherical particles which are still very minute when compared with those that we can see with our eyes, but which have a definite fixed quantity and can be divided into other much smaller particles. The third element . . . consists of particles which are much bulkier or have shapes less suited for motion. From these elements, all the bodies of this universe are composed (*Principles* III 52: AT VIII 105; CSM I 258).

This scheme, Descartes claims in *The World*, will enable us to explain all the various observable qualities of matter 'such as heat, coldness, moisture, dryness and all others, without the need to suppose anything in matter other than the motion, size, shape and arrangement of its parts' (AT XI 26; CSM I 89).

This picture of a vast complexity and diversity arising from simple interactions of corpuscles is distinctly reminiscent of the kind of system proposed by Greek atomists such as Democritus, and graphically described in Lucretius *De Rerum Natura*:

> We teach
> that *body*, firm and everlasting, forms
> those elements of things, and primal seeds,
> whence all this present universe is made.[16]

There are, of course, several respects in which the Cartesian universe differs from that of Democritus and his followers. For example,

Descartes, as already noted, rejects the vacuum or 'void' postulated by the atomists. Moreoever there are, for Descartes, no such things as atoms, or truly indivisible particles. The corpuscles which Descartes invokes to account for the behaviour of his various elements are in no sense 'ultimate'; they are merely portions of matter which happen to be moving together. Further division is always possible, *ad infinitum*:

> It is impossible that there should exist atoms, that is, pieces of matter that are by their very nature indivisible, as some philosophers have imagined. For if there were any atoms, no matter how small we imagined them to be, they would necessarily have to be extended; and hence we could in our thought divide each of them into two or more smaller parts, and hence recognize their divisibility (*Principles* II 20: AT IXB 74; CSM I 231).[17]

Cartesian matter is indefinitely divisible, and this follows logically from its defining characteristic of extension. But despite these important differences between Descartes' physics and that of the early atomists, the comparison remains instructive. As with Democritean physics, the Cartesian theory of the universe is informed by a grand, all-embracing conception of the nature of matter. And as with the Democritean conception, Descartes' science is remarkably schematic – long on generalities, short on detailed prediction and precise verification. Descartes himself claimed that his system was vastly superior to anything that had gone before, both in terms of mathematical precision and experimental confirmation. But it is time to examine how far those claims are justified in practice.

Science, Mathematics and Mechanical Models

As we have seen, Descartes claimed that his reasoning concerning the material universe has the kind of precision and certainty that makes it 'fit to be considered as a mathematical demonstration' (*Principles* II 64). But what exactly is a 'mathematical demonstration'? One feature of the mathematical approach which clearly appealed to Descartes was its rejection of loose qualitative notions in favour of precisely measurable *quantities*. But readers who approach Descartes' scientific writings expecting anything detailed in the way of geometrical measurement, arithmetical calculation or algebraic formulae will to a great extent be disappointed. Indeed, it is precisely the paucity of such mathematical workings that is the striking feature of Descartes' physics, when compared with the work of Galileo, for example. (The comparison with Newton, whose *Principles* were published some 40 years after those of Descartes, is even more striking in this regard.)

This is not to say that mathematical calculation plays no role in Cartesian science. In Part Two of the *Principles*, for example, Descartes' seven rules for determining the speed and direction of bodies after impact all depend on an implicit mathematical formula for the conservation of quantity of motion, measured as the product of size and speed (*Principles* II, 45–52). And in his work on refraction, in the *Optics*, Descartes offers a geometrical analysis which determines the exact relationship between the angle of incidence and the angle of refraction of a light ray (AT VI 100; CSM I 161). But in general, the frequency of precise mathematical analysis is markedly less than one might be led to expect, given the explicit connection which Descartes makes between the study of physics and the 'subject matter of pure mathematics'.[18]

This apparent discrepancy is explained fairly simply. Despite his stress on the mathematical notion of *quantity* as the key to physics, Descartes never commits himself to the thesis that, in order to do good science, one must be able actually to supply detailed formulae for calculation and measurement in respect of each phenomenon to be explained. All that he seems to require is that the properties involved be in principle *capable* of being quantified. What appeals to Descartes about quantifiable properties such as size and shape, is their lack of vagueness, their clarity and distinctness or 'openness' to the attentive mind. It is the elimination of vague qualitative notions such as 'heaviness', 'redness' and 'bitterness' that Descartes above all has in mind when he boasts that his science recognizes 'no matter in corporeal things apart from that which geometers call quantity' (*Principles* II 64).

We thus have to be careful about the claim that is often made that Descartes was a pioneer of the quantitative approach in science. It is certainly true that he appreciated what many distinguished seventeenth-century thinkers such as Francis Bacon failed to see, that future progress in science must lie in moving away from vague qualitative notions and concentrating instead on 'size, shape and movements of particles'.[19] But Descartes' recognition of the importance of 'quantity' does not seem to have gone very much further than that. He does not, for example, seem fully to have shared Galileo's vision that the 'book of nature' was written in a kind of mathematical code, and that if we could only crack that code, we could uncover her ultimate secrets.[20] There is good evidence that Descartes' early fascination for pure mathematics did not last; his enthusiasm for abstract mathematical problems had declined sharply by the early 1630s.[21] And certainly Descartes' own scientific work did not, on the whole, make much of a contribution to mathematical code-cracking. In the century following Descartes' death, the Cartesian system of physics proved remarkably resilient, and it only slowly and gradually gave way to a recognition of the superiority of the Newtonian system.

But the superiority of Newtonian physics lies precisely in that feature which Cartesian physics for the most part lacks – the provision of precise quantitative laws yielding exact predictions about how the universe will behave.

But the question of quantity is not the only, or the most important, respect in which Descartes saw his approach to physics as being a 'mathematical' one. The features which he most frequently stresses when invoking a mathematical model for science are firstly the *simplicity* of subjects like geometry, and secondly their *deductive rigour:*

> These long chains composed of *very simple and easy reasonings* which geometers customarily use to arrive at their most difficult demonstrations gave me occasion to suppose that all the things which can fall under human knowledge are interconnected in the same way. And I thought that provided we refrain from accepting anything as true which is not, and always keep to the *order required for deducing one thing from another*, there can be nothing too remote to be reached in the end, or too well hidden to be discovered (*Discourse*, part II: AT VI 19; CSM I 120: italics supplied).

Now the simplicity and deductive rigour of mathematics is largely a function of its being a 'closed' system, whose demonstrations are independent of experience. In the case of Euclidian geometry, for example, one begins with very simple, supposedly self-evident axioms, and then each subsequent proposition is justified by being shown to follow in a precise step-by-step fashion from the axioms. Is this the model which Descartes wishes to apply to physics? From the examples we have discussed so far – the rejection of atoms, the impossibility of a vacuum, the infinitely extended universe of 'body', it might appear that Descartes proposes to deduce all his results quite independently of experience, simply on the basis of what follows logically from the essential definition of matter as 'extended substance'. And when he tells us that he admits as true only what has been 'deduced evidently from indubitable common notions' (*Principles* II 64), he seems to be implying that physics consists entirely in the unravelling of a series of consequences that follow inevitably from a few self-evident first principles.

There is a fair amount of argumentation in the *Principles* that does conform to this aprioristic model. In Part Two, for example, certain fundamental principles about the nature of motion are deduced purely from first principles – via a consideration of the nature of God:

> God's perfection involves not only his being immutable in himself but also his operating in a manner that is always entirely constant and immutable . . .
> Thus God imparted various motions to the parts of matter when he first

created them and he now preserves all this matter in the same way and by the same process by which he originally created it; and it follows from this that God likewise always preserves the same quantity of motion in matter (*Principles* II 36: AT VIII 61; CSM I 240).

From this Descartes deduces his first law of nature: 'that each and every thing, in so far as it can, always continues in the same state; and thus what is once in motion always continues to move' *Principles* II 37, title). (This, combined with the principle that 'all motion is rectilinear' (the first part of Descartes' second law), is generally considered to be the earliest statement in the history of science of what was to become Newton's law of inertia.)[22]

It is important to realize, however, that Descartes does *not* believe that the whole of physics can be established in this way. Even in his early work, the *Regulae*, which lays so much stress on the deductive model, Descartes had made it clear that science could not be approached on a purely *a priori* basis; it is absurd, he says, to 'expect truth to germinate from our heads like Minerva from the head of Jupiter' (AT X 380; CSM I 21). And later, in the *Discourse*, Descartes explicitly recognizes that what we can deduce *a priori* about the nature of matter is limited to properties of an extremely abstract and general kind:

> The power of nature is so ample and so vast, and my principles so simple and so general, that I notice hardly any particular effect of which I do not know at once that it can be deduced from my principles in many different ways, and my greatest difficulty is usually to discover in which of these ways it depends on them. I know of no other way to discover this than by seeking further observations whose outcomes vary according to which of them provides the correct explanation (AT VI 64; CSM I 144).

So in order to make the transition from general principles to the explanation of particular events, we need, according to Descartes, to rely on 'observations' or, in the original French, *expériences*. This term is frequently used by Descartes to refer to observations made by the scientist. In the Latin texts the corresponding term is *experimenta*; and in his use of both the Latin and the French terms Descartes sometimes comes close to the notion of an 'experiment' in the modern sense. It is worth noticing that the idea of putting something to the *test* is contained in the meaning of the original Latin verb *experior* from which the Latin *experimentum* and the French *expérience* are both derived.[23]

At a level of high generality, then, we can deduce certain abstract structural principles *a priori*; these function, as it were, as the scaffolding of Cartesian physics. But as soon as we wish to construct the detailed explanations of specific phenomena, Descartes moves away from apriorism and towards something which is much closer to the modern idea of a 'hypothetico-deductive' approach. A hypothesis is advanced, and is then tested by seeing whether its observable consequences square with experience.[24] How do we know that there are just three elements in the universe, Descartes was asked by Frans Burman. 'By reasoning', Descartes replied, 'and then by experience which confirms the reasoning' (AT V; CB 74). 'All my conclusions', he wrote ten years earlier, 'are confirmed by true observations' (to Plempius, 3 October 1637: AT I 421; K 38). The whole procedure is summed up with great clarity in Part Three of the *Principles*:

> From what has already been said, we have established that all the bodies in the universe are composed of one and the same matter, which is divisible into indefinitely many parts, and is in fact divided into a large number of parts which move in different directions and have a sort of circular motion; moreover, the same quantity of motion is always preserved in the universe. However, we cannot determine by reason alone how big these pieces of matter are, or how fast they move, or what kinds of circle they describe. Since there are countless different configurations which God might have instituted here, experience alone must teach us which configuration he actually selected in preference to the rest. We are thus free *to make any assumption on these matters, with the sole proviso that all the consequences of our assumption must agree with experience* (*Principles* II 46: AT VIII 100; CSM I 256: italics supplied).

Descartes' official programme for science, then, assigns a crucial role to experience: by appealing to experience we can decide which of the many possible hypotheses consistent with general principles yields the true explanation of a given phenomenon. To leave the matter there, however, gives the impression of a vastly more rigorous system of experimental testing than is in fact to be found in Descartes' scientific practice. If we look at the detailed descriptions and explanations of the structure of the physical world which Descartes offers, the most striking feature of his methodology is the use of *models* and *mechanisms*. The terms 'model' and 'mechanism' are used in a variety of senses by modern philosophers of science, and nowadays the terms often suggest concepts of a highly theoretical kind. But the models and mechanisms which Descartes invokes are disarmingly simple and homely. Perhaps the most famous example is the model of the vortex or whirlpool which is used by Descartes to explain celestial motion. For Descartes, the whole of the celestial matter in which the planets are located turns continuously like a vortex with the sun at its centre:

> In a river there are various places where the water twists around on itself

and forms a whirlpool. If there is flotsam on the water we see it carried around with the whirlpool and in some cases we see it also rotating about its own centre; further, the bits which are nearer the centre of the whirlpool complete a revolution more quickly; and finally, although such flotsam always has a circular motion, it scarcely ever describes a perfect circle, but undergoes some latitudinal and longitudinal deviations. We can without difficulty imagine all this happening in the same way in the case of the planets, and this single account explains all the planetary movements that we observe (*Principles* VIII 30: AT VIII 92; CSM I 254).

It is striking that there is no quantitative mathematics here – no equations, no algebra, not even anything 'mathematical' in the more general structural sense of reasoning which follows a rigorous deductive pattern similar to that found in subjects like geometry. Instead we have a simple everyday phenomenon, familiar from ordinary terrestrial observation, which is used quite literally, as a model for celestial motions. The word 'literally' is in place here, because Descartes is not merely proposing that the motion of the celestial vortex is *analogous* to that of a whirlpool, or that the whirlpool is a useful image for heuristic ˙or expository purposes. He suggests, rather, that the selfsame mechanism which is at work in the case of an ordinary river whirlpool operates in exactly the same fashion, on a cosmic scale.[25]

There are many such models in Descartes' scientific writings. The action of light (which Descartes takes to be explicable in terms of the movement of globules of material of the second element) is described by the model of a number of lead balls arranged in a flask (*Principles* III 63). The 'gravity' or 'heaviness' of terrestrial particles is explained in terms of the pressure exerted from above by other particles, so that terrestrial particles behave in exactly the same fashion as particles or droplets of water in a tub (*Principles* IV 26). Or again, the equilibrium of the particles of celestial matter is explained by reference to the behaviour of air in a bladder or balloon (AT V 174; CB 44; cf. *Principles* III 92). 'The comparisons I use', Descartes wrote to one of his correspondents, 'are, I maintain, the most appropriate means that the human mind can have to explain the truth of questions in physics' (to Morin, 12 September 1638: AT II 368). Later he observed that 'we are not sufficiently accustomed to consider mechanical models, and this is the source of almost all error in philosophy [i.e. natural science]' (AT V 174; CB 44).

Descartes' recognition of the importance of models in scientific explanation represents an important insight. It is by extrapolating from features of the world that we do understand to those that are obscure that scientific progress frequently is made. Indeed one modern philosopher of science has claimed that 'a scientific theory is often nothing but the description and exploitation of some model.'[26] But there remains a serious gulf between Descartes' outlook and that of the modern physicist on the question of how the *applicability* of a given model is established. How does Descartes know that the features present in models like the whirlpool or the balls in the flask are reproduced in the relevant respects in the actual phenomena he is trying to explain? When challenged about his use of models Descartes pointed out that he compared only 'movements with movements and shapes with shapes' (AT II 368; ALQ II 365). The point here seems to be that the laws of matter and motion are uniform throughout the universe, and hence the particles of matter found for example in the celestial vortex can be presumed to operate on the same lines as those in a smaller phenomenon such as a whirlpool. But clearly this does not constitute empirical confirmation that there is a celestial vortex in the first place: this is assumed by the comparison, not established by it. The kind of 'confirmation' which Descartes' models offer is thus of a fairly weak kind. What Descartes has done is to assume that the vortex theory is true, and then point to the presence of a medium-sized terrestrial mechanism that generates results of an approximately similar kind to those observed in the case of planetary motion. We are removed here from the kind of experimental rigour demanded by modern physics.[27] When Descartes says that his explanations are 'confirmed by reliable everyday experience' (*Principles* IV 200), this is certainly not a matter of his being able to specify experiments designed to test whether the predicted results of a given hypothesis actually obtain.

Descartes' overall contribution to the philosophy of science is not easy to assess. It should be clear from what has been said that he was not a rigid deductivist; but it is equally clear that he was not a sophisticated experimentalist. What Cartesian physics offers us is a schematic programme for universal explanation in terms of 'shapes, motions and size of bodies'; and Descartes draws support for his programme from the fact that it seems to be applicable to the medium-sized mechanisms that we see around us. It is in this very general sense that the laws of Cartesian mechanics are confirmed by 'everyday experience'. Descartes himself evidently saw the ultimate justification for his programme as lying in the simplicity and straightforwardness of the properties which it restricted itself to considering. The central feature of good science, as conceived by Descartes, is that it is totally 'above board'. It can avoid any recourse to the occult or mysterious by confining itself to 'the shapes, motions and size of bodies and . . . the necessary results of their mutual interactions in accordance with the laws of mechanics which are confirmed by reliable everyday experience':

Who has ever doubted that bodies move and have various sizes and shapes, and that their various different motions correspond to these differences in size and shape, or who doubts that when bodies collide bigger bodies are divided into smaller ones and change their shape? . . . No one who uses his reason will, I think, deny the advantage of using what happens in large bodies, as perceived by our senses, as a model for our ideas about what happens in tiny bodies which elude our senses merely because of their small size. This is much better than explaining matters by inventing all sorts of strange objects which have no resemblance to what is perceived by the senses, such as 'prime matter', 'substantial forms' and the whole range of qualities that people habitually introduce, all of which are harder to understand than the things they are supposed to explain (*Principles* IV 200–1: AT IXB 318–19; CSM I 286).

The avoidance of mumbo jumbo is, of course, a worthy aim in science. But there is always the risk, with Descartes' model of scientific explanation, of simplicity degenerating into naive oversimplification. The workings of the universe are just not as simple as the workings of whirlpools, or sets of balls in boxes (indeed, since Descartes' time, the 'obviousness' of the mechanisms at work even in these homely examples has largely evaporated with the realization of the complexities at work at the atomic and sub-atomic levels). If modern physicists were to remain faithful to Descartes' programme of purging science of all items that are 'harder to understand than the things they are supposed to explain', then not much would be left of modern physics.

Science and Religion

According to the verdict of his biographer, Adrien Baillet, 'no philosopher ever had a more profound respect for the Deity than Monsieur Descartes'; and there is no good reason to doubt that Descartes approached the study of physics from the standpoint of a sincere believer in God.[28] At a fundamental metaphysical level the very possibility of achieving any genuine knowledge of the material world depended, for Descartes, on prior knowledge of God's existence (see above, chapter 3). Moreover, knowledge of the divine nature played an important role even with respect to the laws of Cartesian physics, for example in the deduction of the laws of motion from the immutability of God (see above pp. 90f). But in spite of all this, there were several respects in which Descartes' account of the physical universe ran the risk of bringing him into conflict with religious orthodoxy. It will be useful to conclude this review of Cartesian science by mentioning some of the principal areas of conflict.

Descartes' general inclination was whenever possible to avoid the danger of conflict with the ecclesiastical authorities. In replying to theological critics of his *Meditations* he insisted that he had 'never become involved in theological studies' except for his 'own private instruction' (Sixth Replies: AT VII 429; CSM II 289). From time to time, however, he is unable to resist such involvement – the best known example being his complex debate with Antoine Arnauld over the thorny question of whether his account of material substance was compatible with the doctrine of transubstantiation in the Eucharist.[29] But such cases were comparatively rare, and in an open letter written to his former teacher Pierre Dinet, the Father Provincial of the Jesuit order in France, Descartes provides this general statement of his outlook:

> I have often declared that I have no desire to meddle in any theological disputes; and since even in philosophy [i.e. natural science] I deal only with matters that are known very clearly by natural reason, these cannot be incompatible with anyone's theology – unless that theology manifestly clashes with the light of reason, which I am sure will not be said by anyone to be true of the theology he professes (AT VII 598; CSM II 394).

Perhaps the best known example of Descartes' caution in such matters is his decision to suppress his treatise *Le Monde* on hearing of the condemnation of Galileo.[30] Even when he was eventually prepared to publish his full account of the physical universe, in the *Principles*, Descartes was fairly circumspect in his discussion of the earth's movement. He is careful to insist that on his account the earth does not move, 'strictly speaking'. This is because X's moving is defined as X's being 'transferred from the vicinity of the bodies with which it is in contact' (*Principles* II 25); yet the earth, Descartes points out, is not transferred from the adjacent portions of the celestial vortex (*Principles* III 28). In spite of this convoluted manoeuvre (the convolutedness is apparent from the fact that Descartes has to admit that in his 'strict' sense, *none* of the planets can be said to move), Descartes does succeed in making his own view on the solar system pretty clear: 'the whole of the celestial matter in which the planets are located turns continuously like a vortex with the sun at its centre' (*Principles* III 30). The earth, moreover, is explicitly included as one of the planets (ibid.). As for the diurnal motion of the earth, Descartes is quite unambiguous in asserting that the earth does indeed rotate daily on its axis (*Principles* III 33). In general, Descartes was fully committed to the new Copernican cosmology, and to its implications for the status of the earth. 'The fact that we think of our own heaven and earth as so large is due to prejudice', Descartes reportedly remarked to Burman. He goes on:

We think of the earth as the end of all things, and do not consider that it too is a planet which moves like Mars, Saturn, etc. – bodies we do not make so much of (AT V 171; CB 40).

In fact Descartes goes beyond Copernicus in recognizing that the sun is only one star among innumerable others, each the centre of its own 'vortex' (*Principles* III 46). Each star, Descartes implies in *Le Monde*, may possess its own planetary system (AT XI 56).

Descartes' unwavering recognition of the relative unimportance of the earth as only one planet revolving round one of infinitely many stars is the most strikingly 'modern' feature of his cosmology. Moreover, his rejection of the old geocentric universe is not just a matter of astronomy. As Descartes saw it, stripping the earth of its status as the centre of all things had vital implications for the place of mankind in the divine plan:

It is a common habit of men to suppose that they are the dearest of God's creatures, and that all things are therefore made for their benefit. They think that their own dwelling place, the earth, is of supreme importance, that it contains everything that exists, and that for its sake everything was created. But what do we know of what God may have created outside the earth, on the stars and so on? How do we know that he has not placed there other creatures, other lives, and other 'men' or at least beings analogous to men . . . ? (AT V 168; CB 36).

Part of the target which Descartes is attacking here is the so-called doctrine of 'final causes'. One of Aristotle's four kinds of reason or explanation was the teleological explanation or 'final cause' – what he called '*that for the sake of which*'. Typically, this kind of explanation involves reference to functions or purposes – flowers have scent *for the sake of* attracting insects; lions have sharp claws *for the sake of* rending their prey. Such explanations were and are extremely common, especially in the biological sciences, and need not imply (nor did they for Aristotle) that all or any of the features of plants and animals are the result of conscious, intentional design.[31] As it developed in medieval and scholastic philosophy, however, the doctrine of 'final causes' implied that an explanation of the structure and behaviour of plants, trees, clouds, planets and everything in nature could in principle be found by looking at the function or purpose of these things in the overall design of a benevolent creator, whose special care was the welfare of mankind. This comfortable and reassuring notion was neatly expressed by Paracelsus in the century prior to Descartes:

It is God's will that nothing remain unknown to man as he walks in the light of nature; for all things belonging to nature exist for the sake of man.[32]

For Descartes, both parts of this claim are simply false. First, though Descartes believes in the 'light of nature' in the sense that he believes that we have the divinely implanted mental capacity to achieve certain and reliable knowledge, he nonetheless believes that there are fixed and unalterable limits to that knowledge; hence it is false that nothing need remain unknown to man. 'We must always remember that our mental capacity is very mediocre . . . Hence we cannot suppose that our mind can grasp the ends which God set before himself in creating the universe' (*Principles* III 2: AT VIII 80; CSM II 248). Secondly, Descartes wholly rejects the idea that all things 'exist for the sake of man': 'It would be the height of presumption to imagine that all things were created by God for our benefit alone' (ibid.).

As a result of this view, Descartes is adamant even in the *Meditations* that 'the customary search for final causes is totally useless in physics' (Fourth Meditation: AT VII 55; CSM II 39). In the Fifth Replies, he puts it even more strongly: 'We cannot pretend that certain of God's purposes are more out in the open than others: all are equally hidden in the inscrutable abyss of his wisdom' (AT VII 375; CSM II 258). This is directly supported in the *Principles* by appeal to the vastness of the rest of the cosmos: 'In the study of physics it would be utterly ridiculous to suppose that all things were made for our benefit since there is no doubt that many things exist or once existed, though they are here no longer, which have never been seen or thought of by any man, and have never been of use to anyone' (*Principles* III 3: AT VIII 81; CSM I 249).

This uncompromising line clashes in a fairly obvious way with the biblical account in Genesis, where God is presented, in Milton's phrase, as creating 'all things for man's delightful use'.[33] Indeed, Descartes came quite close to rejecting the idea of a ready-made creation entirely. The account of the origins of the earth which is given in *Le Monde* is frankly evolutionary: from an initial primeval chaos of randomly moving particles, the parts of the universe will, in accordance with the universal laws of motion, 'disentangle themselves and rearrange themselves in such good order that they will have the form of a quite perfect world' (AT XI 34; CSM I 91). Descartes had, however, maintained the semi-pretense that he was describing not the actual universe but an imaginary 'new world': 'I shall be content to continue with the description I have begun as if my intention was simply to tell you a fable' (AT XI 48; CSM I 98).[34] In the *Principles*, Descartes is more careful to pay lip-service to prevailing orthodoxy:

There is no doubt that the world was created right from the start with all the perfection which it now has. The sun and the earth existed in the beginning and . . . Adam and Eve were born not as babies but as fully grown people. This is the doctrine of the Christian faith and our natural reason convinces us that it was so . . . Nevertheless, if we want to understand the nature of plants or of men, it is much better to consider how they can gradually grow from seeds than to consider how they were created by God in the beginning . . . Thus we may be able to think up certain very simple and easily known principles which can serve, as it were, as the seeds from which we can demonstrate that the stars, the earth and indeed everything we observe in this visible world could have sprung (*Principles* III 45: AT VIII 100; CSM I 256).

Though this sounds like a contortion act, it is not of course beyond the bounds of possibility that Descartes (or any scientist) should regard his theory as having a 'synchronic' rather than a 'diachronic' function – as illuminating the structure of a phenomenon rather than giving an account of its causal genesis. But the general thrust of the explanations given in the *Principles* and elsewhere make it clear that Descartes' aim is indeed a genetic one; we are left in no doubt that a full understanding of a given phemonenon is a matter of understanding how it in fact arose in accordance with the simple and universal principles of Cartesian physics.[35] Descartes was very conscious that his approach might raise difficulties of a theological kind, and in an attempt to give reassurance on this point he had written to Mersenne in 1641 'There will be no problem in adapting theology to my style of philosophy'. He had also promised that his 'Physics' (i.e. the work later published as the *Principles*) would include 'an explanation of the first chapter of Genesis' (28 January 1641: AT III 295; K 93). But some years later, in a revealing exchange with Burman, Descartes in effect admitted that providing such an explanation was a Herculean task which he was not equal to; he is also reported to have added the comment that 'the account of the creation to be found in Genesis is perhaps metaphorical and so ought to be left to the theologians' (AT V 169; CB 37).

Despite Descartes' difficulties over Genesis, and his preference for what may broadly be called an 'evolutionary' approach to cosmology, we never find any suggestion in his writings that this might lead to a wholly materialistic conception of the universe. On the contrary, God's creative power is required to set up the initial system, and to impart all their initial motions to the various parts of matter (*Principles* II 36: AT VIII 61; CSM I 240). Moreover, Descartes subscribed to the orthodox doctrine of God as 'preserver': not only does God create the world, but his continuous agency is required to maintain it in existence from moment to moment (*Principles* II 42: AT VIII 66; CSM I 243). Finally, Descartes never makes the Darwinian move of suggesting that conscious beings might evolve from more primitive life forms. For Descartes, as we shall see in the next chapter, conscious beings are radically different from mere 'extended substance'; in so far as we are thinking things there is a sense in which we lie altogether outside the material universe describable in terms of the laws of Cartesian physics.[36]

But in spite of these qualifications, it is easy to see what Pascal meant by his famous remark 'I cannot forgive Descartes; in all his philosophy he would have been quite willing to dispense with God.'[37] While the Cartesian universe certainly does not dispense with God, the conception of God which it invokes is an austere and in many respects impersonal one. God's ultimate purposes are inscrutable to mankind, and though what we do understand of the universe we understand clearly and distinctly, the vastness and scope of the divine creation is infinitely beyond our power to grasp.[38] The investigation of God's purposes, so far from playing a central role in science, is banished as presumptuous and irrelevant to physics. A firm distinction is made between the proper province of physics and that of theology – the latter being limited to matters of faith, revelation and biblical exegesis (with the last of these probably being restricted to the realm of metaphorical interpretation).[39] Finally, rather than being a garden planted for man's use, the world is seen as arising inevitably, and without any direct reference to the needs of man, simply as a result of the immutable laws of matter and motion.

When challenged by a critic about his rejection of final causes, Descartes wrote:

> It is true that everything was made for God's glory in the sense that we can praise God for all that he has made; and it is true that the sun was made to give us light, in the sense that we see that the sun does in fact give us light. But in metaphysics it would be childish and absurd to assert that God is like a conceited man who has no other goal in building the universe than to be praised by men; or that he made the sun, which is so many times larger than the earth, for no other reason than to give light to men, who occupy so small a part of it (to 'Hyperaspistes', August 1641: AT III 431; K 117).

Pascal might well have been terrified by the new Cartesian-style universe – the 'silent universe of infinite spaces'. But Descartes could reply to his critics that this conception of a majestic cosmos of which man was only a tiny part was far more in keeping with the true grandeur of an infinite creator than the narrowly anthropomorphic and anthropocentric picture which it aimed to replace.[40]

Notes

1 This is a highly compressed summary of an extended train of thought which occupies the whole first half of Meditation Six. Descartes' reasoning makes many false starts, and has many twists and turns along the way, before he reaches the conclusion quoted here. For a more detailed account of the argument see my 'Descartes' Sixth Meditation: the External World, "Nature" and Human Experience' in Vesey.

2 For Plato's insistence on non-temporary properties, see *Republic* 479. Compare Aristotle's account of 'demonstrative knowledge' in *Posterior Analytics* I 4.

3 See Davies, ch. 11. Cf. S. Kripke: 'Science attempts by investigating basic structural traits, to find the nature and thus the essence (in the philosophical sense) of natural kinds.' Essential properties of natural kinds are, for Kripke, necessary (though they must be discovered *a posteriori*, by empirical investigation (Kripke, 136–8).

4 Having commented on the fleeting nature of such qualities as colour, taste, smell, etc., Descartes proposes to set aside 'everything that does not *belong to* (*pertinere ad*) the wax' (AT VII 31; CSM II 20).

5 There are many respects in which Descartes' project in the second half of the *Meditations* turns out to be a kind of theodicy. The problem of human error and how it may be reconciled with the benevolence of God was a major theme of the Fourth Meditation (see ch. 3, above) and it occupies a major part of Descartes' attention in Meditation Six (AT VII 83ff; CSM II 58ff).

6 The latter phrase occurs in the Synopsis to the *Meditations* (AT VII 14; CSM II 10). The Latin term *corpus* is a pitfall for translators of Descartes. Sometimes it means 'body' in this general sense; sometimes a particular body (such as a stone); and sometimes the human body. Context will generally, but not always, resolve the ambiguity (see AT VII 54; CSM II 54, note 2). The lack of a definite or indefinite article in Latin causes similar problems with other key terms in Descartes such as *substantia*, which can mean substance in general, or a particular substance (cf. *Principles* I 63 and 64).

7 To suppose that air is not corporeal, or is a 'mere nothing', is one of the preconceived opinions which Descartes lists as typical of those who have not progressed beyond a conception of the world that is based on the senses (*Principles* I 71).

8 See above, ch. 2, pp. 26f.

9 Descartes eventually proposes an account of colour that makes the colours we perceive dependent on the speeds and motions of the particles of objects. See *Description of the Human Body*: AT XI 255/6; CSM I 323. (One may compare more sophisticated modern explanations in terms of electromagnetic wavelengths of light.) But despite this the notion of a sensible quality involves something irreducibly 'mentalistic' which, for Descartes, is not susceptible of quantitative analysis. See below, ch. 6 pp. 135ff. It should be noted that the terms *qualia* and *quanta* are not Descartes' own. See below, ch. 6, note 8.

10 In Aristotle a substance is that which is a subject of predication, but cannot be predicated of other things; thus an individual horse or man is a substance, but whiteness is not a substance but a predicate (*Categories* 2a 12). Aristotle also suggests, however, that a substance, being an ultimate subject of predication, is something that has independent existence (see *Categories* 1a 24/5 and 2a 13).

11 By God's 'concurrence' is meant the continuous divine action necessary to maintain things in existence: 'An architect is the cause of a house only in the sense of being the cause of its coming into being; hence once the work is done it can remain in existence quite apart from the cause. But the sun is the cause of light, and God of created things not just in the sense that they are the causes of the *coming* into being, but also in the sense that they are causes of their *being*; and hence they must always continue to act on the effect to keep it in existence' (Fifth Replies: AT VII 369; CSM II 254).

12 See note 10 above.

13 There is here a strong anticipation of the Spinozan notion that individual physical things are simply modes of a single substance under the attribute of extension: *Ethics* (c.1665) Bk II P7. The influence of Descartes on Spinoza is particularly strong with respect to the use of terms like 'substance', 'attribute' and 'mode'. (Cf. Descartes' definition of substance as *res quae nulla alia re indiget ad existendum* – 'a thing which depends on no other thing for its existence' – (*Principles* I 51) with what Spinoza says about substance at the start of *Ethics* Bk 1.) For a discussion of the extent to which Descartes' conception of matter as pure extension marked a break with scholastic accounts, see G. Hatfield 'First Philosophy and Natural Philosophy' in Holland, 149ff.

14 Torricelli's invention of the barometer was in 1643; Pascal had the instrument carried up the Puy de Dome and observed that the height of the mercury column diminished, leaving an apparently empty space at the top of the column. Descartes and his supporters countered that from the fact that there was no perceptible matter in the space above the column it did not follow that it was 'empty'. Cf. *Principles* II 17.

15 It is not entirely clear that the property of impenetrability follows inevitably from the pure geometrical notion of three-dimensional extension. Cf. B. Williams: 'It is legitimate to think of two geometrical solids occupying (in one sense) the same space, or parts of them doing so, as when one conceives of two polyhedra constructed on the same base' (Williams, 229). It is perhaps partly for this type of reason that the Corpuscularians such as Boyle working later in the seventeenth century are often described as *adding* the notion of impenetrability to the Cartesian definition of matter as extended and divisible. Cf. Robert Boyle's account of 'one catholic or universal matter common to all bodies, by which I mean a substance extended, divisible and impenetrable' (*Origin of Forms and Qualities* (1666) in Boyle, 18; and cf. M. A. Stewart's comments in his editorial introduction, ibid., xvii).

16

> *Esse ea quae solido atque eterno corpore constent*
> *Semina quae rerum primordiaque esse docemus*
> *Unde omnis rerum nunc constet summa creata*
> (Lucretius, *De Rerum Natura* I 500–3; trans. J. C.)

17 The phrase 'as some philosophers have imagined' is added in the 1647 French version of the *Principles*. Leucippus is reckoned to be the founder of atomism; its chief exponent was Democritus (bn. 460 BC), but it was through Epicurus (bn. 341 BC) that the doctrines of atomism reached Lucretius. Various versions of atomism had, however, been defended by some of Descartes' contemporaries such as Pierre Gassendi, and the reference may well be to them. The passage from the *Principles* goes on to point out that 'even if God has chosen to bring it about that some particle of matter is incapable of being divided into smaller particles, it will not strictly speaking be correct to call this particle indivisible. For by making it indivisible by any of his creatures, God certainly could not take away his own power of dividing it' (AT VIII 51; CSM I 231). However, neither the argument about God's power, nor the earlier point about our ability to divide atoms 'in our thought' would refute an atomist who claimed merely that there are particles which are in fact incapable of being split by any physical force. Cf. ALQ III 166.

18 Fifth Meditation: AT VII 71; CSM II 49. Cf. *Conversation with Burman*: 'The only difference [between mathematics and physics] is that Physics considers its object not just as a true and real entity, but also as something actually and specifically existing. Mathematics on the other hand considers its object merely as possible, i.e. as something which does not actually exist in space but is capable of so doing' (AT V 160; CB 23).

19 Bacon, notoriously, reduced the status of mathematics to that of a mere 'appendix' to science, criticizing the 'daintiness and pride of mathematicians who will needs have this science almost domineer over physic' (*De Dignitate et Augmentiis scientiarum* (1623), in Bacon, 476).

20 See Galileo, VI 232. See also note 34 below.

21 See letter to Mersenne of 15 April 1630, AT I 139. 'I am tired of mathematics and take little account of them now'. By 1638 Descartes was writing to Mersenne 'I have long been protesting that I do not wish to keep working on geometry and I think I can now decently stop it altogether' (letter of 12 September 1638, AT II 361–2). These and other useful sources for Descartes' attitude to mathematics are cited in Clarke, 119.

22 The term 'inertia' was often used in scholastic philosophy to refer to a supposed 'natural' quality of 'inertness' or 'sluggishness' in terrestrial bodies. This notion Descartes firmly rejects (see letter to Mersenne of December 1638, AT II 466–7; ALQ II 113). The key to the modern notion of inertia – viz. the idea that it is a *change* in motion, not motion itself that stands in need of an explanation – is well expressed in *Principles* II 26: 'No more action is required for motion than for rest . . . For example the action needed to move a boat which is at rest in still water is no greater than that needed to stop it suddenly when it is moving . . .' (AT VIII 54; CSM I 234). In fact this idea had been anticipated many years earlier by Galileo: 'A ship that had received some impetus through the tranquil sea would move continually round our globe without ever stopping, and placed at rest would rest for ever' (letter of 1612; Galileo V, 227, cited in Drake, 186). Galileo failed, however, to anticipate the basic principle of Newtonian physics – continuance of motion at uniform speed in a straight line, maintaining instead that 'if natural bodies have it from nature to be moved by any

movement, this can only be circular motion, nor is it possible that nature has given to any of its integral bodies a propensity to be moved in a straight line' (*Reply to Ingoli* (1624); Galileo VI, 558, cited in Drake, 294). Although Descartes anticipates the rectilinear principle, he maintains that bodies interact in such a way that all actual motion must be in a closed curve (*Principles* II 33). For the relative theoretical poverty of Descartes' principle of inertia, see Miller and Miller, 64ff.

23 For an illuminating discussion of Descartes' use of the term *expérience*, see Clarke, 21ff.

24 For more on this interpretation of Cartesian science, see my comments in *Descartes' Conversation with Burman* (CB 112). For Descartes' rejection of the possibility of strict mathematical deductivism in science see letter to Mersenne of 17 May 1638: 'to ask for geometrical demonstrations in the field of physics is to ask the impossible' (AT II 142; K55).

25 Descartes frequently uses the term 'comparison' (Fr. *comparaison*) in connection with his employment of models. See further Clarke, 123ff. But the translation 'analogy' which Clarke employs is a little too weak for what Descartes has in mind. It is of course true that Descartes' comparisons are not supposed to hold in *all* respects. (Cf. the famous comparison between ordinary ocular vision and the transmission of movements via the sticks used by a blind man at *Optics* 6 (AT VI 135; CSM I 169)). But in general, when comparing a model to the phenomenon to be explained, Descartes supposes that the underlying mechanism is identical in both cases. It does not differ 'any more than a large circle differs from a small one' (letter to Morin of 12 September 1638: AT II 367–8).

26 Harré, 174.

27 This is not, of course, to suggest that the models employed by modern science can be verified conclusively; it has long been accepted that this type of positivistic ideal is unattainable. What modern science does in general demand in the assessment of its models, however, is the systematic matching of predicted results against observed results; recognition of the importance of this requirement (grasped, for example, by Galileo) is largely lacking in Descartes.

28 Baillet, II 503. There is a long history, beginning in Descartes' own lifetime, of allegations that Descartes' professed religious belief was insincere or due simply to caution. Some of the accusations were pure calumny (as in the case of the attacks of Voetius of Utrecht; see above, chapter 1 pp. 15ff); but there is no doubt that many saw Descartes' separation of theology and philosophy, and his articulation of a physics based solely on 'matter and motion' as paving the way for a world-view which had no place for God. The reactions of the Cambridge Platonist Henry More (who corresponded with Descartes in the late 1640s) are instructive in this respect: he began by cautiously welcoming Descartes' philosophy (as providing, for example, a defence of the immortality of the soul), but gradually came to see Cartesian cosmology as providing the royal road to atheism. See A. Gabbey 'Philosophia Cartesiana Triumphata: Henry More 1646–1671' in Lennon et al., 171ff.

29 The issue arose because Descartes rejected the scholastic terminology of 'substantial forms' and 'real accidents', and conceived of matter as mere extension, capable of being modified in various ways (see above, pp. 84ff).

Antoine Arnauld, author of the Fourth Objections, asked whether this was consistent with the doctrine of the transubstantiation according to which 'we believe on faith that the substance of the bread is taken away from the bread of the Eucharist, and only the accidents remain' (AT VII 217; CSM II 153). Descartes in his reply makes clear his view that 'the supposition of real accidents is opposed to philosophical principles', but suggests that the theological doctrine of the Eucharist can get along perfectly well without this supposition (AT VII 254f; CSM II 176f). For further details see R. A. Watson, 'Transubstantiation among the Cartesians' in Lennon et al., 127ff.

30 See above, ch. 1, pp. 11f.

31 For Aristotle's account of the 'final cause' or 'that for the sake of which' see *Physics* II 3 and II 8.

32 Paracelsus, I 12 148f.; in Jacobi, 183.

33 *Paradise Lost* (1667) IV 692.

34 It has been suggested that Descartes' description of his account as a 'fable' is not just due to prudence but has an epistemological significance: Descartes is acknowledging the speculative character of his hypotheses, which, when he wrote *Le Monde*, were not yet integrated into a complete philosophical system with indubitable metaphysical foundations. For this view see Collins, 9. Another, more radical, interpretation is that Descartes means to point out that his account may have explanatory value even if it is not literally true. Cf. *Principles* IV 204: 'Just as the same craftsman could make two clocks which tell the time equally well and look completely alike from the outside, but have completely different assemblies of wheels inside, so the supreme craftsman of the world could have produced all that we see in several different ways. I am happy to admit this . . . And by imagining what the various causes are, and considering their results, we shall achieve our aim irrespective of whether these imagined causes are true or false, since the result is taken to be no different, so far as the observable effects are concerned' (AT IXB 321; CSM I 289). In the following article, however, Descartes goes on to record his belief in the literal truth of his account. More recently, the French scholar J.-L. Marion has proposed what may loosely be called a 'semiotic' interpretation of Descartes' talk of his world as a 'fable'. The initial world of shapes and figures is transformed by nature, via a kind of 'coding' process, so as to produce in us observers sensations and images which have no intelligible relation to the real world. The scientist's job is to reconstruct the code, proceeding from effects (sensible images) to their causes (the shapes and figures of the extended world). 'If the true world is then called a fable, this is not because it is illusory but because it is "described" or "represented" (*dit*) by means of the initial figures' (Marion, (II) 252). This seems to be an almost intolerably stretched interpretation of what Descartes may have meant by *fable*; but on the question of the relation between sensible qualities (such as colour) and the intelligible qualities (such as shape) Marion's account appears to be on the right lines: see below, ch. 6 pp. 135ff.

35 Cf. *Discourse* Part 5: 'the nature of things is much easier to conceive if we see them develop gradually than if we consider them only in their completed form' (AT VI 45; CSM I 134). (Descartes is careful however to add the pious qualification that the biblical account is 'much more likely'.) Cf. also

Descartes' comments on animal physiology: a proper understanding of the various bodily functions requires an account of how the animal was originally formed *ab ovo* (*Conversation with Burman*: AT V 171; CB 39; and cf. *Description of Human Body*: AT XI 252; CSM I 321).

36 See ch. 5, pp. 110ff.

37 Pascal, *Pensées* no. 77 (first published 1670).

38 For the vastness of the cosmos, see *Principles* III 1 (AT VIII 80; CSM I 248); and for its indefinite extension, see letter to Chanut of June 1647 (AT V 51; K 221). Descartes normally preferred to use the term 'indefinite' to describe the material universe, reserving the term 'infinite' for God alone (*Principles* I 27: AT VIII 15; CSM I 202).

39 For the distinction between the province of theology and that of philosophy, see *Conversation with Burman*: AT V 159, 176; CB 21, 46 and 115.

40 Pascal *Pensées* no. 206: '*le silence éternel de ces espaces infinis m'effraie*'. Despite the grandeur of the Cartesian system, its stress on the relative insignificance of man, from a cosmological standpoint, may well have contributed to the impersonal, 'deistic' conception of God that became popular in the century following Descartes. Henry More, in his criticisms of Descartes, clearly believed that supporters of the Cartesian system could easily slide into a pantheistic cosmology of the Spinozan type, and thence into atheism. (Cf. More's bitter description of Spinoza as 'a *Jew* first, after a *Cartesian* and now an atheist'; letter of 4 December 1671, cited by A. Gabbey in Lennon et al.) Descartes was challenged by Princess Elizabeth on the question of whether an infinite universe might not threaten the belief in God's particular concern for mankind; he replied 'the greater we esteem the works of God to be, the better we observe the infinity of his power; and the better known this infinity is to us, the more certain we are that it extends even to the most particular actions of human beings' (letter of 6 October 1645: AT IV 315; K 181).

5

Cartesian Man

Men, Machines and Animals

It is sometimes said that Descartes' comprehensive programme for a unified scientific understanding of the world stopped short of including mankind. This is not entirely true. As far as human physiology went, Descartes was adamant that his general explanatory schema was perfectly applicable to the workings of the body; the selfsame laws and principles that govern the operation of astronomical, meteorological or geological events are, Descartes maintains, sufficient to explain the behaviour of the bodily organs.[1] Descartes is brusquely dismissive of those who invoke a 'psyche' or soul to account for such functions as nutrition, digestion and locomotion. In his unfinished treatise, the *Description of the Human Body*, he writes:

> I shall try to give such a full account of the entire bodily machine that we will have no more reason to think that it is our soul which produces in it the movements which we know by experience are not controlled by our will than we have reason to think that there is a soul in a clock which makes it tell the time (AT XI 226; CSM I 315).

Descartes was particularly interested in automatic physical functions – for example, respiration, blinking and swallowing – whose occurrence is largely independent of any conscious process; and his detailed anatomical studies had led him to the correct conclusion that the key to understanding such functions was the nervous system. In place of the modern theory of transmission of electrical impulses, Descartes conceives of neural activity along purely mechanical lines: the nerves are little pipes through which the fast-moving vapour called the 'animal spirits' flows, so as to inflate the muscles and cause movement (*Treatise on Man*: AT XI 165; CSM I 104; *Passions of the Soul*, Part I, art. 11). While inaccurate in its details, the Cartesian theory acted as a stimulus for scientific research by proposing that the human nervous system could be regarded as a mechanism which was as susceptible of detailed investigation as any other physical structure in the universe. Passages like the following are rightly regarded as containing the germ of what is now termed the theory of reflex action:

> When people take a fall and stick out their hands so as to protect their head, it is not reason that instructs them to do this; it is simply that the sight of the impending fall reaches the brain and sends the animal spirits into the nerves in the manner necessary to produce this movement even without any mental volition, just as it would be produced in a machine (AT VII 230; CSM II 161).

The comparison between the human body and a machine shocked some of Descartes' readers; but throughout Descartes' career it remained absolutely central to his physiology. It is to be found in the *Treatise on Man*, written early in the 1630s, and recurs unaltered in the *Description of the Human Body*, written two years before his death. A famous passage in the *Discourse on the Method* sums up the position:

> This [how the animal spirits are sent from the brain to the muscles so as to make the parts of the body move] will not seem at all strange to those who know how many kinds of automatons, or moving machines, the skill of man can construct with the use of very few parts, in comparison with the great multitude of bones, muscles, nerves, arteries, veins and all the other parts that are in the body of any animal. For they will regard this body as a machine which, having been made by the hands of God, is incomparably better ordered than any machine that can be devised by man, and contains in itself movements more wonderful than those in any such machine (AT VI 56; CSM I 139).

In the case of non-human animals, Descartes believed that the model of the machine was *all* that was needed to account for the observed behaviour. The doctrine of the *bête-machine* as it came to be known, gained a distinctly sinister reputation in the century following Descartes: if animals were mere mechanical automata, then Cartesian anatomists could blandly claim that the screams of vivisected animals nailed to their work benches were of no more significance than the chimes of a clock, or the piping of a church organ when certain keys were pressed.[2] Not surprisingly, Descartes is, for this reason, apt to be regarded as something of an ogre by modern animal liberationists. In fact, though, as we shall see when we come to discuss the Cartesian account of sentience, Descartes' views were not always straightforward, or as crude as the machine model initially suggests.

But what of mankind? The doctrine of the *bête–machine*, that animals are purely mechanical automata, implies that it would be possible in principle to construct an artificial machine that was behaviourally indistinguishable from, e.g., a monkey. But if the *bête–machine*, why not the *homme–machine*? Why, as La Mettrie was to propose later in the century, should we not suppose that all human behaviour can be explained on purely mechanical principles in terms of the 'disposition of the internal organs'?[3] Despite his mechanistic approach to physiology, Descartes consistently refuses to go along with this final piece of reductionism. Two of his reasons are set out with great clarity in the *Discourse*:

> If any such machines bore a resemblance to our bodies, and imitated our actions as closely as possible for all practical purposes, we should still have two very certain means of recognizing that they were not real men. The first is that they could never use words or put together other signs as we do in order to declare our thoughts to others. For we can certainly conceive of a machine so constructed that it utters words, and even utters words corresponding to bodily actions causing a change in its organs (e.g. if you touch it in one spot it asks you what you want of it, if you touch it in another it cries out that you are hurting it, and so on). But it is not conceivable that such a machine should produce different arrangements of words so as to give an appropriately meaningful answer to whatever is said in its presence, as the dullest of men can do. Secondly, even though such machines might do some things as well as we do them, or perhaps even better, they would inevitably fail in others, which would reveal that they were acting not through understanding but only from the disposition of their organs. For whereas reason is a universal instrument which can be used in all kinds of situations, these organs need some particular disposition for each particular action; hence it is for all practical purposes impossible for a machine to have enough different organs to make it act in all the contingencies of life in the way in which our reason makes us act (AT VI 56; CSM I 140).

First, a machine could never be a genuine language user; second, a machine's output is geared to a finite range of inputs – it could never have the ability to cope with the indefinitely diverse contingencies of life. There are hints both in the passage quoted above and elsewhere that Descartes regards these two points as closely connected: the second deficiency of the machine entails the first, since if a machine's responses are geared to specific sets of conditions, it must necessarily lack the language-user's ability to respond sensibly to an indefinite range of situations. This is a point which has been taken up in our own day by the linguistic theorist Noam Chomsky. In Chomsky's phrase, genuine linguistic competence is 'stimulus-free'. The range of human linguistic performances is not determined by a range of environmental conditions: 'even at the lowest level of intelligence the characteristic use of language is free and creative . . . in that one can instantaneously interpret an indefinitely large range of utterances . . .'[4] Language, for Descartes as for Chomsky, is unique to man: the universal capacity to respond appropriately to an indefinite range of utterances sets us apart from even the most sophisticated machines. As for the so-called utterances of animals, these, Descartes observes in a letter to the Marquis of Newcastle of 23 November 1646, are not to be counted as genuine language:

> If you teach a magpie to say good-day to its mistress, when it sees her approach, this can only be by making the utterance of the word the expression of one of its passions. For instance, it will be the expression of the hope of eating, if it has always been given a tidbit when it says the word. Similarly, all the things which dogs, horses and monkeys are taught to perform are only the expression of their fear, their hope or their joy . . . But the use of words, so defined, is peculiar to human beings (AT IV 574; K 207).[5]

To say that the capacities of human beings set them apart from animals still leaves it unclear where the explanation for these special capacities lies. Nowadays we are likely to assume (as indeed Chomsky does) that the explanation must ultimately be sought in terms of human brain complexity, and in particular in the structure of the cerebral cortex; and this in turn, we are likely to suppose, must ultimately depend on the genetic make-up of our species. But in Descartes' discussion of the differences between humans and animals, the fact that human beings can think, and express their thoughts in language, is attributed to their being endowed with a 'rational soul' (Fr., *âme rationale*; Lat., *anima rationalis* (*Discourse* Part 6: AT VI 59; CSM I 141; cf. *Treatise on Man*: AT XI 131; CSM I 101).

Nowadays the word 'soul' is most commonly used in religious contexts; the notion which it conjures up is that of the supposedly immaterial, spiritual part of us which, believers in an afterlife maintain, will survive the death of the body. But in seventeenth-century philosophical usage the term 'soul' did not necessarily imply something immaterial and purely spiritual. According to the Aristotelian account of *psyche*, which strongly influenced scholastic philosophy, the relationship of soul to body is defined in terms of the relationship of 'form' to 'matter'; very roughly, to say that the body is 'ensouled' or 'animated' is to say that the matter of the body is organized in such a way that it has the capacity to function in various ways (to digest, to move, to have sensations, to think). Thus for the Aristotelian, talk of 'soul' need not imply any separate or separable spirit; on the contrary the standard Aristotelian approach insists that the soul *qua* form must be embodied in matter in order to produce a living, functioning human being.[6] Moreover, quite apart from the Aristotelian account, there were other more crudely physicalistic models of the soul which were commonly canvassed in Descartes' time. One conventional view was that the soul was 'something tenuous, like a wind or fire or ether' which permeated the more solid parts of the body. (This conception is referred to in passing by Descartes in the Second Meditation: AT VII 26; CSM II 17; see also Gassendi's views in the Fifth Objections: AT VII 260; CSM II 181). From this it may be seen that Descartes's introduction of the term 'rational soul' does not, in and of itself, signal to his readers the thesis that some immaterial non-physical component must be posited in order to explain human capacities.

Nevertheless, Descartes does maintain just such a thesis, and in the passage under discussion he swiftly and explicitly rejects both the Aristotelian model of the soul and any materialistic account. By 'rational soul', he explains, he means not something 'which can be derived in some way from the potentiality of matter' but something which 'must be specially created' (AT VI 59; CSM I 141). At this point we enter the heart of the Cartesian metaphysics of human nature. That which makes us characteristically human, the thinking part of us, is not something which is derivable from, or in any way a function of, our brain structure, or any of our other physiological attributes. It is entirely non-material – a separate and separable spirit, specially implanted in each body by God.

Res Cogitans

Although Descartes' talk of a non-physical soul accords with theology (and he hoped it would please the theologians),[7] the reasons which led him to believe that the thinking part of him was non-material were not theological ones. And indeed the word 'soul' may mislead the modern reader into supposing that that which Descartes considers to be immaterial is 'spiritual' in the narrow sense of having to do with elevated aesthetic, moral or religious sensibilities. In fact, Descartes' 'soul' is by no means confined to the 'soulful' (in the modern sense) aspects of our mind. Quite simply 'soul' (Fr. *âme*, Lat. *anima*) and 'mind' (Fr. *esprit*, Lat. *mens*) are synonymous in Descartes. Both are merely convenient labels for *res cogitans* – that which thinks (AT VII 487; CSM II 329); and what Descartes has in mind here is the whole range of conscious mental activity.

The Argument from Doubt

In Part Four of the *Discourse*, Descartes seems to arrive at the non-materiality of the mind or soul by an application of his standard technique of the method of doubt. Having established that he exists – *je pense, donc je suis* – he goes on to ask what exactly is this 'I' whose existence he is sure of:

> Next, I attentively examined what I was. I saw that while I could pretend that I had no body, and that there was no world and no place for me to be in, I could not for all that pretend that I did not exist . . . From this I knew that I was a substance whose whole essence or nature is simply to think, and which does not require any place or depend on any material thing, in order to exist. Accordingly this 'I' – that is, the soul by which I am what I am – is entirely distinct from the body . . . and would not fail to be whatever it is even if the body did not exist (AT VI 33; CSM I 127).

This argument is paraphrased by Descartes' astute critic Antoine Arnauld as follows: 'I can doubt whether I have body. Yet I cannot doubt that I am, or exist. Therefore I who am doubting and thinking am not a body For, in that case in having doubts about my body I should be having doubts about myself' (Fourth Objections: AT VII 198; CSM II 139). The reasoning may appear plausible at first sight, yet as Arnauld ingeniously proceeds to show, it is quite invalid. Consider a parallel piece of reasoning concerning a right-angled triangle. I may well be able to doubt (especially if I am not too knowledgeable about geometry) that a right-angled triangle has the property of having the square on its hypotenuse equal to the sum of the squares on its other two sides (call this the 'Pythagorean property'). Now from the fact that I am able to doubt that the triangle has the Pythagorean property, it does not at all follow that the triangle lacks it, or that this property is not essential to the triangle. On the contrary, geometers can prove that, irrespective of any doubts I may have, this property is indeed a necessary part of the triangle's essence. So by parity of reasoning it seems perfectly possible that, despite my ability to imagine myself without a body, the body is indeed an essential part of me – something without which I could not exist.

In his Synopsis to the *Meditations*, Descartes specifically refers to the problem of how it is supposed to follow from the fact that he is not aware of anything except thinking as belonging to himself, that nothing else does in fact belong to his nature. Referring to the original passage in the *Discourse*, he says:

> It was not my intention to make those exclusions [i.e. the excluding of anything physical from my essence] in an order corresponding to the actual truth of the matter (which I was not dealing with at that stage) but merely in an order corresponding to my own perception . . . So the sense of the passage was that I was aware of nothing at all that I knew belonged to my essence except that I was a thinking thing . . . (AT VII 8; CSM II 7).

The implication of this somewhat tortuous remark appears to be that in the relevant part of the *Discourse* (and the same would go for the Second Meditation) Descartes is merely recording his subjective perceptions concerning his nature or essence; he is not claiming that these map on to what is objectively the case. He can, using the method of doubt, arrive at a conception of himself which excludes all body; but it remains to be seen whether this conception corresponds to the way things really are. This interpretation is confirmed by some comments on the Second Meditation which Descartes published in 1647: 'When I said that the soul knows itself as an immaterial substance, I did not at all mean an entire negation or exclusion . . . for I said that in spite of this we are not sure that there is nothing material in the soul (AT IX 215; CSM II 276).[8] So whatever he had originally intended by pointing out that he could doubt that he had a body but not that he was thinking, Descartes was eventually clear that this fact, of itself, could not constitute a proof of the immateriality of the soul.

The Argument from Clear and Distinct Perception

Where Descartes does indubitably and unequivocally undertake to prove that the mind or soul is immaterial and 'really distinct' from the body, is in the Sixth Meditation. The proof (generally known as the 'Argument from Clear and Distinct Perception') is as follows:

> I know that everything which I clearly and distinctly understand is capable of being created by God so as to correspond exactly with my understanding of it. Hence the fact that I can clearly and distinctly understand one thing apart from another is enough to make me certain that the two things are distinct since they are capable of being separated, at least by God. Thus, simply by knowing that I exist, and seeing at the same time that absolutely nothing else belongs to my nature or essence except that I am a thinking thing, I can infer correctly that my essence consists solely in the fact that I am a thinking thing . . . I have a clear and distinct idea of myself, in so far as I am simply a thinking, non-extended thing; and on the other hand I have a distinct idea of body, in so far as this is simply an extended, non-thinking thing. And accordingly it is certain that I am really distinct from my body and can exist without it (AT VII 78; CSM II 54).

But does the fact that I can clearly and distinctly perceive mind apart from body show that the two are really distinct? Although the argument appears to be different from the earlier argument from doubt, Arnauld hastens to point out that it appears vulnerable to a very similar objection. Take again the case of our right-angled triangle. Surely one could clearly and distinctly perceive that triangle ABC has the property of being right-angled without clearly and distinctly perceiving that it has the Pythagorean property. So, on Descartes' reasoning, it would seem to follow that the two properties are distinct – that one could exist without the other. Yet in fact, despite my ability to perceive the one property apart from the other, the two are indeed inseparably and essentially linked. Even God could not create a right-angled triangle which lacked the Pythagorean property (cf. Fourth Objections: AT VII 202; CSM II 142).

Descartes, in reply, denied that the parallel was a fair one: 'neither the triangle nor the property can be understood as a complete thing in the way in which mind and body can be so understood' (AT VII 224; CSM II 158). What exactly is meant by this notion of a 'complete thing'? By a 'thing', Descartes explains, he means a substance – something that can exist on its own. And he writes elsewhere that 'the idea of a substance with its extension and shape is a complete idea because I can conceive it alone [i.e. with these attributes and no others]' (letter to Gibieuf of 19 January 1642: AT III 475; K 124). In the case of the mind, Descartes says in the Fourth Replies:

> since that of which I am aware [the attribute of thought] is sufficient to enable me to subsist with it and it alone, I am certain that I could have been created by God without having these other attributes of which I am unaware, and hence that these attributes do not belong to the essence of mind. For if something can exist without some attribute, then it seems to me that that attribute is not included in its essence (AT VII 219; CSM II 155).

Earlier in this passage Descartes had admitted that there may be many properties within him of which he is unaware, and hence he cannot know that his concept of himself is 'adequate' (i.e. contains all the features that actually pertain to him.) But nevertheless his concept of mind is, he maintains, *complete*; for what he is aware of – his thinking – is sufficient for him to exist with this attribute *and this alone*.[9]

The structure on which this reasoning is based seems clear enough: if a substance can exist with feature F and no other features, then it follows that it is, in virtue of having F, a complete substance. Conversely, if I know that a substance can exist without some property G, then I can know that G is no part of its essence. But unfortunately none of this allays the fundamental misgiving which one feels about the premises of Descartes' argument. How does Descartes know that he could continue to exist without a body? He may reply that he would continue to think, and so could still be sure of his existence – he could still assert *cogito ergo sum*. But how can he know that he would continue to think? Might it not be that certain corporeal attributes (e.g. having a brain) are necessary for thinking? Indeed, might not thinking, as various twentieth-century philosophers have suggested, actually be a physical process? (Such a suggestion, though in fairly speculative form, had indeed been made in Descartes' own day.)[10] Part of the problem with Descartes' reasoning here – and it is a pervasive source of difficulty for his account of the mind – is that he conceives of thinking as a totally 'transparent' process; that is, he takes it to comprise no more than what he is directly aware of when he thinks and doubts and meditates. Yet why should it be supposed that thought is something of which we have a transparently clear understanding? Why should it not be the case, as indeed modern scientific research seems increasingly to be discovering, that it is an extremely obscure and complicated process – vastly more difficult to understand than, say, digestion.

The Cartesian might reply here that this does not alter the fact that thinking *qua* thinking (comprising the ponderings and willings and doubtings of which I am immediately aware) is as entirely and transparently clear to me as could be. And it is certainly true, and important, that I have immediate and indubitable access to my thoughts in a way in which I do not have immediate and indubitable access to, say, my digestive processes. In this sense, Descartes may argue, each of us can know with a special certainty that he is a thinking thing. But from the fact that I know I am a thinking thing, it still does not follow that I know that my nature is *simply* to think. To put it another way, it has still to be shown that what *does* the thinking is something which has no essential attributes apart from that of which I am directly aware. This point was well put by Pierre Gassendi in the Fifth Objections:

> When you say that you are a thinking thing, then we know what you are saying, but we knew it already . . . Who doubts that you are thinking? What we were unclear about, what we are looking for, is that inner substance of yours whose property is to think (AT VII 276; CSM II 192).

As Hobbes put it, even more succinctly: 'It may be that the thing that thinks is the subject to which mind, reason or intellect belong, and this subject may be something corporeal' (AT VII 173; CSM II 122). That which does the thinking may well be something corporeal; Descartes has not proved otherwise.

The Divisibility Argument

Descartes' belief that he is 'really distinct from his body and could exist without it' is reinforced by his perception that he *qua* thinking thing is something non-extended, whereas his body shares with corporeal matter in general the attribute of extension. Mind and body, for Descartes, are not merely distinct: they are defined in mutually exclusive terms. Now as we saw when examining Descartes' account of the material universe, the extendedness of body or matter necessarily entails that it is divisible.[11] Mind, by contrast, is of its nature indivisible, as Descartes argues towards the end of the Sixth Meditation:

> There is a great difference between the mind and the body inasmuch as the body is by its very nature always divisible while the mind is utterly indivisible. For when I consider the mind, or myself in so far as I am merely a thinking thing, I am unable to distinguish any parts within myself; I understand myself to be something quite single and complete. Although the whole mind seems to be united to the whole body, I recognize that if a foot or an arm or any other part of the body is cut off nothing has thereby been taken away from the mind (AT VII 86; CSM II 59).

The final part of this argument is curiously sketchy. It may well be the case that one can lose a foot without losing any of one's mental attributes, but it is, to say the least, far from clear that the same is true of the brain. We are now familiar with the fact that damage to the brain (e.g. by a stroke) can diminish mental functioning; and interestingly Descartes himself (as we shall see below) was ready to admit that there were at least some mental activities (such as imagination and sense-perception) in which the brain plays a crucial role. Nevertheless Descartes insists that what he calls 'pure thought' (for example, a volition to contemplate some abstract object, or an abstract perception of the intellect) can occur without any physiological events taking place, in the brain or anywhere else (cf. *Passions* I 20: AT XI 344; CSM I 336). Even if the body is destroyed entirely, the mind or soul is not harmed – it merely leaves the body (cf. *Description of the Human Body*: AT XI 225; CSM I 315). Bodily death, Descartes asserts, is merely a change of shape and configuration in the component parts of the matter of which the body is composed (Synopsis to *Meditations*: AT VII 14; CSM II 10). And 'we have no convincing reason', Descartes writes in the Second Replies, 'to suggest that the death or annihilation of a substance like the mind must result from such a trivial cause as a change of shape, for this is simply a mode, and what is more not a mode of the mind but of the body, which is distinct from the mind' (AT VII 153; CSM II 109).

There is of course ample evidence nowadays, from a range of phenomena (amnesia, senile dementia, coma produced by cerebral trauma and the like), that physical damage to the central nervous system causes mental impairment. And the depressingly probable inference from this must be that the total destruction of the central nervous system will cause total mental extinction. But for Descartes, as for Plato,[12] the doctrine of the immortality of the soul is impervious to this sort of consideration, since the doctrine has already been established on *a priori* grounds, via the claim that the soul is by its very nature quite distinct from the body. (Thus Descartes' insistence that bodily damage does not diminish the mind is not really an independent argument for the thesis of the immateriality of the mind; rather it is a consequence of that thesis.) So firmly committed is Descartes to the view that the thinking part of us is independent from the body, that he is led to make the remarkably counter-intuitive claim that the soul always continues to think – even during the deepest sleep, and even during early infancy (indeed even before birth, when the child is still in the womb) (AT VII 356; CSM II 247f). When challenged about the plausibility of the claim that the soul always thinks, Descartes replies that it *must* be true:

I believe that the soul is always thinking for the same reason as I believe that light is always shining . . . or that extended substance always has extension, and in general that whatever constitutes the nature of a thing always belongs to it as long as it exists. So it would be easier for me to believe that the soul ceased to exist at the times when it is supposed to cease to think than to conceive that it could exist without thought (letter to Gibieuf 19 January 1642; AT III 478; K 125).

What, though, of the claim that the mind is indivisible? Here at least Descartes does seem to have an independent argument for the view that the mind is immaterial (given the premise that matter is necessarily divisible). 'We cannot conceive of half of a mind', writes Descartes in his Synopsis of the *Meditations*, 'while we can always conceive of half of a body, however small' (AT VII 13; CSM II 9). Half a mind does seem an odd notion (we do say things like 'he has only got half a mind since his accident', but this does not imply that the mind has been divided, only that it is functioning less well). But what about *parts* of the mind? In Descartes' time it was conventional (as to some extent it still is) to divide the mind into various faculties – will, understanding, sensation. But Descartes observes that these are not 'parts' of the mind strictly speaking, since 'it is one and the same mind that wills and understands and has sensory perceptions' (Sixth Meditation: AT VII 86; CSM II 59). As it stands, this remark is not very clear; but presumably Descartes means that though my consciousness comprises a whole range of diverse activities, these are all referred to the same 'I'.

But should we accept that the 'I' of consciousness is something simple and indivisible? What of the commonplace fact (which led Plato to divide the soul into parts)[13] that our desires and our reason can pull us in opposite directions – as when one (greedy) part of us says 'take the second cream cake', and another (more prudent) part says 'put it back'? It is of course true that the structure of our language encourages the idea of a single centre of consciousness: it is the singular pronoun 'I' that is the subject both of the desire for the cake and of the resolve to avoid it. Each of us speaks in the first person singular, as a unitary individual, not in the first person plural, as a collectivity. But it is not clear that we are entitled to 'read off' from this linguistic fact any conclusions about the essential indivisibility and unitariness of consciousness. The Cartesian may reply that it is just subjectively evident to each person that he is a single undivided consciousness. But as Hume pointed out, subjective introspection does not, in any straightforward and incontestable way, reveal the presence of a single 'I' or ego.[14] The whole question of the nature of personal identity and individual consciousness has been the subject of intense scrutiny in recent years, and while the results of this work cannot be examined here, it is at least worth noting that the Cartesian picture of the self has come under considerable pressure. Recent empirical research, in particular, has suggested to some philosophers that our mental life may not be nearly as simple and unified as Descartes' account suggests:

> It is possible that the ordinary, simple idea of a single person will come to seem quaint one day, when the complexities of the human control system become clearer, and we become less certain that there is anything very important that we are *one* of.[15]

Whatever the outcome of this debate, however, Descartes' divisibility argument remains flawed. For even if one accepts the unitariness and indivisibility of consciousness, it remains possible that consciousness might be a (unitary and indivisible) property of a physical system. And if that which thinks is a physical thing (a brain, a nervous system, or perhaps a whole person) then even though the attribute of consciousness or thinking may in some sense be indivisible, the thing which does the thinking will of course be divisible, like any other physical thing. Considerations about the alleged unity of consciousness thus fail to establish the Cartesian claim that mental activity belongs to a separate, indivisible thing or substance.

Cartesian Dualism and Its Problems

By 'Cartesian dualism' is meant the thesis that man is a compound of two distinct substances – *res cogitans*, unextended thinking substance, or mind, and *res extensa*, extended corporeal substance, or body. 'Thought and extension', Descartes writes in the *Principles of Philosophy*, 'can be regarded as constituting the natures of intelligent substance and corporeal substance, and then they must be considered as nothing else but thinking substance itself, and extended substance itself – that is, as mind and body' (*Principles* I 63: AT VIII 31; CSM I 215). The central, and most controversial, feature of Descartes' dualism is its insistence on the non-corporeality of the mind, and some of the difficulties of this claim have already emerged. In the light of modern neurophysiological knowledge, the vast majority of scientists and philosophers, and probably most laymen too, would now regard Descartes' claim that an act of thinking or doubting 'needs no place and depends on no material thing' (e.g. requires no brain) as simply preposterous.[16]

A further notorious problem for dualism is the problem of interaction between mind and body. We know from experience that a mental change can cause a physical change (e.g. a desire to ask a question can cause someone's hand to go up); conversely, a physical change (e.g. the pressure of a sharp stone on my foot) can cause a mental change (the decision to remove my foot from the offending object). For such things to be possible, it seems that Descartes must allow some kind of causal flow from mind to body and *vice versa*; indeed he explicitly remarks that we know from our experience that mind acts upon, and is acted upon by, body (to Hyperaspistes August 1641: AT III 424; K 111; cf. to Elizabeth 21 May 1643: AT III 664; K 137). But since mind and body are defined by Descartes in terms of not just distinct but mutually incompatible attributes, it is not easy to see how such causal flow is possible. Normally Descartes holds that causal transactions require some relationship of similarity between effect and cause; but in the case of mind and body this is quite impossible, given the logical gulf between them (defined as they are by Descartes in terms of logically incompatible attributes). It is this problem which has given rise to Gilbert Ryle's celebrated description of the Cartesian account of the mind as the doctrine of the 'ghost in the machine'.[17] If the mind is indeed a ghostly, incorporeal substance, it is very hard to see how it could have the power to push the appropriate causal levers so as to initiate bodily movement. When Frans Burman in his interview with Descartes asked the philosopher 'how can the soul be affected by the body and vice versa when their natures are completely different?', Descartes lamely admitted 'This is very difficult to explain, but here our experience is sufficient, since it is so clear on this point that it cannot be gainsaid' (AT V 163; CB 28).

To this general worry about *how* psycho-physical interaction is possible in Descartes' system may be added a more specific worry about *where* it is supposed to take place. It seems that the soul, being non-corporeal, cannot have a location in the normal sense of occupying space. So where exactly do its transactions with the body occur? Descartes' frequent answer is that the soul is *united* with the body (Sixth Meditation: AT VII 81; CSM II 56); but he later admitted that he had said 'hardly anything' in the *Meditations* to explain what this union amounted to (to Elizabeth 21 May 1634: AT III 664; K 137). In the Sixth Replies, there is an attempt to explain the presence of the soul within the body by reference to the way in which 'gravity' or heaviness is popularly understood to be present in an object:

> Gravity, while remaining coextensive with the heavy body, can exercise all its force in any one part of the body; for if the body were hung from a rope attached to any part of it, it would still pull the rope down with all its force, just as if all the gravity existed in the part actually touching the rope instead of being scattered through the remaining parts. This is exactly the way in which I now understand the mind to be coextensive with the body – the whole mind in the whole body and the whole mind in any one of its parts (AT VII 442; CSM II 298).

The comparison is a curious one, particularly since in his writings on physics Descartes argues that 'gravity' or heaviness is not a real quality at all (AT IXB 8; CSM I 182f). Nor is the talk of the soul being 'coextensive' with the body readily intelligible in the light of Descartes' definition of the soul as an unextended substance. At best then, Descartes does not seem to have provided anything more than an obscure, if vaguely suggestive, analogy; though in his letters he continued to insist that the comparison could be a helpful one.[18]

In the *Passions of the Soul*, however, Descartes develops a much more detailed account of the way in which the soul interacts with the body and he specifically addresses the 'location' problem:

> We need to recognize that although the soul is joined to the whole body, nevertheless there is a certain part of the body where it exercises its functions more particularly than in all the others. It is commonly held that this part is the brain, or perhaps the heart – the brain because the sense organs are related to it, and the heart because we feel the passions as if they were in it. But on carefully examining the matter I think I have clearly established that the part of the body in which the soul directly exercises its functions is not the heart at all, or the whole of the brain. It is rather the innermost part of the brain, which is a certain very small gland situated in

the middle of the brain's substance and above the passage through which the spirits in the brain's anterior cavities communicate with those in its posterior cavities (*Passions* I, 31: AT XI 352; CSM I 340).

A wealth of experimental and observational data led Descartes to the conclusion that the point of interaction between soul and body must be within the brain. His favourite example is the phenomenon of the 'phantom limb' – where an amputee continues to feel pain as if in the hand or foot after its surgical removal. 'The only possible reason for this', writes Descartes, 'is that the nerves which used to go from the brain down to the hand now terminate in the arm near the elbow, and are being agitated by the same sorts of motion as must previously have been set up in the hand, so as to produce in the soul, residing in the brain, the sensation of pain in this or that finger. And this shows clearly that pain in the hand is felt by the soul not because it is present in the hand but because it is present in the brain' (*Principles* IV 196: AT IXB 315; CSM I 284).

As for the choice of a specific gland – Descartes is referring to the pineal gland or *conarion* – as the place where the soul directly exercises its functions, Descartes seems to have arrived at this by the thought that there must be *one* place where the dual data arriving from eyes, ears, etc., are integrated, so as to enable the soul to have a *single* visual or auditory perception:

> There must necessarily be one place where the two images coming through the two eyes, or the two impressions coming from a single object through the double organs of any other sense, can come together in a single image or impression before reaching the soul, so that they do not present to it two objects instead of one (*Passions* I 32: AT XI 353; CSM I 340).

This conclusion was one Descartes had arrived at in his earlier *Treatise on Man* (AT XI 177; CSM I 106); and he wrote in a letter of 1641 that the seat of sensation 'must be very mobile, so as to receive all the impressions coming from the senses, but must be movable only by the spirits transmitting these impressions. Only the *conarion* fits these conditions' (to Mersenne 21 April 1641: AT III 362; K 101).

The soul here seems to be reduced to a kind of homunculus – a little man inside the brain viewing a screen where the images from the optic nerves converge.[19] One feels a certain grudging admiration for Descartes' dogged determination to find a location where his incorporeal soul can exercise its role. But needless to say the thesis that the pineal gland is the 'principal seat' of the soul only postpones, and does not solve, the problem of how psycho-physical interaction is possible. If there is a problem about how an incorporeal soul can act and be acted upon by the body as a whole, there is going to be no less a problem about how an incorporeal soul can produce, and be affected by, movements in the pineal gland.

Sensation and Imagination

Apart from the problems of interaction just discussed, a further troubling feature of Descartes' dualism is what may be called the 'mental-or-physical dilemma'. All human attributes, it seems, must be regarded either as modes of thought, or as modes of extension. Either we are dealing with purely physical or mechanical events like the jostlings and janglings of nerve fibres, or we are dealing with the perceptions of an incorporeal spirit. Yet complex psycho-physical phenomena such as *vision* seem somehow recalcitrant to being classified as either purely mental or purely physical.

It is now time to notice, however, that despite his official dichotomy between mind and matter, Descartes does acknowledge in many places that human experience cannot always be handled in terms of these two rigidly exclusive categories. This point emerges with particular force in connection with Descartes' treatment of what may be called the 'hybrid' faculties of sensation and imagination. This pair makes its appearance early on in the Second Meditation, where Descartes, having established that he exists, ponders on his nature, on *what* he is:

> But what then am I? A thing that thinks. What is that? A thing that doubts, understands, affirms, denies, is willing, is unwilling . . . (AT VII 28; CSM II 19).

So far so good; all the activities listed are straightforward acts of intellection or volition of the kind which Descartes classifies as modifications of a *res cogitans*, a thinking thing. But now two unexpected verbs make their appearance:

> . . . and also imagines and has sensory perceptions (*imaginans quoque et sentiens*).[20]

Now in the context of the Second Meditation, Descartes is not prepared to commit himself to the real, extra-mental existence of any of the objects of sense-perception or imagination; he is still 'setting aside anything which admits of the slightest doubt' (AT VII 24; CSM II 16). It follows that the verbs *sentire* and *imaginare* can here be used only in a very 'thin' sense, to refer to what the subject is indubitably aware of even if no extra-mental objects exist. This is made clear in the *Principles of Philosophy* where (in what is virtually a commentary on this part of the *Meditations*) Descartes says that if we take a sensory act like seeing to apply not to vision as involving bodies but merely to the awareness or the thought that one is seeing, then this will be something that pertains to the mind alone (*Principles* I 9: AT VIII 7; CSM I 195). But even though Descartes is here employing *sentire* and *imaginare* in a very restricted sense, he reveals a certain reluctance to lump them with the other modes of thinking. There is a faint shift of emphasis between the first six members of the list and the last two, a shift which is signalled in the original text by the Latin particle *quoque*, 'also'. A thinking thing is a thing that doubts, understands, affirms, denies, is willing, is unwilling – and also that imagines and has sensory perceptions. The last two verbs are paired together and tacked on to the rest of the list almost as an afterthought. Why should this be?

A possible reason is that Descartes knows that when he is eventually able to examine the true nature of sensation and imagination, he will discover that they have special features that set them apart from the other members of the list. This point cannot be developed in the Second Meditation, but has to wait until the Sixth, when the existence of a non-deceiving God has been established, and the way is open for re-establishing the belief in the existence of bodies in general and one's own body in particular. Descartes is then able to give a much fuller treatment of sensation and imagination, and though these activities are still classified as types of thinking, they are singled out for distinctive treatment: the faculties of sensation and imagination are, says Descartes, 'faculties for certain *special* modes of thinking' (AT VII 78; CSM II 54). When Frans Burman interviewed Descartes in April 1648, he asked the philosopher about this phrase, and Descartes (reportedly) gave the following account of what he meant by a 'special mode of thinking':

When external objects act on my senses, they print on them an idea, or rather a figure of themselves. And when the mind attends to these images imprinted on the gland [i.e. the pineal gland] in this way it is said to have *sense-perception* (*sentire*). When, on the other hand, the images on the gland are imprinted not by external objects but by the mind itself, which fashions and shapes them in the brain in the absence of external objects, then we have *imagination*. The difference between sense-perception and imagination is really just this, that in sense-perception the images are imprinted on the brain by external objects which are actually present, while in the case of imagination the images are imprinted by the mind without any external objects, and with the windows shut, as it were (AT V 162/3, CB 27).

These remarks suggest that the 'specialness' of both imagination and sense-perception consists in the fact that their exercise requires *physiological activity*. The point is not such a straightforward one as may at first appear. Obviously seeing and hearing require eyes and ears; this is an analytic truth. Furthermore, these activities require the possession of optic and auditory nerves – facts which seventeenth-century investigators were beginning to investigate properly for the first time. Descartes was of course very interested in these facts, but they are not the reason for his insistence here that the faculty of sense-perception involves physiological activity; for his claim covers imagination as well as sense-perception, and yet there are no obvious 'organs' or 'nerves' of imagination.[21] The kind of physiological activity Descartes has in mind in this context is not activity of specialized organs or nerve-fibres, but brain activity – movements in the pineal gland at the centre of the brain.

At this point the twentieth-century reader may feel inclined to interject: '*Of course* sense-perception and imagination require the occurrence of brain activity. Descartes may have got the details wrong – he may have talked of movements in the pineal gland rather than electro-chemical changes in the cerebral cortex – but what is so remarkable about his having recognized the principle?' The answer is highy instructive. For we must remember that Descartes, the same Descartes who insists that sense-perception and imagination require the occurrence of physiological events, is quite satisfied – indeed convinced – that doubting, understanding, affirming, denying and willing can often occur as 'pure actions of the soul' – that is, they can occur without any physiological events whatsoever taking place.[22] We thus have a philosophical puzzle on our hands: what convinced Descartes that sensory experience and imagination involve brain activity, when he was quite happy with analyzing doubting, willing and understanding as utterly non-corporeal?

Part of the answer to this lies in some remarkable things which Descartes has to say about the phenomenology of imagination. He notes in the Sixth Meditation that the exercise of the imagination is not at all like that of the pure intellect. When I think of a thousand-sided figure, there are certain properties which I can know with absolute clarity and distinctness that it possesses. (For example, I can demonstrate that it has a thousand angles; and I can prove that this is as true and self-evident as that a triangle has three angles.) But if it is a question not of pure intellection but of imagination, things are very different. Imagination, Descartes notes, requires a 'peculiar mental effort' (AT VII 72; CSM II 51). This is apparent from experience. We can discuss and demonstrate properties of a dodecagon with just as much ease as we can discuss and demonstrate properties of a triangle; but imagining a dodecagon is beyond most of us. Most people can get up to a pentagon or a hexagon, but then it starts to get harder and harder. It is important not to misunderstand Descartes here. He is not, I think, suggesting that purely intellectual acts are always easy and imaginative acts are always hard. Some purely intellectual activities – for example those involved in higher mathematics – are no doubt extremely demanding, while some imaginative acts – imagining a dog for example, or a circle – are no doubt easy enough. What Descartes is appealing to is the inner, phenomenological quality or 'flavour' of an act of imagination: as we picture the pentagon, and then the hexagon, and continue on up to the larger figures, we are conscious each time of a curious 'gap' between our purely intellectual cognition of the figure in question, and our ability to image or visualize it. This strange sensation of having to wait until the figure 'comes' is, Descartes considers, evidence that what is involved is not a pure non-corporeal act of the soul: what is happening is that in order for us to form an image, complicated physical events have to occur in the brain – events which, without practice and effort, we often find it hard to bring about at will. And so this strange sensation of effort we experience when trying to imagine a complex geometrical figure is cited as good evidence that we are not pure *res cogitantes* (thinking things) but that we are somehow united to a sometimes recalcitrant collection of matter – the body: 'When I give more attentive consideration to what imagination is, it seems to be nothing else but an application of the cognitive faculty to a body which is intimately present to it' (Sixth Meditation: AT VII 72; CSM II 50). (The rather more detailed story in the *Conversation with Burman* tells us that imagining involves the mind attempting to fashion actual images in the brain (AT V 162/3; CB 27); a similar story appears in the *Passions of the Soul*, Part I, art. 43: AT XI 361; CSM I 344).

It is interesting that Descartes offers us a precisely similar argument – one based on phenomenological considerations – when he discusses the faculty of sensory awareness (*sentire*) in the Sixth Meditation. On this occasion he focuses not on the 'external senses' – vision, hearing, etc. – but on the 'internal senses' like hunger and thirst. The passage is one of the best known in Descartes:

> Nature teaches me by these sensations of hunger and thirst and so on that I am not merely present in my body as a sailor is present in a ship, but that I am very closely joined, and as it were, intermingled with it, so that I and the body form a unit. If this were not so I who am nothing but a thinking thing would not *feel pain* when the body was hurt, but would *perceive the damage purely by the intellect*, just as a sailor perceives by sight if anything in his ship is broken. Similarly, when the body needed food or drink, I should have explicit understanding of the fact, instead of having confused sensations of hunger and thirst. For these sensations of hunger, thirst, pain

and so on, are nothing but confused modes of thinking which arise from the union and as it were intermingling of the mind with the body (AT VII 81; CSM II 56).

What Descartes is drawing attention to here is the peculiar phenomenology of sensation – its special subjective character as present to our consciousness. This phenomenology is regarded by Descartes as evidence for the fact that sensory awareness, like imagination, does not belong to us *qua* incorporeal 'thinking things', but attaches to us *qua* embodied beings.

It is worth asking here, what things would be like, phenomenologically, for a pure thinking thing (e.g. a spirit or an angel) to which God had temporarily attached a body. The answer which Descartes would appear to offer, on the basis of the passage just quoted, is that the awareness which such a being had of his bodily condition would lack any phenomenological dimension; it would lack any 'colour' or 'flavour'. There would simply be purely intellectual judgements of the kind 'this body needs food', or 'this body is damaged'. Now we human beings make such judgements too: when educated diabetics take a blood sample and analyze it, they know, intellectually, that they require sugar; when I accidentally put my hand on a hot stove, and then inspect the result, I know, intellectually, that tissue damage has occurred. But of course this is not the whole story. The diabetic feels a funny dizzy feeling when his blood sugar is low; I feel a characteristically sickening flash of pain when my hand touches the stove. These sensations cannot, Descartes insists, be clearly and distinctly conceived: sensations like that 'curious tugging of the stomach' which I call 'hunger' (*nescio quae vellicatio ventriculi*; literally the 'I-know-not-what plucking': AT VII 76; CSM II 53), are inherently 'confused', like the strange feeling of effort we have when we try to picture a dodecagon.

The reason for the gap between, on the one hand, understanding, doubting affirming, denying and willing and, on the other hand, imagining and having sensory experiences, now begins to emerge. The last two are not the transparently clear cognitive faculties of a thinking being: they have an inherently confused, indefinable, subjective quality – a quality which betrays the fact that what is involved is not the pure mental activity of an incorporeal mind, but the activity of a hybrid unit, a human being.

Thus the faculties of imagination and sensation are not, for Descartes, straightforwardly 'mental' (after the fashion of, e.g. understanding). For (i) their exercise always requires the occurrence of physiological activity in the brain; and (ii) their characteristic phenomenology ('what it is like' for us to exercise these faculties) suggests that they belong to us not qua minds, but qua embodied beings. The upshot is that there is an important sense in which these faculties cannot properly be accommodated within Descartes' official dualistic schema. They are not readily assignable either to a *res cogitans* or to a *res extensa*.

Cartesian 'Trialism'

It may be seen from the foregoing section that the account of sensation and imagination which Descartes himself provides tends to put his official dualism under considerable pressure. Partly as a result of this, we often see the emergence, in Descartes' writings on human psychology, of a grouping of not two but three notions – not a dualism but what may be called a 'trialism'. In a letter to Elizabeth of 21 May 1643, Descartes speaks of three *primitive* categories or notions in terms of what we think about the world ('models on which all our other knowledge is patterned'). There is extension (comprising shape and motion), which is assignable to the body alone; thought (comprising understanding and volition), which is assignable to the mind alone; and finally there is the notion of the 'union' of body and mind (comprising the results of psycho-physical interactions such as 'sensations and passions'). (AT III 665; K 138. See also letter to Elizabeth of 28 June 1643: AT III 691; K 141). Commentators, it must be said, have expressed some irritation with these remarks: how, it is asked, can a notion be called 'primitive' if it is dependent on a union of two elements? A mule can hardly be called a 'primitive' species if it comes from the union of a horse and an ass. Descartes has perhaps not expressed himself too helpfully here. But something of what he is getting at may become a little clearer in the light of our earlier discussion of the 'hybrid' faculties of sensation and imagination. If sensory experience and imagination cannot properly be treated either simply as modes of extension or simply as modes of thought, then a separate category seems called for. To pursue the mule analogy a little further: this hybrid animal may be the result of a union of two more primitive species, but for all that it has genuine, distinctive properties of its own which cannot satisfactorily be classified either as equine properties or as asinine properties. Thus what Descartes seems to be moving towards when he talks of his three 'primitive notions' is the idea that, though the *subject* of sensations and feelings may not be a primitive substance, the *attributes* of sensation and feeling nonetheless fall into a distinct and irreducible category of their own.

The trialistic grid which appears in the correspondence with Elizabeth is no isolated aberration, but recurs whenever Descartes has to confront the phenomenon of sensory experience. In the Sixth Set of Replies, when prodded by Mersenne and others, Descartes provides an extended discussion of the faculty of sense-perception; and he produces an analysis in terms of not two but three 'grades' of sensory response:

> The first is limited to the immediate stimulation of the bodily organs by external objects; this can consist in nothing but the motion of the particles of the organs and any change of shape and position resulting from this motion. The second grade comprises all the immediate effects produced in the mind as a result of its being united with a bodily organ which is affected in this way; such effects include the sensory perceptions of pain, pleasure, thirst, hunger, colours, sound, taste, smell and the like, which arise from the union and as it were intermingling of the mind and body, as I explained in the Sixth Meditation. The third grade includes all the judgements about things outside us which we have been accustomed to make since childhood (AT VII 436; CSM II 294).

Later on, Descartes provides more detail. Suppose we are looking at some physical object – say a stick. The first grade of sensory response comprises motion in the optic nerves and the brain, which, says Descartes, is common to us and the brutes. The second grade extends to the 'mere perception of the colour and light reflected by the stick' and arises from the fact that the mind is intimately conjoined with the body; 'nothing further should be referred to the sensory faculty if we wish to distinguish it carefully from the intellect.' Lastly, the third grade of sensory response comprises rational judgement about the properties of the stick, e.g. its size, shape and distance from the observer; this, despite the common view, should not be attributed to the sensory faculty but 'depends on the intellect alone'.

What exactly is going on here, and why are we offered this curious threefold pattern instead of (as one might have expected), a simple dualistic analysis of sense-perception into (i) the physical events involved, and (ii) the mental events involved? To answer this it will help to go back to the instructive example of hunger. The standard 'dualistic' conception analyzes hunger in terms of two sets of events – those involving modifications of extension, and those involving modifications of thought. But in fact Descartes recognizes not two but *three* aspects to hunger. Firstly, there are the 'purely physical' events – the shortage of nourishing materials, the contraction of the stomach and so on; these are purely physical in the sense that they could occur in a completely anaesthetized or comatose patient. Thus even an artificially constructed android, Descartes notes, could possess all the physiological functions associated with digestion and nutrition (*Treatise on Man*, AT XI 132ff). Secondly, there are the 'purely intellectual' events which Descartes attributes to the soul. These are completely 'colourless' and dispassionate

Table 1

Extension	Thought	Item
yes	yes	man
yes	no	animal, plant, stone
no	yes	spirit (angel, God)
no	no	nothingness

judgements such as 'my body needs food';[23] to these may be added dispassionate volitions, such as the calm formation of the intention to take food. Thirdly, and quite distinct from the first two, there is that indefinable sensation – what Descartes calls the 'I-know-not-what plucking' – that is the feeling of hunger.[24]

Such 'confused sensations', as Descartes calls them, are, as we have seen, recalcitrant to straightforward classification as modes of thought or of extension. They are not assignable to mind alone or to body alone, but simply arise mysteriously from the 'intermingling' and 'union' of the two (AT VII 81; CSM II 56). To bring this point home, it may be worth providing two illustrative tables. Table 1 represents Descartes' official dualistic classification which provides only two categories, extension and thought. The logically possible permutations of these give us four lines. Notice several unsatisfactory features of this scheme. First, there is no proper place for animals: they are dumped into the non-conscious inanimate world of mere extension. Second, the phenomenon of sensation is, even in the case of man, left out of the picture, unexplained. As we saw in the previous section, it does not belong in any straightforward way under the category of thinking; nor is it a purely physiological phenomenon, such as, e.g., kidney filtration. It just 'arises', inexplicably, when an extended object is 'intermingled' with a thinking being.

Now let us see how the picture looks if sensation is treated as a third category, distinct from extension and thought. We now have not four but eight possibilities, as shown in Table 2. Since sensation is treated as a separate category, this allows for the possibility of thought without sensation and vice versa. That is, it allows for the (not entirely fanciful) possibility of beings with intellect but no sensations or feelings; and it also allows for the possibility which we know to be actualized on this planet, viz. that of beings with feelings and sensations but no thought. Descartes' official dualistic scheme of course rules out this last possibility: the official line is that there are no non-thinking but sentient creatures; animals are mere mechanical automata. But it is interesting

Table 2

Extension	Thought	Sensation	Item
yes	yes	yes	man
yes	yes	no	embodied angel
yes	no	yes	animal
yes	no	no	plant, stone
no	yes	yes	(no examples)
no	yes	no	spirit (God, angel)
no	no	yes	(no examples)
no	no	no	nothingness

that in several places Descartes acknowledges the possibility that sensation might occur without thought. The soulless non-thinking mannikin described in the 1633 *Treatise on Man* is characterized as having a sensory faculty and an imagination by means of which the ideas of 'colours, sounds, tastes and other such qualities' are impressed on the 'common sense' to be subsequently stored in the memory (AT XI 202; CSM I 108). And elsewhere, even in much later writings, Descartes speaks of animals like dogs, monkeys and birds as having sensations and feelings (e.g. visual sensations and internal feelings such as hunger.[25]

Although the model sketched in Table 2 is suggestive in a number of ways, great caution is needed in using it to interpret Descartes' views. Two important caveats, in particular, need to be entered. First, despite the 'trialistic' flavour of his remarks in the letters to Elizabeth and elsewhere, Descartes never formulates the threefold distinction involved in anything like such a schematic way as that presented in Table 2. On the contrary, in the official formulations of his views to be found in his published works, Descartes always adheres firmly to a dualistic account. There are two substances, mind and body, each defined by its 'principal attribute' of thought and extension respectively (*Principles* I, 53). All other properties are 'modes' or modifications of one of these two attributes; and sensations and feelings are officially classified as modes of thinking – albeit rather peculiar ones (*Principles* I, 64 and IV, 193). The official doctrine is firm and unwavering. But for all that, the threefold pattern outlined in Table 2 is consistent with Descartes' frequent recognition of the special character of sensation, and its recalcitrance to straightforward classification under the categories of thought or extension.

The second important caveat to be entered regarding our 'trialistic' schema is this. Although the three categories listed are distinct in the way explicated earlier, nothing that Descartes says, even in his most 'trialistic' moments, suggests that there are three distinct *ontological* categories involved here. That is, Descartes never suggests that the world might contain, in addition to a *res extensa* and a *res cogitans*, a *res sentiens*, or 'sensing thing', i.e. a separate substance which could have sensations without having any physical properties. Not only are there no examples of such beings (as the notes at lines 5 and 7 of Table 2 indicate), but there is every indication that Descartes would have regarded the idea of a non-physical *res sentiens* as absurd. A non-corporeal being (e.g. God) does not, Descartes firmly insists in the *Principles*, have the form of awareness we call sensation or sense-perception; sensory experience is by its very nature a property of embodied beings (*Principles* I 23: AT VIII 13; CSM I 201).[26] It seems, then, that at least one of the categories or notions involved in the trialistic schema is to be construed attributively rather than substantivally. It corresponds to a distinct aspect of a thing's nature, not to a distinct type of thing.

In so far as Descartes recognized a third category or 'primitive notion' alongside thought and extension without proceeding to classify it in terms of a separate substance, this may be regarded as a significant philosophical improvement on his approach when formulating his initial dualistic distinction. For in distinguishing between thought and extension, Descartes invariably insists on 'reifying' the notion of thought in such a way as to create a separate non-corporeal substance; yet while thought is a distinct and in many ways still mysterious aspect of our nature, what seems overwhelmingly clear to us nowadays is that it cannot subsist on its own, but must somehow be a property of a physical system, or be somehow grounded in a physical substrate.

But even if the prevailing modern view, that everything in the universe is ultimately physical, is correct, it remains true that there are three quite distinct ways in which we can think about ourselves as human beings, three quite distinct aspects of our humanity. Firstly, there are those countless vitally important events going on inside our bodies which do not presuppose or require any form of consciousness; secondly, there are all the thoughts, beliefs, desires and intentions which are true of us qua *res cogitantes* – thinking, language-using beings; and thirdly, there are those many curious sensations which are produced by the effects of the external world and the condition of our own bodies – sensations which we can label, but which we cannot properly define or explicate in language. A grasp of this trialistic distinction, which Descartes articulates – or comes close to articulating – on several occasions, seems to be an essential step towards achieving a true understanding of our nature.

Despite these insights, however, Descartes' account of human nature cannot be counted a success. As the texts discussed above show, Descartes was keenly aware of the distinctive character of our sensory experience, and of the ways in which it differs from, on the one hand, pure cogitation and, on the other hand, mere extension. But the official dualistic framework that continued to dominate so much of his thought meant that he was unable to do full justice to the complexities involved here. However vividly our inner experience might tell us that we are embodied creatures, our reason, Descartes continued to insist, tells us that we are 'thinking things', entirely incorporeal and essentially distinct from the body (AT VI 33; CSM I 127. Compare AT XI 283; CSM I 328) The result is a deep tension between what our reason tells us about ourselves and what our ordinary everyday experience tells us (AT V 163; CB 28); and there is a corresponding tension between on the one hand the tidy desire to classify all our human attributes as modifications either of thought or of extension, and on the other hand the recognition that our sensory experience does not straightforwardly belong in either category. Hunger, thirst, pleasure, pain, and the whole complex network of feelings, imaginings and sensory perceptions that we experience every day – these are absolutely fundamental to what it is to be a human being. Descartes' official theory can tell us little more than that all this vivid experience somehow results from the 'intermingling' or 'union' of two utterly alien and incompatible substances. And hence a major part of our human life remains, in the end, a mystery.

Notes

1   Thus the behaviour of the 'fluids and spirits' in the body is explained in terms of the same classification of particles into 'elements' (by shape, size and motion) which Descartes had employed in his account of the solar system. See *Description of the Human Body* Part III (AT XI 247–8; CSM I 319–20) and *Principles* III 52 (AT VIII 105; CSM I 258). For a direct comparison between the vortex theory and animal physiology see *Conversation with Burman*: AT V 171; CB 38f.

2   For the comparison with a church organ see *Treatise on Man*: AT XI 165; CSM I 104. For some of the notorious animal experimentation practised in Holland during the late seventeenth century, see Lindeboom, 61–5.

3   Julian de la Mettrie's celebrated treatise, *L'Homme Machine*, was published in 1747.

4   From 'Knowledge and Language', *Times Literary Supplement*, 15 May 1969; for a more detailed presentation see Chomsky, Part 1.

5   The attribution to animals in this passage of 'fear, hope and joy' contrasts oddly with Descartes' official doctrine that animals are mere mechanical automata, and suggests that though he denied *thought* to them, he was not always entirely clear about whether they could have sensations. See further J. Cottingham, 'A Brute to the Brutes? Descartes' treatment of animals' *Philosophy* 3 (1978) 551ff.

6 Cf. Aristotle *De Anima* Bk II. Aristotle did, however, maintain that pure intellect or *nous* was 'separable' from the body (though not, apparently in such a way as to make individual survival of death a possibility). Cf. *De Anima* III 5.

7 In the Dedicatory Letter to the Dean and Doctors of the Faculty of Theology at the Sorbonne, which was printed at the front of the *Meditations* in 1641, Descartes writes as if proving the immortality of the soul was one of his chief motives in writing (AT VII 2–3; CSM II 3–4). For a more straightforward statement of his aims see Second Replies: AT VII 153; CSM II 108f).

8 This quotation is from Descartes' 'Letter to M. Clerselier' which Descartes published in 1647 as a reply to a lengthy critique of the *Meditations* which Pierre Gassendi had published in 1644. See further CSM II 268 note. In the Second Meditation Descartes had said 'I am *in the strict sense only a thing that thinks*' (AT VII 27; CSM II 18) which does seem to imply a total exclusion of body from his essence. Gassendi had seized on the term 'only' as 'having a restrictive force, excluding limbs etc'; Descartes' attempts to wriggle out of this implication are only partly convincing. (See further notes at CSM II 18 and 276.)

9 For a discussion of the distinction between 'adequate' and 'complete' knowledge, see *Conversation with Burman*: AT V 151; CB 10, and commentary at CB 65ff.

10 Cf. Gassendi's comments in the Fifth Objections: it is not possible to produce a mental operation 'which takes place outside the brain or independently of the brain' (AT VII 269; CSM II 188). Cf. also Hobbes' materialist position at AT VII 173; CSM II 122. For a modern statement of the view that mental processes are physiological processes see Armstrong. For the more recent view that mental states are *functional* states (of a physical system) see Dennett and Shoemaker.

11 See ch. 4, p. 88 above.

12 Compare Plato's argument for the immortality of the soul in *Republic* Bk X: damage to the body cannot destroy the soul, since the soul can only be harmed by its own specific faults (609–10).

13 *Republic* Bk IV (436).

14 *Treatise of Human Nature*; Hume (I), I iv 6.

15 Cf. T. Nagel 'Brain Bisection and the Unity of Consciousness' in Nagel, 164. But for a more conservative (and arguably more judicious) assessment of the philosophical implications of recent findings, see Marks.

16 Shoemaker thus seems right in his recent assessment that 'despite pockets of dualistic belief in the general populace . . . in most popular writings on scientific topics related to the nature of man it tends to be taken for granted that dualism is no longer credible' (Shoemaker, 287).

17 Ryle, 15. For Descartes on causation cf. AT V 156, CB 17: 'It is a common axiom and a true one that the effect is like the cause'.

18 In the letter to Elizabeth of 28 June 1643 Descartes admits that the analogy with gravity is lame, but suggests that it can be a useful way of conceiving of the union of soul and body, provided one is already clear that the two are really distinct substances (AT III 694; K 142). It should be remembered that the term 'gravity' (Lat. *gravitas*) as used by Descartes and his contempo-

raries, does not have its modern (post-Newtonian) connotation of a universal attractive force. It is merely whatever it is that makes bodies 'heavy'. For Descartes' own (purely mechanical) explanation of heaviness see *Principles* IV 20–23 (AT VIII 212; CSM I 268).

19 For this notion, see A. Kenny, 'The Homunculus Fallacy' in Grene (I), 65ff.

20 The Latin verb *sentire* (Fr. *sentir*) is a major headache for translators of Descartes. For *res sentiens* the rendering which is etymologically closest to the Latin is 'a thing that senses'; but 'to sense' in English has the wrong flavour (of an intuitive hunch). Haldane and Ross have 'feels' (Haldane and Ross I, 153); but *sentire* can refer to e.g. visual sensations as well as internal feelings like hunger. Veitch has 'perceives' (Veitch, 89), but this risks confusion with the Latin verb *percipere* which Descartes reserves for purely intellectual forms of cognition. The paraphrase 'perceives by the senses' will normally do for *sentire*, but the context of the Second Meditation requires not an achievement verb (i.e. one which implies successful apprehension of an actually existing object) but some expression which is compatible with the possibility of dreaming and universal deception. Hence the somewhat cumbersome, but unavoidable paraphrase 'has sensory perceptions'.

21 The Aristotelians did talk of a 'common' sensorium which was the organ of the imagination; but they were pretty hazy about its structure and location. See Aristotle *De Anima* III 3, and cf. Descartes *Regulae*, Rule XII: AT X 414; CSM I 41.

22 Willing, it is true, may terminate in a bodily movement (e.g. in the case of a volition to raise the arm). But, says Descartes, some volitions (e.g. the desire to love God) terminate in the soul, in which case they are from start to finish non-corporeal (see *Passions* I 18: AT XI 343; CSM I 335).

23 Strictly speaking, Descartes attributes only pure cognition or mental perception to the intellect; judgement is ascribed to the will (Fourth Meditation: AT VII 56; CSM II 39). When speaking more loosely, however, Descartes uses the term 'intellectual' to cover both volitions and mental perceptions (see AT VII 438; CSM II 295).

24 The sensation is distinct from the bodily events (stomach contractions, etc.) since (a) it could occur without the bodily events (as a result of disease someone might feel hungry even though his stomach was full – see the 'dropsical' patient at AT VII 84; CSM II 58), and (b) the bodily events could occur without the sensation (e.g. in an anaesthetized patient). The sensation is also distinct from the purely intellectual events (such as the judgement that one needs food) since (a) it could occur without the judgement being formed (e.g. in an infant) and (b) the judgement could occur without the sensation (e.g. in a patient deprived of the sensation of hunger by some drug or disease). For further development of this argument see J. Cottingham, 'Cartesian Trialism', *Mind* XCV no. 374 (April 1985) 226f.

25 See note 5 above.

26 A question never directly raised by Descartes is whether God could not endow a non-corporeal being with conscious states which were qualitatively identical to human sensory experiences. The argument from diabolic deception in Meditation One (see above, ch. 2) implies that this is at least a possibility.

6

The Human Condition

Our Perception of the World and What It Is Really Like

There is, for Descartes, a curious gap between what reason tells us about our nature (that we are pure incorporeal minds) and what our everyday experience teaches us – that we are embodied creatures.

> Nature teaches me by these sensations of pain, hunger, thirst, etc. that I am not merely present in my body . . . but very closely joined and as it were intermingled with it, so that I and the body form a unit (AT VII 81; CSM II 56).

Something of this strange gap between what reason tells us about ourselves, and what our experience teaches us, should have emerged in the previous chapter.[1] But there is, on Descartes' view, an equally large, and equally striking gap between our rational understanding of the world (as extended substance characterized purely in terms of size, shape and motion) and our ordinary human experience, via the five senses, of what the world is like.

We have already noted, in discussing Descartes' theory of the physical world, that Descartes does not regard sensible qualities, such as redness, hardness and heaviness, as being really 'in' objects at all. 'Sensory perception does not show us what really exists in things' (*Principles* II 3; and see chapter 4 above, pp. 83f). Part of the reasoning behind this view should now have emerged in the light of our discusson of Descartes's account of sense-perception in chapter 5. Ideas such as our ideas of colours and tastes are for Descartes inherently confused perceptions, arising mysteriously from the intermingling of a thinking substance with corporeal matter. For a pure thinking thing – God or an angel – the physical world would presumably be perceived simply 'as it is' – as moving configurations of matter characterized by the distinct geometrical properties of length, breadth and depth. Human beings, Descartes argues, *can* attain to clear and distinct intellectual perception of these real geometrical properties of things: our ideas of shape (triangularity, circularity) do indeed mirror what the world is really like. But in the case of those further, indistinct ideas which arise from the fact that we are imperfect and limited creatures who are 'intermingled with matter' there is, according to Descartes, no reason to suppose that what we are aware of matches the true nature of reality.

In reaching his view that sensory qualities such as colour, taste and smell 'do not tell us except occasionally and accidentally what external bodies are like, in themselves' (*Principles* II 3), Descartes was strongly influenced by his physiological investigations:

> Regarding light and colour . . . we must suppose our soul to be of such a nature that what makes it have the sensation of light is the force of the movements taking place in the regions of the brain where the optic nerve-fibres originate, and what makes it have the sensation of colour is the manner of these movements. Likewise, the movements in the nerves leading to the ears make the soul hear sounds . . . But in all these there need be no resemblance between the ideas which the soul conceives and the movements which cause these ideas (*Optics*, Section 6: AT VI 130; CSM I 167).[2]

According to Descartes, all that is really happening, from a purely physical point of view, is that motions of matter in the external world impinge on the body and set up further motions there. As a result of this, certain ideas 'arise' in the soul; but there need be no resemblance between the ideas and their cause. In this connection Descartes employs a celebrated simile of a blind man probing the world with a pair of sticks. He is able to differentiate 'trees, rocks, water and similar things', but there is no reason to suppose any resemblance between 'the idea he forms' and 'the resistance or movement of the bodies, which is the sole cause of the sensations he has of them.' In the same way, when the ordinary sighted person sees colours and light, 'there is no reason to conclude . . . that there is something in the objects which resembles the ideas we have of them' (AT VI 85; CSM I 153).

But is this a good argument? Our perceptions of shape and size, no less than our perceptions of colour and taste, seem to depend on just such impingings of matter on our nervous systems; yet the resulting ideas of shape and size *do*, Descartes maintains, correspond to properties that can be attributed to the objects themselves. So the need, in describing the mechanism of sensory perception, to tell a complicated physiological story about movements of nerve fibres cannot, in and of itself, be sufficient to rule out any resemblance between idea and object.

Part of Descartes' answer to this is that matter is by definition that which is extended and has dimensions. So if I have an idea of a sword as being, say, three feet long, then there is no logical bar to supposing that this length is a genuine property of the real sword. But if, by contrast, I have an idea of the sword as being, say, silver-grey, there is, Descartes would claim, no plausible way of cashing out the notion of a resemblance between idea and object. In this connection Descartes compares our ideas of sensible qualities with internal sensations such as the sensation of pain, which no one would claim to be 'in' the object that causes it.

> A sword strikes our body and cuts it; but the ensuing pain is completely different from the local motion of the sword or of the body that is cut – as different as colour or sound or smell or taste. We clearly see, then, that the sensation of pain is elicited in us merely by the local motion of some parts of our body in contact with some other body; so we may conclude that the nature of our mind is such that it can be subject to all the other sensations merely as a result of other local motions (*Principles* IV 197: AT VIII 321; CSM I 284).

What this example seems to show is that there is no easy and automatic route from the presence of a subjective sensation to the attribution of a corresponding quality to an object. As Descartes puts it in the Sixth Meditation: 'Although I feel heat when I go near a fire and feel pain when I go too near, there is no convincing argument for supposing that there is something in the fire which resembles heat, any more than for supposing that there is something in the fire which resembles the pain' (AT VII 83; CSM II 57). But, on reflection, a certain awkwardness about the comparison between pain, on the one hand, and qualities like colour and heat on the other, begins to emerge. Pain is by definition something which is attributable to a conscious subject; so there is no temptation to attribute it to the sword or the fire (indeed such attributions would be literally absurd). But colour and heat are – at least as far as the ordinary rules of language go – things which we attribute not to conscious subjects but to non-conscious objects. It is true that a *sensation* of redness, say, is attributable to a subject: it is I who have the sensation of redness when I see a rose. But the quality of redness, the redness itself, belongs not to me but to the rose; and it is not yet clear, for all his talk about motions of nerve fibres, that Descartes has ruled out of court the notion that redness and heat are real qualities attributable to external objects.

One important reason why Descartes rules such real qualities out of court has to do with his conception of causation. 'Nothing in the effect which was not in the cause' is a fundamental principle which Descartes claims in the *Meditations* to be manifest by the natural light (AT VII 40; CSM II 28). Elsewhere he records his allegiance to the more sweeping and general formulation 'The effect is like the cause' (AT V 156; CB 17). Let us call this the 'Causal Similarity Principle'. Now suppose, for the sake of argument, that the quality of redness is indeed present in the rose. To explain how I am aware of this quality, it would have to be supposed that this quality has the power to set up motions of matter (since physiology tell us that all that actually reaches the brain when we perceive a rose is mere local motions in the nerve fibres). But how could a supposed 'real quality' such as redness have the power to set up something so different from itself? If it had such a power, we would have a causal chain of the following kind:

$$Q \ldots M$$

(where 'Q' stands for the supposed real quality of redness in objects and 'M' stands for the corporeal motions transmitted via the optic nerves). Yet the maxim 'the effect is like the cause' rules out such a causal chain, since there is no intelligible similarity between Q and M. Indeed, there would seem to be no intelligible relationship *at all* between Q and M – it would just be a brute fact that certain 'real qualities' set up certain corporeal motions. Descartes' rejection of occultism, and his rationalistic insistence that causal relationships be transparently perspicuous to the intellect, rule out such brute facts.[3] Here is how Descartes presents this causal argument in *Principles* Part Four, article 198:

> We understand very well how the different size, shape and motion of the particles of one body can produce various local motions in another body. But there is no way of understanding how these same attributes can produce something else *whose nature is quite different from their own* – like the . . . real qualities which many philosophers suppose to inhere in things; *and we cannot understand how these qualities or forms could have the power to produce local motions in other bodies* . . . Not only is this unintelligible but . . . we do not find that anything reaches the brain from the external sense organs except for local motions. In view of this we have every reason to conclude that the properties in external objects to which we apply the terms light, colour, smell, taste, sound, heat and cold, as well as the other tactile qualities . . . are, so far as we can see, simply various dispositions in those objects which make them able to set up various kinds of motions in our nerves (AT VIII 322; CSM I 285; italics supplied).

For Descartes, then, nothing is explained by attributing a real quality of redness to the rose – unless we construe this 'quality' as a disposition of the rose (in virtue of the shape, size and motions of its particles) to set up local motions in our nervous system.[4]

If one accepts this argument (some of its implications will be looked at below), then the original causal chain 'Q . . . M' will ultimately be replaceable by

$$M_1 \ldots M_2$$

(where M_1 represents the corporeal motions to be found in the rose, and M_2 represents the subsequent motions which are eventually set up in the nervous system). The full account of colour perception would thus go something like this:

$$M_1 \ldots M_2 \ldots S$$

(where 'S' is the sensation of redness finally arising in the soul as a result of the various corporeal events first in the environment and second in the nervous system). But this in turn raises an interesting problem for Descartes. How can it be, given his own allegiance to the Causal Similarity Principle, that S appears at the end of a causal chain composed of purely corporeal events? A sensation of redness, on Descartes' own account, has no resemblance at all to the corporeal events going on in the external world and in the nerve fibres; so how can such a sensation 'arise as a result of' or 'be produced by' those events?[5] The answer Descartes sometimes gives is that it is 'ordained by nature' that certain corporeal motions should produce certain sensations or feelings in the soul (*Passions* I, 36: AT XI 357; CSM I 342). By this, however, he cannot mean that there is some discoverable law of nature (of the kind to be found within Cartesian physics) relating corporeal motions to sensations. For sensations *qua* sensations are excluded from Cartesian science;[6] and in any case the Causal Similarity Principle will not allow such radically dissimilar items to be related by an explanatory law. When Descartes uses the phrase 'ordained by nature' in this type of context, what he has in mind is a divine *fiat* – an arrangement specially instituted by the Creator:[7]

> I maintain that when God unites a rational soul to this machine [of the body] . . . he will place its principal seat in the brain, and will make its nature such that the soul will have different sensations corresponding to the different ways in which the entrances to the pores in the internal surface of the brain are opened by means of the nerves (*Treatise on Man*: AT XI 143; CSM I 102).

In creating the human soul, God has simply decreed that a range of '*qualia*', or qualitative sensations of a distinctive kind, should arise in it whenever the brain to which it is joined is stimulated in various ways.[8]

An interesting implication of this theory (and one which is independent of Descartes' theological commitments) is the claim that the correlations between brain events and *qualia* are, so to speak, *arbitrary*. A distant modern analogy which may be illuminating here is that of a computerized display of, for example, a meteorological chart, where the programmers have arranged things in such a way that areas of, say, low pressure show up as red patches on the monitor screen. The choice of red as the display colour is completely arbitrary: there is no natural lawlike correlation between the colour red and low barometric pressure. The programmers have decided to flag low pressure areas by using red, but they could equally well have chosen green, or yellow, or black dots or grey stripes. This is precisely the kind of thing that Descartes takes to be true of the *qualia* which arise in the soul when the brain is stimulated in certain ways. God, the programmer of the human soul, has chosen that certain corporeal events should be 'flagged' for us in certain ways; but he could have chosen a completely different flagging system. This is how Descartes expresses it when discussing pain arising from damage to the foot:

> When the nerves of the foot are set in motion in a violent and unusual manner, this motion, by way of the spinal cord, reaches the inner parts of the brain and thereby gives the mind its signal for having a certain sensation . . . God could have made the nature of man such that this particular motion in the brain indicated something else to the mind. It might for example have made the mind aware of the actual motion occurring in the brain, or in the foot, or in any of the intermediate regions, or it might have indicated something else entirely . . . (Sixth Meditation: AT VII 88; CSM II 60).

There is, for Descartes, no scientific explanation (that is, no explanation in terms of rationally intelligible causal connections) of the flagging system which actually obtains. The only kind of explanation which Descartes regards as appropriate here (a kind of explanation which elsewhere he resolutely avoids) is one in terms of final causes or purposes:

> Any given movement occurring in the part of the brain that immediately affects the mind produces just one corresponding sensation; and . . . the best system that could be devised is that it should produce the one sensation which, of all possible sensations, is most especially and most frequently conducive to the preservation of the healthy man. And experience shows that the sensations which nature has given us are all of this kind; and so there is absolutely nothing to be found in them that does not bear witness to the power and goodness of God (AT VII 87; CSM II 60).

It might be thought that natural selection can play the beneficent role in this system which Descartes assigns to God. Thus any being for whom serious damage to the foot did not give rise to a highly urgent and intrusive sensation of an unwelcome kind would not survive long. So there would seem to be considerable selective pressure in favour of the emergence of certain kinds of *qualia*; and this in turn would seem to offer the hope, ruled out by Descartes, of integrating the realm of subjective sensation into the rest of our scientific account of the world.

It is not clear, however, that this evolutionary approach can explain all the distinctive qualitative aspects of our sensations. Take the case of colours, for example: admittedly, there is likely to be a selective advantage in developing a system of visual perception that is sensitive to variations in spectral wavelength; but nevertheless the *way* in which these differences appear to the subject – the 'mode of presentation' as it may be called – seems to be something that could be arranged in a variety of different ways. It seems possible to imagine cases of 'qualia inversion' or 'qualia variation': I can imagine a being for whom the wavelength of light coming from a rose was 'flagged' in a way that, from the subjective point of view, was quite different from the way in which it is 'flagged' for me (so that if I could get inside this being's consciousness, I would find that his 'mode of presentation' has nothing in common with this characteristic visual sensation of 'redness' which I have on looking at a rose). If this notion of different possible 'modes of presentation' makes sense it seems to lend support to the Cartesian notion that there is a degree of 'arbitrariness' about the subjective character of our sensations.[9]

It may be objected that this appearance of arbitrariness is due to our ignorance of brain physiology: if we understood more about the structure and functioning of the brain, we might be able to show that a neurological configuration of a certain sort must give rise to a qualitative awareness of a certain characteristic kind. There has been considerable debate over this matter in recent philosophy of mind. Some philosophers, taking the line just referred to, have proposed that it should indeed be possible in principle to locate *qualia* firmly within a scientific account of human behaviour and neurophysiology. Others, however, consider that the qualitative character of a subjective experience is something which is *sui generis* and could not be explained or analysed in physicalist terms, no matter how sophisticated our behavioural and neurophysiological understanding were to become.[10] This debate cannot be evaluated here; but enough has perhaps been said to show, first, that there is a genuine problem about how we are to account for the characteristic subjective dimension of our sensory experience, and, second, that the Cartesian thesis that such an account is beyond the reach of normal scientific understanding cannot simply be dismissed out of hand.

What, though, of the central Cartesian doctrine that sensible qualities such as colour, taste, smell, heat, heaviness and so on are not really 'in' objects in any straightforward sense? If asked to express a view on this doctrine, it seems likely that most natural scientists working today would say they were broadly in agreement with it; analytic philosophers, by contrast, have, partly for historical reasons, tended to be highly suspicious of it. Historically, the best known version of the doctrine is that of Locke, who distinguishes between 'primary' qualities such as shape (supposed to be really in objects) and 'secondary' qualities such as colour (which are not supposed to be in objects in a way which matches our ideas of them).[11] But Locke's account was subjected to a blistering attack by Berkeley, which has greatly influenced subsequent philosophical thinking, and it is still common nowadays to hear the judgement that there is no valid reason for introducing the primary/secondary distinction. Many, indeed, see the whole attempt to distinguish primary from secondary qualities as the result of a philosophical confusion – the confusion of supposing that scientific problems about the mechanisms of sensory perception can cast doubt on our attribution of predicates like 'red' to objects. On this 'common sense' view, the attribution of such predicates is perfectly clear and unproblematic, being governed by standard rules of language with which every normal speaker is quite well acquainted.[12]

But whatever may be the case with regard to Locke (and recent scholarship has suggested that some of the standard Berkeleian objections are misplaced), it is hard to convict Descartes' reasoning of any simple-minded philosophical confusions.[13] It would certainly be a violation of a perfectly sound rule of language to say that roses are not 'really' red; but Descartes does not say that. What he does say is that we are in error if we suppose that there is any direct resemblance between the subjective sensation of redness and the events and properties of the external world, and of our nervous systems, which give rise to that sensation (cf. *Principles* I 68: AT VIII 33; CSM I 217 and *Principles* I 70: AT VIII 34; CSM I 218).

A general and more worrying objection to Descartes' approach to sensible qualities is that the whole notion of the world 'as it is' independently of our experience is an incoherent one. How, it may be asked, can Descartes know that the physical world 'really' consists of motions of matter and nothing else? How can he have the right to claim that is how the world would be perceived by God, or an angel? Is it not a nonsense to suggest that we human beings can attain to such a 'God's eye view', which takes them beyond mere appearances to 'things in themselves'.[14]

Descartes himself never had to confront quite this type of objection; indeed it is an objection of a peculiarly modern, or certainly post-Kantian, kind. But it seems possible to construct a response that is at any rate true to the spirit of what Descartes is trying to do with his distinction between the way the world appears to the senses and the way it really is. What the defender of Descartes must say is that there is every reason to believe first that there is something 'subjective' about our human perspective on things, and second (though this is more difficult) that we can manage to get beyond it. On the first point, if the 'mode of presentation' of colours, tastes, etc. is, at it seems to be, the result of the particular way our sense organs are constructed, then we can make good sense of the idea that other beings, with radically different sense organs, would perceive the world in a quite different way from us. The naive realist who simply says 'roses are red and there's an end on't' seems to be glossing over the very real possibility that the 'subjective grid' of different kinds of perceivers might be radically different.[15]

On the second, point, which relates to the alleged impossibility of attaining a 'God's eye view' of reality, Descartes' own reply would have been to assert that God has implanted in our souls the seeds of truth about the universe. In our innate mathematical concepts, in particular, we have, Descartes would claim, the divinely bestowed apparatus for understanding the world 'as it really is'.[16] Even without God and innate ideas, however, it seems possible to make some sense of the idea of an 'absolute conception' of the world, independent of the varieties of subjective experience. Such a conception would (as one distinguished present-day philosopher has suggested) be one which progressively tried to free itself from the limitations of local perspectives and modes of presentation, so as to arrive at a description of reality which any rational inhabitant of the universe might be expected to agree on, irrespective of the peculiarities of his sensory apparatus.[17] It would take us too far from the present purpose to evaluate the prospects for this programme of reaching out to an 'absolute conception'; but it is not an obviously incoherent programme. It need not involve the absurdity of our trying to 'step outside our conceptual scheme' and compare it with 'reality'. What it would involve is an attempt to identify those features of our conceptual scheme that are bound up with local distortions and modal peculiarities, and then move beyond these to a more neutral and universal perspective. As Descartes expresses it, it would involve a recognition of the 'gap' that exists between those features of our representation of the world that must be 'referred to the senses' and those more universal and abstract mathematical properties that the intellect can 'distinctly perceive' (*Principles* I, 69: AT VIII 33; CSM I 217). There may be many approaches to specifying the 'gap' to which Descartes refers, and Descartes' own approach may not be the best. But without a recognition of something analogous to the gap which Descartes proposes, it is not easy to see how one could construct a viable model for what it is to have a scientific understanding of the universe.[18]

Innate Ideas

The Cartesian method for arriving at a true understanding of reality requires us to 'lay aside all our preconceived opinions', 'lead the mind away from the senses' and 'give our attention in an orderly way to the notions that we have within us' (*Principles* I 75: AT VIII 38; CSM I 221; cf. Synopsis to *Meditations*: AT VII 12; CSM II 9). That philosophy should begin with a turning inwards of the mind upon itself is perhaps the most characteristic feature of Descartes' thinking, and its best known manifestation is of course the Cogito – the mind's initial apprehension of its own existence.[19] But the 'turning inwards' is much more pervasive than that. Even when we wish to proceed beyond ourselves, in order to discover the nature of extramental reality, we must still, according to Descartes, begin by directing our attention inwards, to the innate notions that we find within our minds.

The 'first and most important' of these 'true ideas that are innate in us', says Descartes, is the idea of God. Not all of us reflect properly on this idea and what it implies, but Descartes insists that if we were not 'overwhelmed by preconceived opinions' and if the images of things perceived by the senses did not 'besiege our thought on every side' we would be able to reflect on this idea, and as a result come to acknowledge the existence of its author sooner and more easily than anything else (AT VII 68/9; CSM II 47).[20] Having achieved knowledge of God we can proceed to knowledge of external reality, but even here the focus will still be inwards. We must, Descartes tells us, mistrust what might seem our most obvious and direct link with external reality, the senses, and rely instead on the truths which God has implanted in our souls (cf. *Principles* II 3: AT VIII 42; CSM I 224). The most important of these ideas are the mathematical concepts which enable us to understand the extended, corporeal universe.

The doctrine of innate ideas has a long philosophical ancestry. The claim that certain mathematical ideas are innate is to be found in Plato, who argued that these ideas cannot have been acquired via the senses; instead, they are present in us from birth – the soul 'recollects' them from a prior existence. The curious doctrine of recollection goes some way to accommodating a fact that might seem an obvious objection to the innateness doctrine, namely that infants clearly do not come into the world with actual explicit awareness of the truths of mathematics; the child has to be *taught* such geometrical propositions as the proposition that the angle in a semi-circle is a right angle. The Platonic theory acknowledges that effort is required to 'recollect' such truths; they are 'in the mind' all right, but it may need a skilled Socratic midwife to 'draw them out'.[21] Descartes' rather different explanation of the child's lack of actual explicit awareness of these truths is that the mind in infancy is swamped with bodily stimuli, and so is prevented from attending to its innate ideas: 'In early childhood the mind was so closely tied to the body that it had no leisure for any thoughts except those by means of which it had sensory awareness of what was happening to the body' (*Principles* I 71: AT VIII 35; CSM I 218). 'The body is always a hindrance to the mind in thinking,' Descartes is reported to have remarked to Burman, 'and this is especially true in youth' (AT V 150; CB 8). In a letter of 1641, Descartes gives the following more detailed account:

> It seems reasonable to think that a mind newly united to an infant's body is wholly occupied in perceiving or feeling the ideas of pain, pleasure, heat, cold and other similar ideas which arise from its union and intermingling with the body. Nonetheless, it has inside itself the ideas of God, itself, and all such truths as are called self-evident, in the same way as adult human beings have when they are not attending to them. It does not acquire these ideas later on, as it grows older (AT III 424; K 111).

An interesting question arises from this passage as to what exactly is meant by saying that an idea is 'in the mind'. In his definition of 'idea' in the Second Replies, Descartes states that an idea is the 'form of any given thought, immediate perception of which makes me aware of that thought'; and a 'thought' is defined as that which is 'in us in such a way that we are immediately aware of it' (AT VII 160; CSM II 113). But clearly at any given time we can only be aware of a tiny fraction of the ideas that are in us (for example, the reader has the idea of the number seven, but was not explicitly thinking of this number until he lighted on this sentence). So to say 'S has an idea of X' clearly cannot entail that S is now actually aware of X, or thinking of X; what seems to be meant instead is that S can, as it were, 'call up' the appropriate information if required. Sometimes Descartes uses the metaphor of a storehouse or 'treasure house' in this connection. Discussing the innate idea of God he says:

> It is not necessary that I ever light upon any thought of God; but whenever I do choose to think of the first and supreme being, and bring forth the idea of God from the treasure house of my mind, as it were, it is necessary that I attribute all perfections to him (AT VII 67; CSM II 46).

The possession of an idea, then, is to be construed in a 'dispositional' rather than an 'occurrent' sense: to say that we have an innate idea of X is to say that we can, by appropriate reflection, come to recognize certain truths involving the concept of X. The qualification 'by appropriate reflection' is important: the infant, beset on every side with bodily stimuli, is simply not in a position to reflect on anything; and even the adult may be preoccupied with preconceived opinions based on the senses, and so never give any time to the sort of reflection that would reveal truths about God or about mathematics. I may never reflect on the concept of a triangle, says Descartes, but when I do so, I will recognize that the angles of a triangle equal two right angles (AT VII 67; CSM II 47).[22]

In using the term 'idea', Descartes seems to shift between talking about concepts and talking about propositions: is he saying that the concept of a triangle is innate, or that we have innate knowledge of the proposition that the angles of a triangle equal 180°? The answer seems to be: 'both' – and the elasticity in shifting from concepts to propositions is characteristic. In his discussion of the mind's intuition of the 'simple natures' in the *Regulae*, Descartes had been quite happy to include under one label both concepts (such as extension) and propositions (such as the fundamental axioms of logic) (AT X 419; CSM I 45). Descartes' claim is that the simple 'intuition' or perception of the intellect enables us both to be aware of certain fundamental concepts or categories of thought, and also to perceive self-evident connections and relationships between those concepts. There is a close link between this claim and Descartes' innateness doctrine, the content of which comes down to this: God has structured our minds in such a way that intellectual reflection alone, without the need for information derived from the senses, will enable us to achieve knowledge of the fundamental structure of reality.[23]

The fundamental building blocks of science may be innate for Descartes, but as we have seen in discussing his theory of the physical universe, he does not propose to deduce the whole of science from first principles.[24] In the *Meditations*, Descartes classifies our ideas into three groups: innate, 'adventitious' (i.e. entering the mind from some outside source) and 'fictitious' (made up or invented). My idea of the sun is an example of an adventitious idea; examples of fictitious ideas are ideas of mythological creatures such as sirens or hippogriffs, which the mind has artificially constructed (AT VII 38; CSM II 26). How this relates to the way in which our knowledge of physics is built up would seem to be as follows: our fundamental understanding of three-dimensional matter or 'body in general' is furnished by the (divinely implanted) innate idea of extension; but our understanding of the particular configuration of the solar system, for example, would depend at least partly on adventitious ideas. (In the same way, our idea of what a particular town is like is adventitious: AT V 165; CB 31).

It might seem tempting to conclude from this that while mathematical ideas are innate, sensory ideas (such as those of colour, taste and smell) are adventitious. It is certainly true that Descartes regards our ideas of colours, tastes etc. as arising in the mind as a result of external stimuli, while he regards our ideas of triangles, squares etc. as independent of corporeal events (so that if the mind were entirely removed from the body, it would still be furnished with those ideas: AT III 424; K 111). But to call our ideas of colour 'adventitious' might nevertheless be misleading if it were taken to imply that such ideas 'come into the mind from outside' in some straightforward or simplistic sense (as for example, air comes into the lungs from outside). As we have seen in discussing Descartes' theory of the external world, Descartes does not regard colours, tastes, etc. as being 'in' objects at all. We have also seen that Descartes' theory of sense-perception asserts that there is no natural relation between the movements of particles in the external world or our nervous systems and the occurrence of our ideas of colour and other sensible qualities; the relationship is an 'arbitrary' one, and depends on God's having decreed that a certain idea should 'arise' in our consciousness when a certain stimulus occurs.[25]

This kind of reflection on the nature of sensory perception led Descartes (in a short paper entitled *Comments on a Certain Broadsheet*, written in reply to Regius in 1647)[26] to point out that there was a certain sense in which all ideas, even sensory ideas, are innate:

> If we bear in mind the scope of our senses and what it is exactly that reaches our faculty of thinking by way of them, we must admit that in no case are the ideas of things presented to us by the senses just as we form them in our thinking. So much so that there is nothing in our ideas which is not innate to the mind or the faculty of thinking, with the sole exception of those circumstances which relate to experience, such as the fact that we judge that this or that idea which we now have immediately before our mind refers to a certain thing situated outside us . . . Nothing reaches our mind from external objects through the sense organs except certain corporeal motions . . . But neither the motions themselves, nor the figures arising from them are conceived by us exactly as they occur in the sense-organs . . . Hence it follows that the very ideas of the motions themselves and of the figures are innate in us. The ideas of pain, colours, sounds and the like must be all the more innate, if, on the occasion of certain corporeal motions, our mind is to be capable of representing them to us, for there is no similarity between these ideas and the corporeal motions . . . (AT VIII B 359; CSM I 304).

Sense-perception, then, is certainly not a matter of the simple 'reception' of ideas from the outside world; and we know from several other passages that Descartes had nothing but scorn for such naive scholastic theories as the doctrine of 'intentional forms' according to which material objects were supposed to transmit 'forms', 'semblances', 'phantasms' or 'images' of themselves to the perceiver. Descartes believed that an accurate investigation of how outside stimuli affect the brain via the nervous sytem would forever banish such crude accounts of 'little images flitting through the air' as he scathingly termed them (*Optics*: AT VI 85; CSM I 154). Although Descartes uses the language of 'ideas' in describing how we represent the world to ourselves, he points out that there are many ways of representing (for example the way in which a sign or word represents its object), and hence that talk of images copied from, or transmitted by, objects is unnecessary as well as being suspect from a physiological point of view (*Optics*: AT VI 112; CSM I 165). The upshot is that our sensory ideas should not strictly be thought of as 'coming from' the external world at all; their character is to be explained by reference to the innate (divinely ordained) structure of the human mind.

This pervasively 'innate' element in our human sensory perceptions does not, however, undermine Descartes' initial distinction between 'innate' and 'adventitious' ideas; for we can still distinguish between those abstract concepts with which the intellect is supposedly furnished independently of the body and those which are ordained to arise in the mind as the result of stimulation of the sense-organs. But Descartes' observations about the nature of our sensory ideas do highlight a curious feature of the human situation as he conceives it. The advent of a systematic physiology of sense-perception marks for Descartes the demise of the naive view that our senses provide us with images that straightforwardly copy reality. And with the demise of that naive view, humans become in a sense cut off from the world outside: what might seem their most obvious link with that world – the data of the five senses – has to be mistrusted, as providing only a confused, obscure and imperfect representation of what the world is like (AT VII 80; CSM II 55). But to compensate, as it were, for the imperfection of our sensory information, we have the clear and distinct perceptions of the intellect, implanted in our souls by the Creator himself, and therefore guaranteed to reflect accurately the structure of reality.

This kind of 'dualism' between senses and intellect in Descartes is in accord with the Platonic, or Neoplatonic, tradition which, consciously or not, influenced much of his thinking. The notion that illumination is to be had by turning away from the senses goes back to Plato, and the contrast between the ordinary visible light of the physical world and the intelligible light emanating from God is a major theme in such writers as Plotinus and Augustine.[27] Some echoes of this may perhaps be seen in the 'turn inwards' that is so characteristic of Descartes' philosophy: both the first steps of his metaphysics, and the general doctrine of innate ideas, invite us to turn away from the visible light – the ordinary world perceived by the senses – to the innate *lux rationis*, the intellectual light implanted in our minds by the Creator. Descartes is certainly no mystic, and one of his main motivations in philosophy is a robust desire for enduring progress in the physical sciences (AT IXB 15ff; CSM I 186ff). But it remains one of the remarkable paradoxes of Cartesian philosophy that in order to construct a reliable and informative account of the physical world we are urged first to turn away from it.

Freedom and Reason

If the fundamental ideas enabling us to understand the world are implanted in our minds by God, and if the modes of awareness that arise in our consciousness as a result of sensory stimulation are also determined by God, then this seems to make not just our existence but the very structure of our thought and consciousness dependent in a very detailed way on the power of the Creator. And a natural question to arise from this is: what kind of freedom if any, does this leave us with?

A cursory reading of Descartes' comments on human freedom might suggest that we have a very considerable and extensive power of free choice. Our will or freedom of choice is so great, says Descartes in Meditation Four, that the idea of any greater faculty is beyond my grasp; so much so that it is above all in virtue of the will that I understand myself to bear the image and likeness of God (AT VII 57; CSM II 40). Such language, comparing the human will to that of the deity, might well suggest that humans have an independent contra-causal power of willing; and in the *Principles*, Descartes goes so far as to suggest that our will is not even limited by the preordaining power of God (*Principles* I 41; AT VIII 20; CSM I 206).[28] Certainly the prevailing interpretation of Descartes' views in the latter half of the seventeenth century was that he had a strongly indeterministic or 'hard-libertarian' conception of the freedom of the will: Spinoza criticized Descartes for believing in 'absolute' free will, and Leibniz remarked that Descartes required a 'freedom for which there is no need by insisting that the actions of the will of man are entirely undetermined – a thing which never happens'.[29]

Under closer scrutiny, however, Descartes' views on freedom turn out to diverge considerably from the indeterministic line which Spinoza and Leibniz took him to be maintaining. Within a few lines of the passage from the *Principles* about God's power not restricting our freedom, Descartes goes on to note that the freedom we have merely 'enables us to abstain from believing what is *not* certain or fully examined.' In the case of truths which *are* clearly and distinctly perceived, he goes on to explain, we are quite unable to resist giving our assent (*Principles* I 39 and 43: AT VIII 20/21; CSM I 206/7). Once the intellect has turned towards the truths implanted in it by God, and once it achieves a clear and distinct perception of them, then assent is inevitable and automatic. 'A great light in the intellect gives rise to a great propensity in the will,' says Descartes in the Fourth Meditation, and 'I cannot but judge that what I understand very clearly is true' (AT VII 58/9; CSM II 40).

So what is it to be free according to Descartes? Are we free when our will is fully determined, and its assent necessitated, by our intellectual perception? The (perhaps surprising) answer given in the *Meditations* is a definite *yes*. 'The more I incline in one direction, either because I understand that reasons of goodness and truth point that way, or because of a divinely produced disposition of my inmost thought, the freer is my choice' (*Meditation Four*: AT VII 58; CSM II 40). Cartesian freedom, then, is not an absolute or contra-causal power; on the contrary it is the spontaneous assent that is irresistibly determined by the perceptions of the intellect.[30]

What, though, of the case where our intellectual perception is hazy? In such cases Descartes certainly believes that we have power to withhold assent – and indeed the Cartesian programme for the scrutinizing of preconceived opinions and the avoidance of rash and precipitate judgements requires that in such cases the enlightened philosopher will exercise his will – restraining his assent until he has perceived things clearly.[31] It is worth adding, however, that although Descartes believes we are free to withhold our assent in the case of unclear perceptions, he does not wish to set very much store by this type of case as a demonstration of the freedom of the will. Quite the reverse in fact:

> The indifference I feel when there is no reason pushing me in one direction rather than another is the lowest grade of freedom; it is evidence not of any perfection of freedom but rather of a defect in knowledge or a kind of negation (AT VII 58; CSM II 40).

So, according to Descartes, the fact that we can be in a situation where either of two alternatives seems equally likely, or where there is no conclusive reason for assenting to one rather than the other, hardly provides an impressive demonstration of the greatness of human freedom. It is true that we have the power to withhold assent in such a situation, but the fact that we find ourselves in such a situation at all demonstrates, says Descartes, not any 'perfection of freedom' but merely a 'defect in knowledge'. True freedom, he goes on to say later in the Fourth Meditation is *in inverse proportion to indifference* (AT VII 59; CSM II 41). (By 'indifference' in this context, Descartes means that state where the perceptions of the intellect are not clear enough to determine the will either to assent or to deny a given proposition.)[32]

Descartes' conception of freedom thus turns out to be 'rationalistic' in the sense that, like Spinoza and Leibniz, he sees our freedom not as something opposed to the dictates of reason, but as subordinate to them. Our freedom consists not in some contra-causal power of accepting or rejecting a proposition, but in the spontaneous and irresistible impulse to assent to what the intellect recognizes with such clarity and distinctness that no other course is possible. Moreover, when our perceptions are unclear, we do not make good use of our freedom by jumping in and giving our assent on one side or the other. If in the absence of clear and distinct perception we go ahead and make a judgement, then Descartes insists that this is to abuse our powers of judgement *even if the belief is true*. For in such a case if we stumble on the truth it is 'purely by accident' and this in no way mitigates the fact that our belief is improperly grounded (*Principles* I 44). Where two alternatives present themselves, true freedom for Descartes is to be achieved by searching for a perception which is so clear and distinct that one of the two proposed alternatives ceases, and ceases dramatically, to be equally attractive: 'indifference' is dispelled, the equilibrium shattered, and one of the two alternatives – the correct one – simply compels our assent.

It should be clear from all this that the role of God in Descartes' account of human freedom is a dominant one. The truth has been determined from eternity by God, who is the author not just of what is the case but also of what is possible.[33] Our intellects are the divinely bestowed apparatus for recognizing the truth, and God has furnished them with ideas whose clear perception leaves no room for anything but assent. The introduction of God here, as elsewhere in Descartes' philosophy, is no routine manoeuvre or pious concession to theological orthodoxy: it is central to the system. It would however be a mistake to conclude from this that Descartes' account of freedom has nothing of importance to contribute to a secular account of the human situation. In insisting that a decision taken in a state of 'indifference' involves the 'lowest grade of freedom, and not any perfection of free will' Descartes has highlighted an important point – that if an act of will is to count as a rational human decision, it must be made because 'reasons of truth or goodness point that way.' Genuine freedom, it seems, cannot be some contra-casual power of just 'deciding', *ex nihilo*, in favour of some one of two alternatives. Our human situation is such that either we must make our choices out of habit or some blind impulse, or else we will strive to make them depend on a rational grasp of the relevant facts. There is much to be said for Descartes' insistence that the truly free agent is one for whom the 'determination of the will' is always generated by the 'prior perception of the intellect' (AT VII 60; CSM II 41).

The Good Life

Though Descartes' contribution to the philosophy of knowledge can scarcely be exaggerated, his contribution to the philosophy of practice is generally regarded as negligible. He is reported to have declared that he 'did not like writing on ethics' and that the 'provisional moral code' which he inserted into the *Discourse on the Method* was merely inserted out of caution, lest it be thought that by introducing a method which called everything into doubt he was subverting conventional morality (AT V 178; CB 49).[34]

Nevertheless, in Descartes' famous metaphor, 'morals' does find its place alongside mechanics and medicine as one of the fruit-bearing branches of the tree of knowledge of which metaphysics are the roots and physics the trunk. Morality is even described as the 'ultimate level of wisdom' (AT IXB 15; CSM I 186). It is important, however, not to construe the term 'morality' in too modernistic a way. Nowadays philosophers tend to conceive of 'morals' either from a Kantian perspective (as being concerned with the 'moral law' and the nature of duty and obligation), or from a utilitarian perspective (as being concerned with the 'foundations of morality' and the evaluation of the consequences of our actions); alternatively perhaps, the subject may be seen from an analytic perspective (as being concerned with the logic and semantics of ethical language). There is little evidence of much interest in any of these areas on the part of Descartes; and it seems clear that what he means by 'ethics' is something closer to what Aristotle meant – the science of how best to enjoy a fulfilled and rewarding life.[35] Descartes was convinced that his scientific system could provide practical benefits which would make for a more worthwhile life: in place of the 'speculative philosophy' taught by the Schoolmen, Descartes claimed to offer a 'practical philosophy' that would ultimately make us 'masters and possessors of nature' (AT VI 62; CSM I 142). Amongst the other benefits he envisaged was the possibility of prolonging life (see AT V 178; CB 50) and of improving physical and mental health – the 'chief blessing and foundation of all other blessings in life' (AT VI 62; cf letter to Newcastle of October 1645: AT IV 329; K 184).[36]

On the question of how the individual should best conduct himself so as to live a worthwhile life, Descartes conducted an extended correspondence with Princess Elizabeth of Bohemia after suggesting to her, in July 1645, that they should read and discuss together Seneca's *De Vita Beata*. Commenting on Seneca's title, Descartes wrote: '*Vivere beate*, to live happily, is to have a perfectly content and satisfied mind (AT IV 262: K 164). The key to such satisfaction, Descartes repeatedly observes, is the right use of reason – and it is on this that the 'supreme felicity of man depends' (AT IV 267; K 166). And the chief obstacle to such a rationally guided life is that we are beset by human passions which 'often represent to us the goods to whose pursuit they impel us as being much greater than they really are' (AT IV 295; K 173). The problem of the conquest of the passions had been a major topic for moral philosophers from the stoics onwards; and a decade or so after Descartes' death it was to become one of the principle themes of Spinoza's *magnus opus*, the *Ethics*. Descartes' chief contribution in this area (apart from the letters to Elizabeth) is to be found in his last published work, the *Passions of the Soul*.

The *Passions* is an important work because it goes a considerable way to counteracting the narrowly intellectualistic conception of man as essentially a 'thinking thing' which is uppermost in the *Meditations* and other metaphysical writings. It is in the *Passions* that Descartes brings us closest to a conception of man as an embodied being, a creature of flesh and blood; and such is the human condition, he argues, that we cannot hope for fulfilment if we confine our attention to the mental part of us alone: 'The soul can have pleasures of its own. But the pleasures common to it and the body depend entirely on the passions, so that persons whom the passions can move most deeply are capable of enjoying the sweetest pleasures of this life' (AT XI 488; CSM I 404).

By a 'passion' in the broadest sense Descartes means anything that *happens* to the soul as opposed to what it actively *does*. Thus a volition is an 'action' of the soul, since 'we experience it as proceeding directly from our soul and depending on it alone', whereas a perception is a 'passion', since it involves the soul's taking in or 'receiving' some representation (*Passions* I 17: AT XI 342; CSM I 335). In the more specific sense in which Descartes uses the term, however, a passion is an emotion or feeling that arises in the soul when it is acted upon *by the body*; and Descartes lists six principal examples of passions in this specific psycho-physical sense – wonder, love, hatred, desire, joy and sadness (*Passions* I 69). Other passions are analysed as modifications and combinations of the six primary passions; thus anger is described as a violent kind of hatred combined with a desire involving self-love (*Passions* III 199).

Given that we experience a passion such as anger as something that 'happens to us' – the emotion rises up in us in a way that is seemingly independent of our will – how can we achieve the rational control over the passions that is the hallmark of the happy man? Descartes' answer to this question is sometimes taken to be that we just have to exercise our will and decide to override the passions. Thus Spinoza criticizes Descartes for holding that 'there is no soul so weak that it cannot acquire an absolute power over its passions'; and he refers disparagingly to the doctrine that the passions 'depend entirely on our will and we can control them absolutely'.[37] The notion of such absolute control does indeed seem absurd; one cannot simply stop feeling frightened or angry by deciding to do so. But Spinoza seems to have misunderstood Descartes in attributing to him the view that we can achieve this kind of control. For Descartes explicitly says in *Passions* I 45 that 'our passions cannot be directly aroused or suppressed by the action of the will . . . For example in order to arouse boldness and suppress fear in ourselves it is not sufficient to have the volition to do so.' The passions can be controlled only *indirectly* (AT XI 363; CSM I 345).

Descartes goes on to explain the reason for our lack of direct voluntary control over the passions. The passions are caused and maintained by physiological events – disturbances in heart, blood and 'animal spirits'; and physiological events of this sort are not under the direct control of the will (*Passions* I 46). Descartes goes on to observe, however, that it is possible by careful training to set up habitual associations between certain thoughts and certain movements in the pineal gland, which will in turn generate certain movements of the 'animal spirits'; once these associative networks are laid down, we will possess an indirect control over the passions.[38]

This account appears at first sight to be inextricably dependent on Descartes' mind–body dualism, and in particular on the strange notion of the soul's interacting with the body via the pineal gland. Certainly Spinoza was quick to pour scorn on the curious psycho-physical transactions which are invoked here. 'I should very much like to know,' he observed drily, 'how many degrees of motion the Mind can give to that pineal gland and how great a force is required to hold it in suspense.'[39] The picture of volitions pushing against the pineal gland from one side while animal spirits push against it from another does indeed look like the 'ghost in the machine' at its most bizarre; and one would certainly not want to defend everything Descartes says either about volitions or psycho-physical interactions in general. But in the particular case of the control of the passions, Spinoza has considerably underestimated the subtlety of Descartes' position. The point is not that the animal spirits generating fear are bubbling up on one side, and the volition to be brave is exerting pressure on the other side. As we have already seen, it is no use, according to Descartes, to just directly 'will' that the passion of fear should abate. I cannot directly will that the agitation of the animal spirits should cease (in modern terms, I cannot will that my pulse should slow or that my adrenalin levels should go down). What I *can* do, according to Descartes, is to set up an habitual response whereby some mental performance which *is* under my control will trigger some automatic reduction in the agitation of the spirits (adrenalin levels, or whatever).

Descartes compares the way in which the decision to pronounce a word will automatically produce certain muscle contractions in the tongue which it would have been difficult or impossible to produce directly by the command of the will. Another example: 'dilate your pupils' is a command we cannot obey directly; but we can manage to comply indirectly by deciding to look at a distant object (*Passions* I 47; Descartes goes on to make a comparison with the way in which animals are trained: *Passions* I 50). Thus, supposing that one was menaced by a wild animal, the Cartesian technique would not be to just try and *will* the fear to subside; rather one should have trained oneself in such a way that some voluntary act (perhaps deep breathing, or the repeating of a mantra) will automatically have the desired effect. Notice that the inherent plausibility of this account is not affected by the question of whether the mind–body dualism which Spinoza so bitterly criticizes is tenable. For whatever the status of volitions (i.e. whether they are wholly incorporeal events, or whether they are events in the cerebral cortex), it undoubtedly remains true that one cannot directly will passions such as fear to subside, yet one can decide to train oneself in such a way that a passion subsides or is reduced automatically by the performance of certain actions that are within voluntary control.

'The chief use of wisdom', wrote Descartes at the end of the *Passions*, 'lies in its teaching us to be masters of our passions'. But such mastery was not, for Descartes, a matter of our standing wholly outside the world of natural causes, still less of our trying to override such causes by an arbitrary exercise of will. Just as, in his account of human freedom, Descartes acknowledges that the will must be guided by the rational perceptions of the intellect, so in his account of how we should conduct our lives, Descartes acknowledges the need for a rational understanding of the network of physiological causes, for the most part operating independently of our will, which condition so many aspects of our human nature.

As for what that nature is, however, Descartes' position never achieves real stability. The clarity of vision which made him such an original metaphysician, and which led him to formulate the ambitious goal of a transparently accessible and all-embracing system of science, ultimately clouded over when he came to confront the human condition. Essentially incorporeal beings, mysteriously intermingled with a body which obeys the laws of extended matter, we nonetheless vividly experience, as a result of that intermingling, emotions and sensations which can be responsible for some of the sweetest and most bitter experiences of our human life (AT XI 488; CSM I 404). Since Descartes put those feelings and emotions beyond the reach of rational science, his programme for philosophical enlightenment can never wholly encompass this vital aspect of our humanity. The best we can do is to investigate the bodily events which give rise to our passions, and hope that such an investigation will enable us to develop indirect techniques for controlling them.

Descartes allowed in correspondence that his comprehensive design for an all-embracing scientific system might not succeed in encompassing all aspects of human nature. 'There is' he admitted, 'a very great distance between the general account of the heavens and earth which I tried to convey in my *Principles*, and the detailed knowledge of the nature of man' (AT IV 441; K 196). In the face of these difficulties, Descartes sometimes appeared tempted by a retreat into a kind of mysticism: in a latter to Chanut he suggested that the soul 'detached from the traffic of the senses' should devote itself to the loving contemplation of the divine intelligence, of which it is a faint and imperfect emanation (AT IV 608; K 212).[40] But in general, Descartes retained a robust confidence in the abundant benefits, both theoretical and practical, which his philosophical system would eventually yield, bringing us in time to 'the highest level of wisdom' and to 'supreme perfection and felicity of life' (AT IXB 20; CSM I 190).

Today we are beset by doubts both about the epistemological status of the scientific programme which Descartes helped to inaugurate, and about its supposed benefits; few are entirely confident either about the objective basis of our scientific knowledge, or about its unqualified capacity to improve the lot of mankind. But neither have we abandoned entirely the grand Cartesian vision of the possibility of a unified understanding of reality – the conviction that 'all the items of knowledge which lie within reach of the human mind are linked together by a marvellous bond' (AT X 496; CSM II 400). The Cartesian vision has not lost its power to inspire us; and it probably never will.

Notes

1 See above, ch. 5 pp. 122ff. For a full account of the 'gap' between what reason tells us about ourselves and what experiences tells us, see J. Cottingham, 'Descartes' Sixth Meditation: The external world, "nature" and human experience' in Vesey.

2 For Descartes' (bizarre) theory of what is really going on in the external world when we perceive colours, see *Description of Human Body*: AT XI 255f; CSM I 323.

3 For Descartes' rejection of occultism see *Principles* IV 187: AT VIII 314; CSM I 279. For the transparent accessibility of all science to the human intellect, if rightly directed, see *Search for Truth*: AT X 496–7; CSM II 400/1. It has recently been argued that there was no clear demarcation between occultist and non-occultist modes of thought in the seventeenth century. See G. Ross

'Occultism and Philosophy' in Holland, 95ff. But whatever may be the case with other writers, the distinction in Descartes is clear and explicit.

4   An unmistakably clear anticipation of Locke's concept of the 'secondary' quality. See John Locke, *Essay concerning Human Understanding* (1690) II viii 10. For a lucid exposition of Locke's account, see Alexander, ch. 5.

5   For such causal language see *Optics* 6: AT VI 130; CSM I 167, and *Passions* I 36 and 37.

6   Scientific explanation, as understood by Descartes, restricts itself to a consideration of 'divisions, shapes and motions' (*Principles* II 64). See ch. 4, above.

7   The famous phrase *Deus sive Natura* ('God or nature') is widely attributed to Spinoza. But in fact Descartes comes close in some places to using the terms 'God' and 'nature' almost equivalently; and the actual phrase *Deus sive Natura* is used by him at *Principles* I 28 (AT VIII 15; CSM I 202).

8   The term *qualia* is not, of course, due to Descartes himself, but has become a convenient label in modern discussions on philosophy of the mind to refer to the 'qualitative' aspects of our perceptual experience. Examples of 'qualia' would be the characteristic smell of a rose, or the distinctive taste of an orange as experienced by the perceiving subject (for this usage see Shoemaker, ch. 9). (In Latin *quale* (plural *qualia*) means 'of a certain kind or quality', just as *quantum* (plural *quanta*) refers to a certain amount.)

9   The phrase 'modes of presentation' is coined by C. McGinn, though his usage is somewhat different from that in the text. See McGinn, ch. 5; cf. also the term *Darstellungsweise* as used by writers such as Frege and Wittgenstein. The notion of 'qualia' inversion appears to be been suggested first by Locke, who raised the possibility that 'the idea that a *Violet* produces in one Man's Mind' might be the same as that which 'a *Marigold* produced in another Man's' (*An Essay concerning Human Understanding* (1690), II xxxii 15). Some modern philosophers, particularly those influenced by Wittgenstein's argument that the meaning of terms in the language cannot be fixed by reference to a purely private occurrence or event (see note 31, ch. 2, above), have denied that such a notion makes sense. Shoemaker, however, arguing from the easier case of intra-subjective qualia-inversion (roughly: I wake up one morning and find that marigolds look the way violets looked to me yesterday), has maintained convincingly that there are no sound reasons for ruling it out as incoherent. See Shoemaker, ch. 15.

10 For an attempt to locate qualia within a scientific account of human functioning see Shoemaker, ch. 9. For the view that the subjective character of experience cannot be captured by a behavioural or neurophysiological account, compare Nagel 'What is it like to be a bat?' in Nagel, ch. 12.

11 Strictly, qualities are, for Locke, in objects while ideas are in the mind. But in the case of colours Locke holds that all that is 'in' the object is 'a power it has by reason of its . . . primary qualities to operate on our senses and thereby produce in us different ideas' (*Essay concerning Human Understanding* II viii 23). That there need be no resemblance between our idea and what is in the object is stated in *Essay* II viii 13: it is no more impossible 'that God should annex Ideas to notions with which they have no similitude than that he should annex the Idea of Pain to a notion of a piece of Steel dividing our Flesh, with which that idea hath no resemblance.'

12   For Berkeley's criticism of Locke see G. Berkeley, *Principles of Human Knowledge* (1710), Section 9. For the 'common sense' view of colour attribution, see Ryle, 208ff.

13   For the weakness of some of Berkeley's criticisms, see Alexander, ch. 10. To say that Descartes is innocent of radical philosophical confusion on the primary/secondary distinction is not to say that all his arguments for the distinction are adequate. See Kenny, 208ff. For a more radical critique of the primary/secondary distinction, see Putnam, ch. 3. See also P. Hacker 'Are Secondary Qualities relative?' *Mind* 1986 pp. 180ff.

14   Compare Kant's strictures against the supposition that we can attain to knowledge of 'Things in Themselves' (Kant, A49/B66). For a more recent critique of the 'absolute' conception, see Richard Rorty: 'The application of honorifics such as 'objective' is never any more than the expression of the hope for agreement among inquirers. We need to give up the idea that our criteria of successful inquiry are not just *our criteria but also the right* criteria, *nature's* criteria, the criteria which will lead us to the *truth*' (Rorty, 335, 299).

15   For this notion see McGinn, 140ff.

16   See the next section of this chapter for more on the innateness doctrine and the use to which Descartes puts it.

17   For this conception see Williams, chs. 8 and 10. The notion of an 'absolute' conception of the universe need not require divinely guaranteed innate ideas, since it might be claimed instead that there are certain fundamental truths of logic and mathematics (e.g. the laws of identity and non-contradiction) which are fundamental not just for our local cultural or human perspective, but for any system of thought.

18   For a possible alternative model of understanding which restricts itself to what may be called 'internalist' criteria of justification, see Rorty, ch. 8. For the distinction between 'externalist' and 'internalist' perspectives and a searching critique of the 'externalist' approach, see Putnam, ch. 3.

19   See above, ch. 2, pp. 35ff.

20   For the details of the arguments offered by Descartes to prove God's existence, see above, ch. 3.

21   Se Plato, *Theaetetus* 147; *Meno* 81.

22   Note that the talk of 'dispositional' knowledge does not reduce to the weaker claim (which even anti-innatists would support) that we have the *capacity* to acquire certain kinds of knowledge. Descartes' insistence that the child actually *has* the ideas and does 'not acquire them later on' (AT III 424; K 111) implies that the information is now present – not in the sense that the child need actually be aware of it, but in the sense that by appropriate reflection he could call it forth. (Contrast CB xxxiiiff., which unfortunately tends to gloss over the distinction between a positive disposition and a mere capacity. See also Williams, 134; Clarke, 52). In a passage whose import is not entirely clear Descartes himself compares our possession of innate ideas with a disposition to contract a disease possessed by babies of certain families (AT VIIIB 358; CSM I 303). The point here, I take it, is not the weak one that the child *can* catch the disease, but that it now actually possesses within it some inherited defect which means that it is likely, when the appropriate circumstances arise, to contract the illness.

23   For 'intuition' in the *Regulae*, see above, ch. 2 pp. 25f. The connection

between what Descartes says about simple natures and what he says about innate ideas is well brought out by D. M. Clarke; see Clarke, ch. 3.

24 See above, ch. 4, p. 91ff; for the notion that what is innate is merely the fundamental elements or 'building blocks' from which more complex knowledge is later constructed, see CB xxxvf.

25 See above, ch. 4, pp. 83ff; ch. 6, pp. 139ff.

26 For Regius, see above ch. 1, p. 26. For the circumstances surrounding the 'Comments on a Certain Broadsheet' (often known in English by the bizarre title 'Notes against a Programme' – a slavishly literal rendering of the Latin *Notae in programma quoddam*) see CSM I 293.

27 See above, ch. 2, note 9.

28 In the passage cited Descartes asserts: 'It is difficult to grasp how the power of God leaves the free actions of men undetermined'. Picot's French version puts the matter even more emphatically and talks of the power of God leaving the actions of men 'entirely free and undetermined' (*'entièrement libres et indéterminés*: AT IXB 42; ALQ III 115). This almost suggests that 'free' for Descartes *means* undetermined – a highly misleading impression, as will be argued shortly. For the relation between God' decrees and the actions of his subjects, see further the letter to Elizabeth of January 1646: AT IV 352ff; K 188ff).

29 Spinoza *Ethics* II 48; Leibniz *Theodicy* (1710) *Preliminary Discourse*, § 69.

30 Descartes at one point appears to suggest that we do have the power to refuse to assent to a clearly perceived truth. See letter of 9 February 1645: AT IV 173; K 160. However, the most plausible interpretation of this text is that Descartes means to say only that we have the power to withhold our assent to a truth once perceived *at some later date*; at the time when a given proposition is actually being clearly and distinctly perceived, assent is unavoidable. See further A. Kenny 'Descartes on the Will' in Butler, 24ff.

31 For the Cartesian rule for the avoidance of error, see above, ch. 3, pp. 64ff.

32 The term 'liberty of indifference' was traditionally used in the schools to refer to an independent contra-causal power of willing ('which means a negation of necessity and causes' as Hume later put it: *Treatise of Human Nature* III ii 2). It is in this sense that God is said by Descartes to act with 'maximum indifference' (AT V 166; CB 33). But in the passage under discussion from the Fourth Meditation, where Descartes says that indifference is the 'lowest grade of freedom', he is using the term in a rather different sense, to refer to the state of mind we are in when the reasons in favour of each of two alternatives appear to be equally balanced, and so we feel no rational pull towards either. The 'indifference' that applies to God's actions (viz. an absolute contra-causal power) is thus different from anything to be found in the human case. For humans, either assent is necessitated by clear perception of the intellect (in which case there is no power to do otherwise), or else our perceptions are unclear, in which case we are 'indifferent' in the low-grade sense of not seeing clearly what to do (so that any decision must either be postponed or based on blind irrational impulse).

33 'God's will is the cause not only of what is actual and to come, but also of what is possible and of the simple natures' (AT V 160; CB 22). See also AT VII 432; CSM II 291, and the passages referred to above at ch. 3, note 12.

34 For a different view of Descartes' attitude to the *morale provisoire* which he included in the *Discourse* see Gilson, 234; compare the commentary at CB 118f.

35 The object of ethics, for Aristotle, is *eudaimonia*, often translated 'happiness' but perhaps better explicated in terms of the idea of a flourishing, successful or worthwhile life; see *Nicomachean Ethics*, Bk I.

36 With hindsight, and in the light of our current ecological crisis, the Cartesian vision of men as 'masters and possessors of nature' may seem to take on a somewhat sinister tone. For some critics this is no accident; there are those who see Descartes' whole approach to the natural world as leading to the alienation of man from nature. For this view see Grene (II), esp. ch. 3.

37 *Ethics* Part V, Preface; in Spinoza, II 277.

38 For a discussion of 'associative networks', and an attempt to explain them in terms of brain events, see letter to Chaunt of 6 June 1647: 'The objects which strike our senses by means of the nerves move certain parts of our brain and there make certain folds . . .; the place where the folds were made has a tendency to be folded again in the same manner by another object resembling even incompletely the original object. For instance when I was a child I loved a girl of my own age who had a slight squint. The impression made by sight in my brain when I looked at her cross eyes became so closely connected to the simultaneous impression arousing in me the passion of love, that for a long time after when I saw cross-eyed persons, I felt a special inclination to love them simply because they had this defect' (AT V 57; K 224).

39 Spinoza, II 180.

40 Letter of 1 February 1647. There is more than a hint in this letter of the idea of the *amor intellectuali Dei* – the 'intellectual love of God' which Spinoza, later in the century, was to present as the highest degree of human fulfilment. (See Spinoza, *Ethics*, Part V.)

Appendix: Descartes' Dreams

The following account is translated from Book I chapter 1 of Adrien Baillet's *La Vie de Monsieur Des-Cartes*, published in 1691. It purports to be based on material, in a section entitled *Olympica*, from Descartes' early notebooks, which were found among his papers at Stockholm shortly after his death. The account, not readily available in English, is bizarre enough to have a certain curiosity value in its own right. It also has some philosophical relevance to the famous 'dreaming argument' in the First Meditation, since it implies, first, that dreams can be intensely vivid and relatively coherent experiences, and, second and more important, that the dreamer can, while still asleep, reflect on his experiences and entertain doubts as to whether is awake or asleep. For the dreaming argument, see chapter 2, pp. 31f. above; for the events leading up to the dreams, see chapter 1, p. 9, above.

He [Descartes] tells us that on the tenth of November 1619 [after a day's philosophical meditation in his stove-heated room which left him in a state of great mental agitation] he went to bed 'quite filled with this mental excitement' and preoccupied with the thought that 'that day he had discovered the foundations of a wonderful system of knowledge'. He then had three consecutive dreams in one night, which he imagined could only have come from above. After falling asleep, his imagination was assailed with the impression of several phantoms, which came up to him and terrified him to such an extent that (thinking himself to be walking along a street) he was obliged to cross over onto the left side, in order to proceed to the place where he wanted to go; for he felt such a great weakness on his right side that he could not stand up. Being ashamed to walk in such a fashion, he made an effort to stand upright, but he felt a violent wind which swept him round in a kind of whirlpool, making him spin round three or four times on his left foot. But this was still not what terrified him most. The difficulty which he had in standing made him believe that he would fall down at each step, until he noticed a college that opened onto his road, and went in to find a refuge and a remedy for his trouble. He tried to reach the college chapel, where his first thought was to go and pray; but noticing that he had passed someone whom he knew without greeting him, he decided to turn back to pay his respects, and was violently pushed back by the wind which blew against the chapel. At the same time, he saw in the middle of the college quadrangle someone else who addressed him by name in very civil and obliging terms, and told him that if he wanted to look for Monsieur N., he had something to give him. M. Descartes imagined that this was a melon brought from some foreign country. But what surprised him more was to see that the people who gathered round the man to talk were upright and steady on their feet, while, on the same ground, he was still bent double and reeling, although the wind which had tried to blow him over several times had much lessened. On this thought he awoke, and felt at once a sharp pain which made him fear that it was the doing of some evil demon who had wanted to deceive him. At once he turned onto his right side, for it was on his left side that he had gone to sleep and had the dream. He offered a prayer to God to ask to be protected from the bad effect of his dream and to be preserved from all the ills which might be hanging over him as a punishment for his sins – sins which he recognized could be serious enough to bring thunderbolts down on his head, despite the fact that he had hitherto lived a life which was irreproachable enough in the eyes of men.

In this situation he fell asleep again after an interval of two hours spent in various reflections on the goods and ills of this world. At once another dream came to him in which he thought he heard a loud and violent noise which he took for a thunderclap. The terror which he felt at this woke him up at once, and opening his eyes he saw many fiery sparks scattered throughout the room. This had happened to him several times before, and it was not very unusual for him to wake up in the middle of the night with flashes in his eyes bright enough to enable him to glimpse the objects closest to him. But this time he wanted to have recourse to reasoning drawn from philosophy, and was able to draw conclusions which were more favourable for his state of mind, after observing, on first opening and shutting his eyes, the quality of the forms which were represented to him. Thus the terror he felt subsided, and he went back to sleep with a considerable sense of calmness.

A moment later he had a third dream, which contained nothing terrible like the first two. In this third dream he found a book on his table, though without knowing who had put it there. He opened it and, seeing that it was a *Dictionary*, he was struck with the hope that it might be very useful to him. At the same instant, he found another book, also new to him; and again he did not know how it had got there. He found that it was a collection of the poems of different authors entitled *Corpus Poetarum*. He was curious to read something, and opening the book he came to the verse '*Quod vitae sectabor iter?*' ['What road in life shall I follow?'] At the same instant he saw a man whom he did not know, but who gave him a piece of verse beginning *Est et Non*, saying it was an excellent poem. M. Descartes told him he knew it was, and that the piece came from the *Odes* of Ausonius, who was in the anthology of poets that was on the table. He wanted to show the man the piece, and he began to leaf through the book, whose contents and layout he seemed to have a perfect knowledge of. While he was looking for the place, the man asked him where he had got the book, and M. Descartes replied that he could not tell him how he had got it, but that a moment earlier he had been holding another book which had disappeared without his knowing who had brought it or who had taken it away. He had not yet finished his search when he saw the book appear once more at the other end of the table. But he found that the *Dictionary* was no longer complete, as it had been when he saw it before. Meanwhile, he came to the poems of Ausonius in the anthology he was leafing through, but could not find the piece beginning *Est et Non*; so he told the man that he knew an even better poem from the same poet, beginning *Quod vitae sectabor iter?* The man asked him to look for it, and Descartes was starting to do so when he came upon several engraved miniature portraits. This told him that the book was a very fine one, but was not the same edition as the one he knew. At this point, the books and the man disappeared, and faded from his imagination, but without waking him up. The curious point about this was that, being in doubt as to whether what he had just seen was a dream or a vision, not only did he decide while still asleep that it was a dream, but he even decided on the interpretation before waking up. He considered that the *Dictionary* signified all the sciences collected together, and that the anthology entitled *Corpus Poetarum* indicated more particularly, and in a more distinct manner, philosophy and wisdom combined. For he reckoned that it was not very surprising to realize that even the lighter poets are full of more serious, sensitive and better expressed thoughts than those to be found in the writings of the philosophers. He attributed this remarkable fact to the divine origin of enthusiasm and the power of the imagination, which makes the seeds of wisdom (which are found in the minds of all men like the sparks of fire in flints) emerge with much more ease and clarity than can be accomplished by the reasoning of the philosophers. Continuing to interpret his dream while asleep, M. Descartes thought that the verse beginning *Quod vitae sectabor iter?*, which dealt with uncertainty about the type of life one should choose, stood for the good advice of a person of wisdom, or even for moral theology. Thereupon, still in doubt as to whether he was dreaming or meditating, he woke up quite calmly, and opening his eyes, continued the interpretation of his dream along similar lines. The collected poets in the anthology he took to signify revelation and enthusiasm, with which he had some hope of seeing himself blessed. The piece of verse *Est et Non* – the 'yes and no' of Pythagoras – he took to stand for truth and falsity in human knowledge and the secular sciences. Seeing that the interpretation of all these things seemed to him to work out so well, he was confident enough to convince himself that it was indeed the spirit of truth that had chosen to open to him the treasures of all the sciences by means of this dream. It only remained to explain the miniature portraits that he had found in the second book; and he ceased to look for the explanation of this after receiving a visit from an Italian painter on the following day.

The last dream, which contained only very pleasant and agreeable matters, he took to represent the future; its purpose was to show him what would happen to him in the remainder of his life. But he took the two previous dreams as threatening warnings concerning his past life, which could not have been as innocent before God as it had been in the eyes of men. He thought that this was the reason for the terror and fright which accompanied these two dreams. The melon which had been offered to him in the first dream signified, he decided, the charms of solitude, but as seen in the context of purely human concerns. The wind which pushed him towards the college chapel, when he had a pain in his right side, was the evil demon which was trying to hurl him by force into a place where he planned to go of his own accord. This was why God did not permit his advancing any further, and why he allowed himself to be swept away towards a holy place by a Spirit which God had not sent – though he was quite convinced that it was the spirit of God which had made him take his first steps towards the chapel. The terror with which he was struck in the second dream represented, in his interpretation, the pangs of his conscience concerning the sins which he might have committed during the course of his life up till that time. The thunderclap which he had heard was the sign of the spirit of truth which was descending to take possession of him.

References

The following list gives details of books referred to in the notes. It is not intended to be a guide to the literature on Descartes (which would require a whole volume in its own right).

Alexander, P., *Ideas, Qualities and Corpuscles* (Cambridge: Cambridge University Press, 1985).

Anscombe, E. and Geach, P. T. (trs), *Descartes' Philosophical Writings* (London: Nelson, 1969).

Armstrong, D. M., *A Materialist Theory of the Mind* (London: Routledge, 1968).

Austin, J. L., *Sense and Sensibilia* (London: OUP, 1962).

Bacon, Francis, *The Philosophical Works of Francis Bacon* ed. J. M. Robertson (London: Longmans, 1905).

Baillet, A., *La Vie de Monsieur Des-Cartes* (Paris: Horthemels, 1691). Photographic reprint Hildesheim: Georg Olms, 1972.

Berkeley, George, *Berkeley's Philosophical Works* ed. D. M. Armstrong (London: Macmillan, 1965).

Boyle, R., *Selected philosophical papers of Robert Boyle* ed. M. A. Stewart (Manchester: Manchester University Press, 1979).

Bridoux, A. (ed.), *Descartes, Oeuvres et Lettres* (Paris: Gallimard, 1937).

Butler, R. J. (ed.), *Cartesian Studies* (Oxford: Blackwell, 1972).

Chomsky, N., *Language and Mind* (New York: Harcourt, Brace & World, 1968).

Clarke, D. M., *Descartes' Philosophy of Science* (Manchester: Manchester University Press, 1982).

Collins, J., *Descartes' Philosophy of Nature* (American Philosophical Quarterly Monograph, Oxford: Blackwell, 1971).

Craven, J. B., *Dr Robert Fludd* (Kirkwall: Occult Research Press, 1902).

Curley, E. M., *Descartes against the Sceptics* (Oxford: Blackwell, 1978).

Davies, P., *God and the New Physics* (Harmondsworth: Penguin, 1983).

Dennett, D., *Brainstorms* (Hassocks, Sussex: Harvester, 1978).

Doney, W. (ed.), *Descartes, A Collection of Critical Essays* (London: Macmillan, 1968).

Drake, S., *Galileo at Work* (Chicago: University of Chicago Press, 1978).

Frankfurt, H. G., *Demons, Dreamers and Madmen: The Defence of Reason in Descartes' Meditations* (New York: Bobbs-Merrill, 1970).

Galileo, Galilei, *Le Opere*, ed. A. Favaro (Florence: Barbera, 1889–1901, reprinted 1968).

Gilson, E. (ed.), *René Descartes, Discourse de la Méthode, texte et commentaire* (Paris: Vrin, 1925).

Gouhier, H., *Essais sur Descartes* (Paris: Vrin, 1949).

Green, C. E., *Lucid Dreams* (Oxford: Institute of Psychophysical Research, 1968).

Grene, M. (I) (ed.), *Interpretations of Life and Mind* (London: Routledge, 1972).

Grene, M. (II), *Descartes* (Brighton: Harvester, 1985).

Gueroult, M., *Descartes selon l'ordre des raisons* (Paris: Montaigne, 1952; 2nd edn 1968). References in the notes are to translation by R. Ariew: *Descartes' Philosophy Interpreted according to the order of reasons* (Minneapolis: University of Minnesota Press, 1983).

Haldane, E. S. and Ross, G. T. R. (trs)., *The Philosophical Works of Descartes* (Cambridge: Cambridge University Press, 1911).

Harré, R., *The Philosophies of Science* (London: Oxford University Press, 1972).

Holland, A. J. (ed.), *Philosophy, Its History and Historiography* (Dordrecht: Reidel, 1985).

Hooker, M. (ed.), *Descartes, Critical and Interpretive Essays* (Baltimore: Johns Hopkins, 1978).

Hume, David (I), *A Treatise of Human Nature* (1739–40) ed. L. A. Selby-Bigge (Oxford: Oxford University Press, revised 1975).

Hume, David (II), *Enquiry concerning Human Understanding* (1748) ed. L. A. Selby-Bigge (Oxford: Oxford University Press, revised 1975).

Jacobi, J. (ed.), *Parcelsus: Selected Writings* tr. N. Guterman (London: Routledge, 1951).

Kant, Immanuel, *Critique of Pure Reason* (1781) tr. N. Kemp Smith (New York: Macmillan, 1965).

Kenny, A., *Descartes* (New York: Random House, 1968).

Kripke, S., *Naming and Necessity* (Oxford: Blackwell, revised 1980).

Lennon, T. M. et al. (eds), *Problems of Cartesianism* Montreal and Kingston: McGill–Queens University Press, 1982).

Lindeboom, G. A., *Descartes and Medicine* (Amsterdam: Radopi, 1979).

Locke, John, *Essay concerning Human Understanding* (1690) ed. P. M. Nidditch (Oxford: Clarendon, 1975).

Marion, J.-L. (I), *Sur l'ontologie grise de Descartes* (Paris: Vrin, 1975).

Marion, J.-L. (II), *Sur la théologie blanche de Descartes* (Paris: Presses Universitaries de France, 1981).

Marks, C., *Commissurotomy, Brain Bisection and the Unity of Consciousness* (Cambridge, Mass.: MIT Press, 1981).

Miller, V. R. and Miller, R. P. (trs)., *Descartes, Principles of Philosophy* (Dordrecht: Reidel, 1983).

McGinn, C., *The Subjective View* (Oxford: Oxford University Press, 1983).

Nagel, T., *Mortal Questions* (Cambridge: Cambridge University Press, 1979).

Paracelsus, *Sämtliche Werke*, ed. K. Sudhoff and W. Matthiessen (Munich: Barth, 1922–5, and Berlin: Oldebourg, 1928–33).

Pascal, *Oeuvres*, ed. L. Brunschvieg (Paris: Hachette, 1904).

Popkin, R. H., *The History of Scepticism from Erasmus to Descartes* (New York: Harper & Row, 1964).

Putnam, H., *Reason, Truth and History* (Cambridge: Cambridge University Press, 1981).

Rorty, R., *Philosophy and the Mirror of Nature* (Oxford: Blackwell, 1980).

Ryle, G., *The Concept of Mind* (London: Hutchinson, 1949).

Shea, W. R., *Galileo's Intellectual Revolution* (London: Macmillan, 1972).

Shoemaker, S., *Identity, Cause and Mind* (Cambridge: Cambridge University Press, 1984).

Spinoza, Benedictus, *Opera*, ed. C. Gebhardt (Heidelberg: Carl Winters, 1925), 4 vols.

Veitch, J., *Descartes, Discourse on Method, Meditations and Principles* (London: Dent, 1912).

Vesey, G. (ed.), *Philosophers Ancient and Modern*. Royal Institute of Philosophy Lectures, 1985–6 (Cambridge: Cambridge University Press, 1987).

Williams, B., *Descartes, The Project of Pure Enquiry* (Harmondsworth: Penguin, 1978).

Wilson, M., *Descartes* (London: Routledge, 1978).

Wittgenstein, L., *Philosophical Investigations (Philosophische Untersuchungen)* 1953, trs. G. E. M. Anscombe (Oxford: Blackwell, 1953, and New York: Macmillan, 1958).

Index